FIGHT
THE
RIGHT

ALSO BY WARREN KINSELLA

The War Room
Fury's Hour
Unholy Alliances
Kicking Ass in Canadian Politics
Party Favours
Web of Hate

FIGHT THE RIGHT

☆ ☆ ☆ A MANUAL FOR SURVIVING THE COMING CONSERVATIVE APOCALYPSE ☆ ☆ ☆

WARREN KINSELLA

Random House Canada

PUBLISHED BY RANDOM HOUSE CANADA

Copyright © 2012 Warren Kinsella

www.randomhouse.ca

Library and Archives Canada Cataloguing in Publication

Kinsella, Warren, 1960–
    Fight the right / Warren Kinsella.

Issued also in electronic format.

ISBN 978-0-307-36165-3

    1. Conservatism—Canada. 2. Right and left (Political science)—Canada. 3. Conservative Party of Canada. 4. Politics, Practical—Canada. 5. Canada—Politics and government—2006–. I. Title.

JC573.2.C3K55 2012   320.520971   C2012-902049-4

Text and cover design by Terri Nimmo

Cover image: © David M. Schrader | Dreamstime.com

Printed and bound in the United States of America

10 9 8 7 6 5 4 3 2 1

To Emma, Ben, Sam and Jake

C0NTENTS

INTRODUCTION

The conservative species is, increasingly, dominating a fragile political environment. Liberal flora and fauna are being harmed.
Herewith, an examination and an assessment of their dastardly manipulations of language and values. Also, a brief discussion of what progressives and liberals must do to ensure the survival of their own species, a subject-matter that will be expanded upon in this slender manual.
Finally, a call to action: one to rouse the liberal species from its slumber.

Fight the Right!

Because, whether you like it or not—and the polls say quite a few of us don't like it—conservatives, large and small *c*, are winning.

Everywhere you look these days, conservatives are winning elections, winning power, winning control. Nationally, locally, the story is the same: angry white men on the Right are ascendant. The Left, meanwhile, seems to be increasingly divided and dispirited, and rapidly losing ground.

Conservatives are on the march for all sorts of reasons. They're well funded, thanks to their well-heeled corporate backers. They're better organized than at any time in their history. The corporate, right-wing media adore them. The politics and economics of the era seemingly favour them. And—up here in Canada, at least—conservatives have benefited from schisms and squabbling on the Left. Liberals, lefties and progressives all continue to scrap over shrinking political real estate. The Right, meanwhile, reaps the benefits.

Everywhere you look, these days, conservatives abound, and they are bad news. As will be shown in due course, they ruin economies and social balance. They pit one class against another. They discriminate. They are nasty, brutish and short-sighted.

There's a rising rightist tide, all right, one that can't be disputed. Just about everywhere in the West, conservatives dominate the discourse. In the U.S., Gallup polls suggest that nearly half of Americans consider themselves conservative or *very* conservative—while only a puny 20 percent now self-identify as liberal. In Canada, conservatives and/or the Conservative Party dominate at almost every level of government, from one coast to another. Meanwhile, most of the European Union is governed from the Right, too, with nearly all of the EU's 27 member states embracing the Right or, sometimes, the further right.

From Rome to Riga, from Maine to Miami, from Whitehorse to Witless Bay, conservatives are on the march. They're not very good at governing, but they've gotten particularly good at winning power. What, if anything, can be done?

Well, we can fight the Right, for starters.

Thus, this book.

☆ ☆ ☆

Fight the Right is a handbook of sorts. It's a handbook on how to understand and ultimately survive the mean and nasty conservative era in which we find ourselves. It's a guide on how to keep sane, when all those around you seemingly are not—and when power seems to reside with a few (ostensibly) red-necked, knuckle-dragging mouth-breathers who want to take us back to the Dark Ages, or worse. It's a manual, quite literally, on how to push back against the rising rightist tide, and win.

I've been around liberal (small and large *l*) campaigns for all of my adult life, and a good part of my teenage years, too. I've been privileged to be an advisor to lots of winning progressives, from Prime Minister Jean Chrétien to Bobby Kennedy Jr. I've helped out trade unions, NGOs, associations and individuals over the years. And while I've been fortunate to be part of a few wins, I've had my share of losses. You learn a lot from losing.

What I've learned along the way are a few things about how to take on the Right and how to beat them at their own game. *Fight the Right* is designed to help progressives better compre-hend their adversary, and then to go on and defeat conservatives wherever the battle is taking shape. On the campaign trail. In the legislature or the council chamber. In TV and radio news-rooms, where shrill right-wing voices increasingly dominate. In the pages of our newspapers, which overwhelmingly favour the Right. Wherever conservative cabals are targeting average citi-zens and hard-working families, this book will try to provide a way to give the bullies a taste of their own medicine.

Salvation lies in understanding. The surest way to defeat your adversary, as John Stuart Mill says, is to first understand them: "[Cicero] has left it on record that he always studied his adversary's case with as great, if not with still greater, intensity than even his own. He who knows only his own side of the case, knows little of that." In other words, the best way to stop losing to conservatives is to figure out why they keep win-ning. This book is all about following Mill's sage advice.

Thus, *Fight the Right* will take a look at *why* conservatives are winning and *how* they have radically changed their approach to politics in order to do so. Mainly, I'll argue that conservatives have stolen the two things that liberals used to own: values and language. Without knowing how to appeal to the values of average citizens—and lacking the very words to do so—progressives are forever doomed to failure. The only way to seize victory is to appeal to people's hearts as well as their minds. Conservatives know this, and—for a few years, now—they have been rigorously applying it in every campaign.

Fight the Right will also map out some of the issues that conservatives have in their crosshairs, as well as what we progressives have done wrong—and what the Right has done, well, right. From conservatives' perspective, victory hasn't yet been secured; to them, there is still much to be done. There are those things that they like (armies and generals, tax cuts for the rich, guns, big corporations and people who think just like them) and those things they don't (abortion, social justice, gays and lesbians, diversity, the United Nations, culture and people who don't think like them at all). To conservatives, it's total victory or nothing. For progressives, whether they like it or not, the war is already underway. For progressives to pretend otherwise only helps the other side to win.

Having examined what a conservative is, how a conservative behaves, and how conservatives win, this book will then describe the ways in which conservatives can be beaten into submission by smart progressives. Values and language aren't just part of a winning strategy, I'll argue. They *are* the winning strategy.

Because—truly—conservatives can be beaten! Conservatives can be vanquished! Despite their arrogance, despite their current political successes, conservatives are not without crucial weaknesses. They adore big money, for sure, just as they adore big business and a big biased media—and they are ready, willing and able to use both to crush progressives seeking justice and fairness. But the greatest threat to conservative hegemony is a populist opposition. That is, average citizens coming together in common purpose, and using common-sense messages to mobilize the masses. By taking back values, by taking back words, liberals can once again start beating conservatives.

☆ ☆ ☆

It was the Year of Our Lord 2000, and as he jogged, kickboxed and roller-bladed across the hinterland—always with a helpful photographer in tow!—Canadian Alliance leadership candidate Stockwell Day blathered on, cheerfully, about all sorts of things.

Just stick a microphone before him and he would pipe up about what he was against (gun control, abortion, gays and lesbians, the Playboy Channel, multiculturalism and subsidies to what he ominously referred to as "special interest groups"). He would also prattle on about what he was for (guns, armies and generals, sex offender registries, flat taxes, "choice" in health care and prosecuting disobedient fourteen-year-olds as adults).

Between kickboxing matches, Day would mutter darkly about the conspiracies being promulgated by unseen forces of "political correctness." At one of the interminable, coma-inducing Canadian Alliance leadership debates, Day scolded fellow leadership aspirants Tom Long and Keith Martin for suggesting that a stridently anti-abortion platform is a one-way ticket to electoral oblivion. Said Day, as he wagged a telegenic finger at his adversaries: "This discussion will not tear a political party apart. Your comments are well intended, but [you are] not understanding that we are actually moving out of the era of fear of political correctness. That era is on its last legs. My campaign has proven that."

Note that important phrase: "the era of fear of political correctness." What Day was saying, it seemed, was that Long and

Martin were censorious, statist, culture-loving, One World Government lackeys, bent on curtailing discussion about the surefire vote-winner that is abortion. Something like that.

As in any conservative sophist's war, definitions are important. "Political correctness," *The Concise Oxford Dictionary of Politics* informs us, "was an influential movement on U.S. campuses beginning in the late 1980s [which] sought changes in undergraduate curricula to emphasize the roles of women, non-white people, and homosexuals in history and culture, and attacked the domination of Western culture by dead white European males." Oxford went on to note that political correctness was in full retreat by the early 1990s. But that did not deter the (now-defunct) Canadian Alliance's champion of dead white European males, Stockwell Day, from tilting away at the PC windmill.

Having spent more than two decades chronicling the activities of Canada's political right, I have noted that, of all of the many and varied enemies regularly excoriated by right-wingers, *political correctness* tops the hit parade. Whenever a rightist is critiqued for something they have said or written, the outraged respondent inevitably charges that he or she (but usually he) is being victimized by satanic PC inquisitors.

For example: in postings to the Freedom Site, Canada's favoured Internet address for Holocaust deniers and white supremacists, political correctness is vilified over and over and over. At the far-right Western Canada Concept's website, meanwhile—where Day's deceased father, Stockwell Day Sr., could once coincidentally be found referring to homosexuals as "sodomites"—political correctness is vilified, ad nauseam, in the party's official organ. The WCC's leader, whom the elder Stockwell Day referred to as his "captain," was Douglas H. Christie, lawyer to Jim Keegstra, Ernst Zundel and assorted anti-Semitic lunatics.

Braying about political correctness is most often done for a couple of reasons. Sometimes, it is done by intolerant people hoping to give a patina of respectability to their intolerance—to wit, "This may not be politically correct, but I think all refugees should be thrown in detention when they arrive here." (Interestingly, that was precisely Alliance candidate Tom Long's stated position.) Other times, it is done by conservative politicians to chill legitimate criticism of their views on issues like abortion, sexual orientation or something else.

What criticism was Stockwell Day Jr. attempting to forestall, or prevent, with his vituperations of political correctness? Perhaps it was his statement, in a February 1992 issue of *Alberta Report*, that homosexuality was "a mental disorder." Or perhaps it was his June 1995 declaration at an Alberta Progressive Conservative Party convention: "Women who become pregnant through rape or incest should not qualify for government-funded abortions." Or perhaps it was his April 1995 conclusion, found in an *Edmonton Journal* profile, that abortions are not "medically required." Or perhaps it was even the revelation, made by award-winning journalist Gordon Laird, that Stockwell Day—as a pastor—included the aforementioned Holocaust-denying Keegstra in a men-only prayer group in Alberta in the 1980s.

We cannot know for certain, of course. All we can know with confidence is that criticizing these sorts of views, made by someone then seeking the highest office in the land, is not "political correctness." It is merely *the right thing to do*. Conservatives such as Stockwell Day—who would go on to win the Canadian Alliance leadership, and then get his electoral ass handed to him by my former boss, Liberal leader Jean Chrétien—have a great preoccupation with language. They, more than many liberals and progressives, know the tremendous importance of language in shaping and framing the outlines of political debate. Thus, "global warming" becomes the slightly more benign "climate change." Something like "oil drilling" becomes "energy exploration." Or "estate tax" is transformed into "death tax." It's never "tax reform," it's "tax simplification." It's not government "outsourcing"—instead, it's government "innovation." It's never "undocumented workers," naturally—it's "illegal" aliens or refugees. And so on and so on.

"Political correctness," however, is the phrase that is near the very apex of the decades-long conservative campaign to manipulate language to their partisan advantage, because it is the very thing that permits them to give voice to whatever bit of nastiness is rolling around inside their conservative craniums. Whenever conservatives wish to say something bigoted, or mean or stupid about something they hate (*vide supra*, abortion, social justice, gays and lesbians, diversity, the United Nations, culture, people who don't look like them), they will therefore respond to inevitable criticism by dismissing it as political correctness. And, since they are the defenders of "freedom of speech" (there's that ever-useful "freedom" word, which, as we will see, conservatives deploy with great frequency), if you are politically correct, you are against freedom. Even worse: you are a "censor."

But that's just language. Wait'll you see what conservatives have to say about *values*, and how that they have come to dominate that debate, too.

☆ ☆ ☆

Whose values are your values? Conservatives, increasingly, think your values are theirs. Just ask them.

In October 2011, for example, hundreds of Republican activists gathered in Washington, D.C., for what was billed as the Values Voter Summit. It was the biggest gathering of the religious right in the U.S. in a long time, and just about every single GOP presidential candidate was in attendance. The presidential contenders—along with a bevy of congressional leaders, and a parade of televangelists—addressed the rapt delegates for two straight days.

Among the "values" being mooted was the notion that the United States was a "Christian nation." Bryan Fischer, from the American Family Association, said over and over that the U.S. constitution did not protect the religious liberty of non-Christians—including Mormons (Mitt Romney, the guy who would go on to win the Republican nomination, is one). Meanwhile, a Baptist pastor attracted quite a bit of attention when he declared that Texas Governor Rick Perry was a "genuine" Christian—presumably because his values were the right ones. Romney, said the megachurch pastor, belonged to "a cult." Nice.

But that's not all that took place at the Values Voter Summit. One after another, conservative leaders lined up in front of microphones to deplore the repeal of a ban on openly gay and lesbian people in the armed forces. Not surprisingly, lots of them took swings at same-sex marriage, too. The American Family Association's Fischer, to rousing applause, declared that America needed a president "who will treat homosexual behavior not as a political cause at all but as a threat to public health." (Asked about the Occupier camps then dominating the news in D.C. and elsewhere, Fischer said that liberals are "driven by angry, bitter, acquisitive greed for the wealth of productive Americans.") One conservative writer suggested it was not possible to be conservative and support gay marriage; it was akin to being a "liberal who likes tax cuts."

Presidential candidate and former House Speaker Newt Gingrich stated that conservatives in the legislative and executive branches of government should simply ignore judicial rulings they didn't like. Another presidential aspirant, ultramontanist Rick Santorum, insisted the "pursuit of happiness" stuff in the Declaration of Independence didn't actually mean happiness for *everyone*: instead, it meant adhering to conservative values and doing "the morally right thing." Finally, there was Rep. Steve King, who said the United States was actually created by God, personally. America was "built by His hand," said King—adding the heretofore unknown fact that the Declaration of Independence was typed up by the Almighty, Himself, and that the founding fathers were God's earthly instruments, kind of like Jesus had been. Who knew?

Conservatives like the ones gathered at the Values Summit believe their values are American values because, well, they are. That's just the way it goes, and if you don't like it, you're with the terrorists.

But fair's fair. It's not a uniquely *American* conservative point of view. Up here in the Great White North as well, conservatives have been claiming for years that conservative and Canadian values are interchangeable—after all, how else do they keep winning election campaigns, right? So, right after the 2011 federal election campaign, Prime Minister Stephen Harper made his annual visit to the family-friendly Calgary Stampede. There, beneath a stetson, he bashed his opponents (as expected) and insisted his Conservatives are super-duper winners (ditto). But then he said this: "Conservative values are Canadian values." And "Canadian values are Conservative values."

Hoo boy! When he uttered that little syllogism, the progressive side of the commentariat promptly went bananas. Liberal leader Bob Rae—whose party Harper amusingly described as being as relevant as "disco balls and bell bottoms"—declared that Harper was sounding pretty arrogant, which was true. One of the *Globe and Mail's* resident greybeards, Lawrence Martin, agreed (and the *Globe* would certainly know arrogance when it sees it). So did a Saskatoon *StarPhoenix* columnist, who opined it reeked of "annoying arrogance." In the *Winnipeg Free*

Press, Frances Russell—not a noted Harper cheerleader—concurrent that the Stampede tub-thumper was a lot of triumphalism, hubris and arrogance. You get the picture: arrogant.

It was indeed arrogant to say Conservative values and Canadian values are the same thing. (Although, truth be told, I thought Harper's crack about disco balls and bell bottoms was pretty funny, coming as it does from a guy so square he needs to walk around the block to turn over in bed.) So when Harper's Stampede stump-speech and his values claim came up during my appearance on Krista Erickson's Sun News Network show, I shrugged. "Meh," I said. First off, I reminded her, I am a Calgarian who—like most sane Calgarians—is no fan of the Stampede. The Stampede, I suggested, is mostly an opportunity for uptight businessmen and repressed easterners to descend on downtown Calgary, drink too much, contract venereal diseases and throw up in public. "If you're a true Calgarian, Stampede's a good time to leave town," I said to my horrified host.

Second, I suggested, Canadian conservative politicians have been claiming their party's values are identical to Canadians' values since Jesus was a little feller. Before he became prime minister in 1978, Brian Mulroney gave a speech in honour of a conservative bagman suggesting that Tory values were "real values" and Canadians deserved "no less." In the same vein, the aforementioned Stockwell Day once speechified as Canadian Alliance leader that "new leadership"—that is to say, *his*—was needed to reflect Canadians' values. Ditto Preston Manning, the former Reform Party boss, and Harper and Day's predecessor, who made the same claim: "As conservative values become more Canadian values . . . that's something conservatives should be happy about."

It's the same, in fact, for every other recently minted Conservative leader to emerge from Alberta (as all of them do). Conservative politicians can always be seen insisting that theirs are identical to yours, because they know that whoever controls the values debate tends to always win.

That doesn't mean we progressives should let them, of course. If we want to start winning—if we want to defeat the conservative hordes—we need to show that we, too, have the values that resonate with ordinary folks. That means getting better at appealing to the hearts and minds of voters, and our fellow citizens. For progressives, it's a valuable endeavour, you might say.

☆ ☆ ☆

Along with the right words, and better focus on values, progressives also need an alternative narrative. More particularly, we need a narrative that *connects* with the values of citizens in a way that they understand.

The great global recession of 2008–2009—and the cataclysm of despair that it unleashed—has receded somewhat. But its effects are still felt all over, and nowhere as much as among what we once called the middle class. Foreclosures, layoffs and broken dreams are everywhere to be seen. The ongoing legacy of the recession is pain and misery, and a rising tide of anger.

Where, in the midst of all of this, has been the Left? What have liberals had to say about all of this gloom and despair? Mostly, nothing. Progressives have been virtually invisible at the very time when the old dogmas and old fixes of the Right are, to many, a cruel joke. Don't just take my word for it: ask former conservative muse Francis Fukuyama. In a remarkable February 2012 essay about this failure of progressives to rally to the side of the battered middle class, the Stanford Senior Fellow wrote: "Something strange is going on in the world today. . . . Despite widespread anger at Wall Street bailouts, there has been no great upsurge of Left-wing American populism in response. It is conceivable that the Occupy Wall Street movement will gain traction, but the most dynamic recent populist movement to date has been the Right-wing Tea Party. Something similar is true in Europe as well, where the Left is anemic and Right-wing populist parties are on the move."

Fukuyama is an acclaimed author and a political economist. At one time, he had also been classified as a neoconservative, but he came to reject that label. An early enthusiast of Reaganism, Fukuyama broke from Bush-era conservatism over its undisguised Islamophobia and its wild misadventures in places like Iraq. History, he has said, "cannot be pushed along by the application of power and will"—a notion that, to a conservative, sounds positively heretical. But in his 2012 essay, which appeared in *Foreign Affairs* magazine, Fukuyama does not sing any paeans to progressives, either: he does not hesitate to dispassionately rebuke the Left for its own lapses, which are, unfortunately, myriad.

"There are several reasons for [the] lack of Left-wing mobilization," writes Fukuyama, "but chief among them is *a failure in the realm of ideas*. For the past generation, the ideological high ground on economic issues has been held by a libertarian Right."

What does that mean? It means, as my conservative friend Kory Teneycke told me one day, that "ideas are the hard part." It also means that Western democracy and the middle class that at one time gave it purpose and legitimacy are at risk of vanishing entirely if the Left does not get its act together. For instance: median incomes in the United States and other Western democracies have been stagnating since the 1970s. "[The middle class] may today benefit from cheap cell phones, inexpensive clothing, and Facebook, but they increasingly cannot *afford* their own homes, or health insurance, or comfortable pensions when they retire," Fukuyama writes.

The centre of capitalism, as everyone from the Occupiers to the billionaires gathered at Davos have lately observed, cannot hold. To many, it is a well-intentioned but essentially failed theory. But the Left, Fukuyama declares, is absent from this crucial discussion and is also AWOL from offering cogent alternatives. "One of the most puzzling features of the world in the aftermath of the financial crisis," he says, "is that, so far, populism has taken primarily a Right-wing form, not a Left-wing one. In the United States, for example, although the Tea Party is anti-elitist in its rhetoric, its members vote for conservative politicians who serve the interests of precisely those financiers and corporate elites they claim to despise."

The academic Left, the feminist theorists, the postmodernists and the professional multiculturalism advocates all have plenty to say, Fukuyama concedes, but not to those they most need to achieve real democratic and economic change. "It is impossible to generate a mass progressive movement," Fukuyama dryly notes, "on the basis of such a motley coalition: most of the working- and lower-middle-class citizens victimized by the system are culturally conservative, and would be embarrassed to be seen in the presence of allies like this." Richard Nixon, as many others have written, knew this first and best. It was one of the ways in which Tricky Dick and his ilk were able to demonize and marginalize liberalism. It was cynical and dishonest, but it was also undeniably effective.

The biggest problem for the Left, Fukuyama would agree, is a lack of credibility, a lack of authenticity—and the lack of a values-enriched narrative. What is needed is an ideology for the future. Fukuyama, again: "Politically, the new ideology would need to reassert the supremacy of democratic politics over economics and legitim[ize] government as an expression of the public interest. . . . It would have to argue forthrightly for more [wealth] redistribution and present a realistic route to ending interest groups' domination of politics." Sounds like a liberal, doesn't he?

The task, of course, is immense, and the rewards uncertain. Why bother? Because, according to Fukuyama, "Inequality will continue to worsen. The current concentration of wealth has already become self-reinforcing: the financial sector has used its lobbying clout to avoid more onerous forms of regulation. Schools for the well-off are better than ever; those for everyone else continue to deteriorate. Elites in all societies use their superior access to the political system to protect their interests." The Left must step up. "[A populist and progressive] mobilization will not happen," cautions Fukuyama, "as long as the middle classes of the developed world remain enthralled by the narrative of the past generation. *The alternative narrative* is out there, waiting to be born."

☆ ☆ ☆

With the right words, with the right values—with the alternative narrative—progressives can overpower conservatives. But not while they fight among themselves. In the U.S., the 2008 victory of Barack Obama brought together the warring factions of the Democratic Party for the first time in a long time. But in Canada, New Democrats and Liberals stubbornly refuse to co-operate with one another. And it is conservatives, and the Conservatives, who reap the benefits.

Because, let there be no doubt: a fractured Left benefits only a unified Right. So, when Liberal leader Michael Ignatieff had a chance to effectively eliminate NDP leader Jack Layton as the only other progressive choice; when he had a historic opening to bring together the Left; when Ignatieff had an opportunity, long before the May 2011 election, to craft a deal with the NDP for co-operation, or a coalition or even a merger, he emphatically said no. In June 2010, with his former leadership rivals Bob Rae and Dominic LeBlanc standing behind him in a House of Commons hallway, nodding like bobble-head dolls, Ignatieff declared that he wanted nothing to do with the NDP. Forming an alliance with the NDP was "ridiculous," he snorted.

Not quite. But that declaration gave Stephen Harper, and Conservatives, what they most desired. And for good measure, Harper once again invoked the spectre of the "Liberal-socialist-separatist coalition" on the very first day of the historic 2011 campaign, just to seal the deal. Once again, Ignatieff meekly fell into line. The Liberal Party "will not enter a coalition with other federalist parties," Ignatieff croaked. If it hadn't had such brutal consequences, Ignatieff's willingness to dance to Harper's tune would have been comical.

As the Democrats have shown in the U.S., in crass political terms, co-operation on the Left makes eminent sense. The Canadian Conservatives' grip on power is maintained, more than anything else, by the inability of progressives to come together. For the past three federal general elections, Harper has remained in office with the support of less than 40 percent of the electorate. If some, or all, of the other 60-odd percent were to come together in a single, formidable force, the Conservatives would be defeated. Period.

A united Liberal–New Democratic option would also benefit both parties, by neatly offsetting each other's weaknesses. Liberals have *gravitas* and experience in governing, skills the federal New Democrats still lack. The NDP has a robust fundraising capacity and a strong relationship with its grassroots, both lingering Grit deficiencies. In policy terms, more unites the two parties than divides them. New Democrats are, as Jean Chrétien likes to say, mainly "Liberals in a hurry." A united progressive party—a Liberal-Democratic Party, perhaps— acknowledges a natural evolution in politics, towards a binary political universe. A united Left is commonplace in most other Western democracies, like the U.S. What's unusual is that it hasn't yet happened in the Great White North.

All of which, naturally, must entertain conservatives like Stephen Harper a great deal. A few days after the May 2011 general election that saw him finally secure a comfortable majority government, in fact, one could almost picture Harper sitting up at the prime ministerial retreat at Harrington Lake and reading the papers. And having a good old chuckle.

And who could blame him? In one newspaper, there was interim Liberal leader Bob Rae, saying a merger of his party and the NDP is a work of "fiction" and something no Liberal wants to talk about. (That would be the same Bob Rae who, the day after his party was reduced to a rump in the House of Commons, said it wasn't such a bad idea at all.) In another paper, there was former Liberal leader Michael Ignatieff—on the grim morning after the Liberal Party's May 2 rout—pouring cold water on the merger idea. (And the week before, there was the selfsame Michael Ignatieff musing on his Facebook page about how the Grits and Dippers now needed to consider coming together.) Senior Liberal MP Ralph Goodale? Hated the idea. Senior Liberal MP Denis Coderre? Loved it. For a Liberal who might still feel confused by all of this, rest assured: the NDP were pretty confused, too.

While just after the 2011 election, Jack Layton was against working with the Liberals, just after the 2009 election, Layton had been all for it and had worked energetically to cobble together a progressive governing coalition. Other Dippers were similarly inconsistent. New Democrat party president Brian Topp—who is one of the brainiest political backroom boys around, and who in March 2012 lost his months-long quest to win Jack Layton's job as NDP leader—sounded distinctly unenthusiastic about getting together with the despised Liberals when asked about it during the interminable NDP leadership slog. (This would be the same Topp who was at the forefront of the 2008 NDP-Liberal talks that very nearly resulted in a coalition government. He even wrote a book about it.) Prominent NDP MP Pat Martin? He used to be utterly silent on the subject, but now was saying he was all for it. Dyspeptic NDP leader Thomas Mulcair? In 2010, he was "categorically" against such an idea. A year later, Ottawa media noted, Mulcair could be seen leaving the door open. And so on and so on.

To repeat: Stephen Harper and his gang must be having a good old laugh about what they are seeing across the aisle. In the view of many—such as Jean Chrétien plus former NDP luminaries Ed Broadbent and Roy Romanow—progressives need to come together for the good of the country. To those Liberals and New Democrats who still fulminate against bringing progressives together, remember this: Messrs. Chrétien, Broadbent and Romanow have forgotten more about politics than you will ever know. In politics, experience and winning count. Each of those men were winners. And each one knows that, as long as Canadian progressives remain divided, it's Stephen Harper who will keep on winning.

The one federal Liberals and New Democrats should look to for inspiration in all of this, ironically enough, is Harper himself. He may be a democracy-stomping autocrat, but Harper's no fool. He watched the divided Right get its face rubbed in the proverbial dirt by Liberals in 1993, 1997 and 2000. He knew his fellow conservatives would never win power if they didn't unify. So around 2005, he brought together the warring Reform, Alliance, and PC tribes—and he won government very shortly afterwards. That, more than anything else he has done, is Harper's greatest achievement. It's a lesson the Left needs to learn.

It's also, by the way, why Harper has expended so much of his time demonizing co-operation on the Left. He knows it is the only thing that can dislodge his grip on power. Brilliantly, he made "coalition" a dirty word—even when polls consistently showed that Canadians thought the NDP and the Liberals should come together.

In the U.S., Democrats are more unified than they have been in many years. The factional battles of the past are, for now, a memory. But up north, conservatives continue to win not simply because they have a better command of values and words. They win because they've gotten their act together, and we on the Left haven't.

Three years ago, I was in New York City to meet Bobby Kennedy Jr. Bobby looks so much like his dad, it can almost take your breath away. Unlike his father, however, Bobby Jr. hasn't pursued the political avocation. He's a law professor and a prominent environmental activist. But he still likes to talk about politics, and knows quite a bit about the Canadian political scene.

"So," he said, "the New Democrats are off on their own, and you Liberals are off on your own, right?"

I nodded.

"Why?" he asked.

I shrugged.

"Doesn't that just mean that the Conservatives are going to win again?" he asked, rhetorically.

"For sure," I said. "As long as progressives continue to fight with each other, he'll win."

Bobby Kennedy Jr. shook his head, marvelling. He didn't say anything else. He didn't need to.

And so, three years later, the farce that is Canadian progressive politics continues apace. Liberals and New Democrats persist in fighting among themselves, while Harper's regime giddily reaps the benefits. Even with the robocall election fraud scandal, Harper retains the loyalty of the 30-plus percent who classify themselves as hard-core conservatives. Progressives, meanwhile, remain powerless—despite the fact that 60 percent of the electorate favour them. The sad saga continues. Not long ago, speaking to a group of students in Victoria, Liberal MP Justin Trudeau said this: "If by 2015, with the election approaching, and neither party has gotten its act together enough to shine and to be the obvious alternative, then there will be a lot of pressure for us to start looking at that. I think there is not anyone in Parliament, outside the Conservative Party of Canada, that is willing to risk seeing Stephen Harper become prime minister one more time."

Within hours, a nameless factotum working for interim Liberal leader Bob Rae swiftly disavowed Trudeau: "A coalition is not on the agenda for the Liberal Party of Canada. Period." Meanwhile, NDP leadership candidate Nathan Cullen had made comments similar to Trudeau's. Days before the March 2012 NDP leadership convention, Cullen said: "[We need to tell] Canadians that we are going to put country ahead of party. I got into politics to be the official government . . . I think [co-operation with the Liberals] gives us the best shot." But the NDP establishment—of which Rae used to be a prominent part—wouldn't embrace Cullen's point of view, either. NDP leader Thomas Mulcair, who even used to be a Liberal cabinet minister, was now categorical: "The 'no' is categorical, absolute, irrefutable and non-negotiable. It's no. End of story. Full stop."

Rae, Mulcair and others are dreaming in Technicolor if they think that continuing to split the progressive vote is going to change the outcome in 2015, however. Conservatives will never, ever abandon Harper; it is their ideological make-up. Despite a multitude of scandals under his watch, Harper can always count on the thirty-plus points his loyalists give him. Harper can also count on the generous assistance of the Liberal and New Democrat establishment. As long as the likes of Bob Rae and Thomas Mulcair are running the progressive show, in fact, Stephen Harper hasn't got a care in the world. Back at our meeting a few years ago, Bobby Kennedy Jr. shook his head. "Can't they somehow be persuaded to work together?" he asked.

"Nope," I said. "They're too goddamn stupid."

☆ ☆ ☆

Values. Words.

Those two things—along with their unity and discipline, and their noted ability to take partisan advantage of progressive civil wars—account for much of the conservative movement's current undeniable success. By making their appeals to voters more understandable and persuasive—by using language in such a way that it is understood by the greatest number, and not just a chosen few—conservatives dominate the discourse. By rebranding the extremism that is latent in their own value system, and by manipulating the values of voters, as Richard Nixon did so artfully, conservatives now tower above the ideological landscape in a way that no one, least of all liberals, saw coming.

But George Lakoff did.

I encounter Lakoff, Berkeley professor and all-round smart guy, in a noisy Los Angeles café. The muzak is too loud, but Lakoff—who is sought for his insights by progressives across Europe and the Americas—is smiling. Among progressives, at least, he is a much-admired and much-quoted celebrity. For many years, he had been teaching at Berkeley, writing about mathematics, about language and about the way the human brain works. He was a respected linguist and cognitive scientist. More than a decade ago, however, he started to pay closer attention to the way in which our minds are political—and the way politics works in our minds. His reflections set off a revolution, of sorts, and he became eagerly sought after by academics, journalists and everyone from Dr. Oz to the *Huffington Post*.

Asked when, precisely, conservatives stole words and values away from previously dominant liberals, Lakoff nailed it down to the day, almost.

"It goes back to 1967," he says, matter-of-factly. "Back in 1964, Lyndon Johnson beat Barry Goldwater very badly [in the U.S. presidential race]. Johnson got something like 63 percent of the vote, and Goldwater got 37 percent—and at that point, most Americans wanted to be 'liberal,' and 'conservative' was a scary word. Especially among poorer people and working people, many of whom were unionized. So working people saw themselves as liberals." Richard Nixon, with his tiny black heart and endless scheming, took notice. While a certifiable crook, the Republican presidential candidate was no fool. Having been beaten by John F. Kennedy—a *Catholic!* a telegenic liberal *Catholic!*—Nixon knew that he needed to capture the support of working families who had elevated Kennedy and Johnson to the White House. With the assistance of key advisors like future Fox News supremo Roger Ailes, Nixon devoted himself to changing perceptions of conservatism and, by extension, liberalism.

Says Lakoff: "Nixon assigned Roger Ailes to figure out how to get working people to vote Republican. Using research, they realized that three important changes had taken place between 1964 and 1967. The first concerned the antiwar movement. A lot of working people had been in the military, and they resented antiwar politicians and students. They saw it as antimilitary and therefore anti-American and maybe even communism. So Nixon ran as the anticommunist."

Lakoff says the next thing Nixon did concerned women—and women's role in a progressive society. "They noticed the rise of feminism, and they noticed that a lot of working men were traditionalists. They were traditional fathers at home. And they were threatened by what they saw as radical feminism—and so Nixon ran on traditional family values."

The third and final element of the Republican strategy focused another emotionally charged issue: racial equality. "Nixon and Ailes focused on the civil rights movement that had happened around 1965," Lakoff says. "There were riots in Detroit and Los Angeles, and there were a lot of working people in the South who were still racist. And so Nixon ran on what he called law and order, and against civil rights.

"As a result of those three things, they got working people—working people who were actually liberals to start with—to become conservatives."

But that wasn't enough, apparently. With conservatives—like Stephen Harper in Canada and George W. Bush in the U.S.—it is never enough to simply win. It's necessary to utterly wipe out all progressive opposition, too. To shred them, and disperse their remains to the winds. For instance, one of Harper's candid former senior advisors, Keith Beardsley, says this of his former boss: "He hates the Liberal Party, and I would say his aim from day one—and I don't think anyone would disagree—was to break the brand. The long-term strategy, that was it." A former Conservative cabinet minister agrees: Harper and his conservative cabal "viscerally hat[ed] their political opposition. Sometimes it was just startling to me."

None of this surprises Lakoff. "Conservatives had to put down liberalism. They created an important message—the message that liberals were elitists. They were 'smart-pants' types, and they didn't really know the real world. And they looked down on working people. That's when conservative populism really started, and they've all been pushing it since 1967."

Lakoff pauses, seemingly to listen to the music in the café. "And liberals didn't really seem to have any idea that this had happened, or what to do about it. And it is still the one thing that Barack Obama and many others do not understand."

☆ ☆ ☆

Understanding that those of us on the progressive side of the spectrum are presently on the losing side of the argument is crucial. Without that understanding, and without a collective commitment to changing our strategy (that is, our goal) and our tactics (that is, the things we do to achieve the strategy), we are doomed to an eternity of living in the mean, miserly ninth circle of hell that is conservative rule. That is our fate, if we don't fight back.

Fight back! Fight the Right! This book is not for the skittish or the faint-of-heart. Conservatives didn't assume their position of supremacy by playing nice. They analyzed liberal successes and losses, they copied the tactics they could, they adapted to what they couldn't, and then they set about transforming the body politic in the Americas and Western Europe. Given the near-total dominance conservatives now enjoy in different political and media environments, *Fight the Right* takes the position that the war will not be won by polite letters to the editor, or well-intentioned Facebook pages, or kind-hearted petitions that go precisely nowhere. With simplicity, repetition and volume—and with a carefully crafted message that appeals to the heart as well as the mind—progressives can overwhelm the enemy, once again, and win.

Fight the Right!

HOW TO IDENTIFY A CONSERVATIVE

*The conservative species—its dominant characteristics and traits.
Through careful study in its natural habitat, and not-inconsiderable
experience from direct encounters, the author has assembled handy tips
on how to recognize and categorize the conservative species.
What is a conservative? What isn't? Are they safe to eat? (No.)
A practical psychological profile.*

———

S o, what the hell is a conservative, anyway?

Good question. Hacks and flaks use the word all the time
these days—to describe political parties, to describe politicians,
to describe someone's position on the ideological spectrum.
Because conservatives increasingly dominate our politics, the
word gets used a lot. But is it the right word? That is, are the
people being called conservative (mainly by journalists, because
journalists are in the shorthand business) truly conservative?

We indisputably live in a conservative era. In Europe, for the
first time in generations, conservative political parties tower
over the landscape. We've had David Cameron in Britain,
Angela Merkel in Germany, Nicolas Sarkozy in France, Silvio

Berlusconi in Italy—along with conservative dominance in Finland, Sweden, Denmark, the Netherlands, Austria, Poland and Belgium. The European Union, its ongoing economic predicaments aside, has been an overwhelmingly conservative union since 2005.

In the Americas, it's the same. To be sure, Barack Obama came to power four years ago promising progressives lots of change and hope, but even his most ardent fans acknowledge that Obama hasn't delivered either. His predecessor permitted Wall Street to do whatever it wanted to do, leading to economic ruin for millions of Americans, and for America itself. Obama hasn't yet followed through on his promises of fundamental fiscal and economic reform, and the billionaire bankers are still getting their million-dollar bonuses. The Bush regime wars, meanwhile, didn't end as quickly as voters had been led to believe. Obama may call himself a Democrat, but—to some of his disappointed electors—he has shown the instincts of a Republican, a conservative.

In the Great White North, of course, conservatives—or men and women who can be fairly described as such—rule from coast to coast. In B.C., in Alberta, in Saskatchewan, in the Atlantic, and of course federally: conservatives take different names, sometimes, but conservatives they remain.

Sometimes, the conservative appellation gets appended to people and philosophies that could not be more different. In Canada, both Joe Clark and Stephen Harper have been described as conservatives, and both have been the leaders of Conservative parties, but the philosophies and approaches of the two men are wildly different. Clark is a true "progressive" conservative, that oxymoronic label that federal and provincial Canadian conservatives affixed to themselves for decades. He (and they) believed that government could be a force for good, and that government had a moral obligation to help those who most needed it.

In this way, he was a liberal in disguise. Harper, however, is from an entirely different school: he is a self-professed Reformer, an unrepentant libertarian who seems to despise government even as he schemes to control it. He has presided over an administration that seems to revel in picking fights with those with less power. It was no surprise that Joe Clark voted for Stephen Harper's Liberal opponent, and not Harper.

It may be that "conservative" has become a term that doesn't really mean much anymore, if it ever did. But there are views that you can fairly assign to the new-era conservatives found across Europe and the Americas. There are certain things that they all seem to believe in. Less government. Less taxation. Less regulation. Less, or no, gun control. No enthusiasm for the United Nations, or human rights, or same-sex marriage; no wall between church and state, but plenty of walls between communities. More lip service to religion, more "rights" for the propertied classes, more oil drilling, more law and order, and more defence spending.

To know these new-era conservatives is to dislike what they stand for. Herewith, an attempt to know them better.

☆ ☆ ☆

In the sunny, hopeful days following Barack Obama's big win in 2008—and in the unlikely event the newly minted U.S. president was thinking about Canada—I thought I would pick up the Blackberry (a Canadian invention, by the way, and one that Obama had been photographed with many times in the early days of his presidency) and thumb out a political memo. It was about what Obama, then still a certifiable progressive, should know about the Stephen Harper Conservative government—Harper being the guy Obama amusingly described in an August 2007 Democratic candidates' debate as "the president of Canada."

Obama was ribbed about that mistake, and he made amends, but here's the funny thing: he probably had it right the first time. Stephen Harper is the prime minister of Canada, but in both style and content, he and his team appear to harbour a desire to lead the United States of Canada. In that regard, they are true conservatives, since many conservatives disdain the country they live in and often seem to like other (more conservative) countries better.

The Canadian Conservative leader oversees a government that is more than pro-Republican. It is, arguably, the world's first Republican government-in-exile. Anti-Kyoto, anti-abortion, anti-gun control, anticulture, antigovernment: all that Harper's guys (and they *are* mainly guys) seem to favour are tax cuts and the use of God as a policy instrument. Oh, and the war in Iraq. They were all for that, as seen in March 2003 when Harper famously remarked that those Canadians who did not support that war were "gutless." So one presumes that Obama, too, was "gutless," seeing as how he opposed the Iraq war.

Some months before the 2008 election, Obama's Republican opponent, John McCain, came to Ottawa, Canada's snow-bound national capital. Hundreds of Harper-regime apparatchiks turned out in their finest blue ties and ten-piece suits. It was a veritable neoconservative love-in, with Conservative Party campaign bosses in attendance. Party spokesmen observed that if Canadian Liberals and American Democrats can fraternize, then so, too, can conservatives from both sides of the border. Fair enough.

But the Republican-Conservative relationship goes beyond policy footsie. The two parties are like two hormonal teenagers in perpetual lip-lock, and it's evident that they share the same political DNA. Republican political consultants regularly ply their trade with Conservatives up in Canuckistan, and one U.S.-obsessed Conservative prime minister—Brian Mulroney—was a regular sleep-over guest at the Bush compound in Kennebunkport, Maine. On almost any issue, the Republicans and the Conservatives are virtually indistinguishable. All that kept the Harperites from realizing their innermost Republican fantasies, in fact, was their chronic inability to achieve a parliamentary majority for five long years.

Ascertaining what the Canadian Conservatives think about progressives generally and Democrats in particular isn't difficult to do. In February 2008, to the astonishment of the U.S. media, senior Harper-regime staffers were involved in what came to be known up north as NAFTAgate: they leaked the news that folks from Obama's campaign team had privately met with them and they suggested that Obama was lying about trade in order to curry favour in swing states like Ohio. Hillary Clinton, then Obama's principal opponent for the Democratic crown, had a field day with the controversy: Obama was depicted for the first time as dishonest, and Harper was forced to apologize. It was a big mess, but it was also revealing. It laid bare the truth about conservatives: to them, ideological purity counts for more than common sense. They are even prepared to jeopardize trade-related jobs and prosperity—and sabotage good diplomatic relations—to stick it to a liberal.

Apologies notwithstanding, quite a few Canadian progressives believed NAFTAgate was no accident. It was, they surmised, a deliberate attempt to sabotage Obama's campaign from afar and assist his Republican opponent. Plenty of conservatives hate the likes of Barack Obama. To them, Obama represented their darkest, deepest fear: a black man with power. No, worse: a powerful black man with a Muslim-sounding name.

Canadian liberals like me are unashamed of our historic friendship with American Democrats, to be sure. Our two parties share some of the same values and principles, and some of our leaders—most recently Bill Clinton and Jean

Chrétien—have been allies and friends. At the political level, we have occasionally helped each other during times spent in political exile: such as in 1993, when senior Democrats advised us about setting up our campaign war room; in 2002 and 2003, when Obama's chief strategist, David Axelrod, was a consultant to the Ontario Liberals; and in 2007 and 2008, when hundreds of Canadian Liberals travelled to the U.S. (on their own dime) to work for Obama. But at the end of the day, Canadian Liberals aren't a branch-plant operation of the U.S. Democratic Party. Unlike the symbiotic relationship that exists between Canadian and American conservatives.

Canada's Conservatives, however, are not friends to Democrats in the U.S. Not even close. And if anyone is at all uncertain about that, I recommend calling pretty much anyone up here in Canada. One might even start with that conservative who presently rules from Ottawa—you know, President Harper.

☆ ☆ ☆

Now, don't get me wrong. I don't necessarily hate conservatives. I'll have a beer or two with conservatives. I have worked with conservatives. I have employed conservatives. I have befriended conservatives. I have even dated conservatives—and once, I married a lovely woman who (wisely) dumped her conservatism and, eventually (also wisely), me. Conservatives are fine, as dinner companions or even life companions.

But conservatives cannot be trusted with power.

Now, as noted, not every conservative is evil. Not every conservative lacks a soul. But power transforms them. When they possess power, the record shows that the policies conservatives espouse will inevitably favour the rich over the poor. They will pick the powerful over the powerless. They will assist owners, but not the labourers. Old over new; more of the same instead of change. They will side with developers and industrialists, but rarely the environment and environmental-ists. Men over women; "unborn" but not the "born." The Right will toss around billions to purchase fighter jets, but not nearly as much to fund nurses. They can be counted on to embrace secrecy and subterfuge, but rarely openness and can-dour. Selfishness instead of empathy. In almost every respect, in virtually every way, power-wielding conservatives make powerfully bad choices.

Let me give you a fairly recent example. It's not on par with the outbreak of war, and nobody died. But it is very revealing. It provides a true glimpse into the conservative mind, I think.

Me being a Canadian—and Canada being currently run by Conservatives—I paid close attention to what the Conservatives did in the 2011 federal election campaign. I'm a liberal, and a Liberal, and I can't help myself. When Conservatives are in power, I am filled with dread and revulsion, and I cannot tear my eyes away. It's like being at a slasher movie, except that it goes on way longer.

Now, for the purposes of this tale, I define a liberal as some-one who believes in protection of citizens by government. A conservative, on the other hand, is someone who wants citi-zens to be protected *from* government. Conservatives say they believe in liberty and in freedom. They don't believe those things come from governments. They believe those things are taken away by governments.

I have a slightly more benign view of government. I think government can be the source of much good in society; if done right, it gives us the ability to help those who need help. But conservatives worry that governments do more harm than good. Often, they consider government to be corrupt and evil.

Anyway, to ensure that I'm accurately describing what con-servatives feel about government, I found some pretty good quotes. They were about what a conservative is and what freedom is, and they were spoken by former Canadian Conservative prime minister John Diefenbaker. Around my house as I was growing up, we held Dief in pretty high regard, even though we were all Liberals. He was a Conservative, but he was also a *progressive* conservative. When he died in 1979, I remember my dad getting a bit misty-eyed: coming from the prairies, Diefenbaker appreciated the things that government could, and should, do for the citizens they serve. Here's what the giant of Canadian conservatism said: "Freedom is the right to be wrong, not the right to do wrong."

If you were to ask Diefenbaker's ideological heirs in Ottawa today if they still believe those words, they wouldn't hesitate. They would say *yes*: this is the credo by which we still live. Absolutely. Freedom, freedom, freedom: it's the word they use the most. Freedom is important to them.

And I'd say: "Tell that to Awish Aslam." Aslam, as quite a few Canadians learned in the spring of 2011, was a University of Western Ontario student. She didn't look very scary. Maybe a hundred pounds, soaking wet. She wore a veil, and she wasn't white. One Sunday during the election campaign, Aslam and a friend went to a Conservative Party rally in London, Ontario. They signed up to attend the event with the assistance of the friend's father, who was a Conservative supporter. About thirty minutes after their arrival, a party organizer carrying a clipboard asked the pair to step out to talk. A burly RCMP officer in a suit came, too.

The guy with the clipboard slipped away, and the police officer suddenly ripped the name tags off the two girls. "You are no longer welcome here," he said.

When they asked why—Aslam, stunned, was crying—the Mountie said: "We know you have ties to the Liberal Party through Facebook." And then he kicked them out.

It turns out Aslam—like a lot of young people—liked to

get her picture taken with well-known people, which she'd then post online. So when Aslam had had her picture taken with the Liberal Party's leader, she naturally put it up on the social networking site. The Conservative Party, or the RCMP (or both), saw that picture and decided Aslam and her friend were a real and present danger to, um, *something*. Agents of the governing Conservatives, or agents of the federal police force (or both), had been creeping a kid's Facebook profile. I'm not making this up, as much as I wish I was.

What was surprising about all of this—what was jaw-droppingly shocking, truth be told—was that conservatives and Conservatives always like to claim that theirs is the ideology of freedom. Freedom of religion. Freedom of the press. Freedom of speech. Conservatives will always say—as no less than John Diefenbaker said once—they believe in freedom of speech and freedom of assembly. That would include, one assumes, the freedom to get your picture taken with a famous person (like Aslam did) and not be punished for it by a police officer.

If you are a conservative and you're reading this, you likely won't be so concerned that a party official wanted to eliminate the possibility of trouble-making at a Conservative rally. That's understandable, and plenty of conservative friends told me so. But if you are a conservative, small or large c, doesn't it worry you that the RCMP—gun-toting agents of the state, paid for by the taxpayers whom conservatives profess to respect—are behaving that way with a kid? Does it, in any way, sound like "freedom" to you?

☆ ☆ ☆

"Happiness is a trick."

That's what Greg Lyle, a conservative and a Conservative, said to me. It was spring, the birds were chirping, we were in cramped, smelly campaign room on the Left Coast, and Lyle—a veteran of countless conservative campaigns in Canada, the U.S. and Europe—had been explaining what separates conservatives (like him) from liberals (like me).

"Happiness is a trick," he repeated. "True conservatives know that. We plan for disaster, and are always pleasantly surprised when it doesn't happen."

Lyle continued as I listened, perplexed. He is a smart fellow, a pollster and a strategist, and we had come together— improbably—to toil on behalf of British Columbia Liberals. The B.C. Liberals, as I would shortly discover, weren't nearly as liberal as me, but political life is sometimes filled with such unpleasant surprises.

His battered shoes perched on his cluttered desktop, his hands clasped behind his head, Lyle smiled beatifically. If one believes that all of human existence is mean and miserly, as conservatives do, said Lyle, then one becomes understandably suspicious of governments or political parties bearing gifts. One becomes distrustful of anyone, in fact, who claims that true happiness is achievable, let alone plausible. It's every man (and man) for themselves, and one should generally order one's affairs to achieve maximum personal benefit. Anyone who believes otherwise is delusional—or worse, a liberal. Liberals are always chirping about the greater good, and always blithely asserting that happiness is achieved when the circumstances of every person are improved.

"But that's a crock," said Lyle. "Ask any conservative."

I was struck mute. It was 1996: I've toiled on many campaigns since, but I've yet to stumble upon as a pithy, or as accurate, a summation of the conservative credo than Greg Lyle's. There's a myriad of conservative species: theocons and neocons, movement conservatives, crunchy conservatives, paleoconservatives, fiscal conservatives, social conservatives, and so on and so on. But in Lyle's view, they are all brought together by a single, unifying notion. That happiness is unachievable. That it is a mirage. That it is, as he asserted, a trick.

When you understand that, perhaps, you understand quite a bit of what it means to be a conservative. (Parenthetically, it also explains why conservatives favour country music: it's the musical genre that takes the position that happiness is a ruse and that you shouldn't be surprised when shit happens. It's also the musical genre of white people who lack rhythm or self-awareness. In other words, conservatives.)

A lot of conservatives—not all of them, but enough of them—are miserable, and they consider it their divine role to make everyone else miserable, too. Conservatives are not happy, paradoxically, until their co-citizens are as unhappy as they are. If that sounds a bit uncharitable, then listen to the wisdom of Jonah Goldberg. Goldberg is the *sine qua non* of modern American conservatism, and he is the online editor of the conservative house organ, the *National Review*. He is also the son of Lucianne Goldberg, the Republican Party dirty trickster who conjured up the Monica Lewinsky scandal in order to topple the Goldbergs' hated nemesis, Bill Clinton.

"Conservatism," declares Goldberg, "in its most naked form is amoral."

As definitions go, I wouldn't change a word.

Certainly, as Goldberg notes, conservatism is more than simply amoral—and, ipso facto, the ideology of misery. There are certain key characteristics one can always ascribe to conservatism and conservatives, he says. Conservatives are also "deeply suspicious" about the power of the state. They prefer "liberty over equality." They are "patriots." They are attached to, and believe in, established institutions and hierarchies. They are "suspicious" about the idea of progress (conservatives, apparently, are suspicious a lot). Finally, Goldberg says, conservatives are "elitists." And an elitist merely accepts the notion that "some people are going to be better at a given thing than other people."

As a liberal, I interpret Goldberg's definition in this way: conservatives are solipsistic, sophistic snobs. They hate government working for the greater good. They hate change—but they love power, they love those fellow conservatives who exercise power, and they are generally indifferent to intolerance. And, per my friend Greg Lyle, conservatives cling to the view that happiness is a trick.

Now, at this point, you may be wondering why a book called *Fight the Right* is so preoccupied with the dimmest, dankest recesses of conservative craniums. You have dealt with conservatives; perhaps, you have battled conservatives. You know them. Why spend so much time labouring to define their joyless ideology and their parsimonious psychological profile? Simple. Because, per John Stuart Mill, you can't beat 'em until you know 'em.

The best way to stop losing, always, is to understand why the other guy keeps winning. When pondering the current ascendancy of the Right, it's positively crucial. Given the fact that the conservative voting base has historically always been smaller—and given the fact that progressives have traditionally been fortunate enough to count on two-thirds of citizens to lean their way—how is it that conservative causes increasingly dominate at all levels of government? How is it that they stole winning away from liberals? What do they think? More specifically, who are they?

If you were to sit down with a pile of dictionaries, and attempt to scrabble together a working definition of "conservative"— and its ideological reverse, "progressive"—you'd end up getting pretty frustrated pretty quickly. Incongruous definitions abound. For me, meanwhile, a progressive is a person who, as the moniker implies, accepts that things change, and that it is possible and indeed advisable to pilot the change in a direction that benefits the greatest number. Conservatives are the opposite. They deny change. They oppose change. They work to keep it from happening—or, at least, they work to ensure that change should reflect the priorities of an affluent few. Them, in other words.

Conservatives favour the status quo, another couple of words that may see you heading towards the dictionary. "Status quo": whatever it is, it doesn't exist, because the real world is in a continual state of flux. It's a Latin phrase, meaning the current state of affairs, the dominant reality. Logically, it's an impossibility, because current affairs are perpetually changing. Notwithstanding that, the conservative priority is to preserve it, but only the status quo as *they* see it.

Remember William F. Buckley Jr.? The conservative oracle? The Rightest Diety? In the inaugural issue of his hallowed conservative journal, the *National Review*, Buckley wrote that a conservative's purpose is to "stand athwart history, yelling stop." Coming from the conservative who is the *primus inter pares*, that is a definition to clip and tape to the fridge door. Conservatives are *against history*, sayeth he.

Now, a conservative would say that a liberal should never be asked to define a conservative. Liberals will always choose the definition that makes *them* look good, they'll say, and they've got a point. So let's go at our definitional task in a different way. Now that we have a broad definition of the conservatives, let's reverse-engineer it. Let's examine a set of issues, and then ascertain the conservative and liberal positions most commonly associated with them. When you think about it, in fact, one of the simplest ways to distinguish between a conservative and a liberal is to look at where they stand on the issues that matter to people. Here are some of the top ones, in alphabetical order.

ABORTION: We liberals and progressives believe that a woman has the right to decide what happens to her body. It's *her* body, after all. We also believe that governments should provide reasonable access to abortion. Many conservatives, meanwhile, don't. They don't think a woman has the right to choose what happens to her body. A lot of them believe a fetus—even one that is the product of incest and rape—is a person and deserves protection. And wherever it's happening, they want to defund government support for abortion. Thus, this from former governor Mike Huckabee during the 2008 presidential race: America has to import so many workers because "for the last thirty-five years we have aborted more than a million people who would have been in our workforce."

AFFIRMATIVE ACTION: We progressives know that there was discrimination and bigotry in our collective past. It's a fact. People were deprived of opportunities because of the colour of their skin, or their religion, or the way they looked or who they had sex with. Some people were slaves, in fact. So we believe that all of us—and all governments—have an obligation to make up for that and to make the day-to-day grind of existence a bit fairer. Conservatives, however, hate the idea of giving anyone a hand in landing a job or getting into a school. They think individuals should make it on their own, without any help from anyone at all. And they don't think the discrimination and bigotry that took place in the past has anything to do with them. To them, it's all just a lot of whining by whiners. Per Rick Santorum: "I don't want to make black people's lives better by giving them somebody else's money."

DEATH PENALTY: We liberals mostly think it doesn't work. To us, it's cruel and unusual punishment. And in an imperfect justice system, every execution carries with it the risk of killing an innocent person. Conservatives, naturally, like capital punishment a great deal. To them it isn't cruel, it isn't unusual, and it's what you deserve if you take a white person's life. And if mistakes get made? *Whatever.* So, for those who break the law by buying and smoking marijuana, Newt Gingrich declares: "I have made the decision that I love our children enough that we will kill you if you do this."

ECONOMY: For most of us liberals, a market economy is probably best—but we Liberals support a market economy in which government provides oversight, and which is amenable to change. Former Liberal Party leader John Turner had one of the pithiest descriptions of this position: "Capitalism with a big heart." Government needs to level the playing field, we believe, motivated by the public interest. Conservatives, on the other hand, think the unrestrained "free" market is the best way to go. They believe that the market shouldn't be burdened by much, or any, government interference. Let the market decide, they say. Businesses are smarter than people, they say. Thus, Ronald Reagan's timeless words of wisdom: "I am not worried about the deficit. It is big enough to take care of itself."

EDUCATION: Public schools and publicly funded schools are preferable—for students and for society. That's what we progressives generally think, even though some of us have been educated in both public and private systems. The focus needs to be on better test results, smaller class sizes, and a curriculum that is modern and progressive. Many cons, however, support vouchers to create market-style competition between schools. They don't like sex education, they don't like the liberal arts, and they want schools to be models of discipline (sometimes corporal discipline), where students are taught the basics and nothing else. It seems that if they could get away with it, some of them would also like to see prayer in public schools, and perhaps even a bit of bit of old-time segregation, too. This from the Cornerstone Church's Rev. John Hagee, who endorsed John McCain during the 2008 presidential race: "As soon as Jesus sits on his throne he's gonna rule the world with a rod of iron. That means he's gonna make the ACLU do what he wants them to. That means you're not gonna have to ask if you can pray in public school. We will live by the law of God and no other law."

ENERGY: Oil is a disappearing resource, and it isn't as clean as we'd like it to be, either. Progressives think governments need to encourage—and in some cases, subsidize—alternative energy sources, like wind, solar, biomass and so on. Conservatives, on the other hand, think burning coal is just fine—and they support drilling, mining and digging for resources wherever they might be found. Including in the middle of the ocean. Pipelines through wildlife preserves? No problem. Shipping oil in big tankers that can sink? Go for it. Opposing public involvement in any energy utility, ever, under any circumstances? Absolutely! Big oil companies should be permitted to charge whatever the market will bear, say cons, and those same companies should be taxed even less than average citizens. As Sarah Palin asked, fittingly, on Twitter: "Extreme Greenies: see now why we push 'drill, baby, drill' of known reserves & promising finds in safe onshore places like [the Alaska National Wildlife refuge]? Now do you get it?" Er, no.

GLOBAL WARMING: We progressives agree: climate change and extreme weather are largely caused by greater reliance on fossil fuels. They're caused by burning coal, oil and natural gas without regard to the consequences. Lots of folks on the Left think we need to reduce carbon emissions, urgently, if we are to save the planet for future generations. Conservatives, meanwhile, holler that climate change is bunk. They claim that global temperature changes are normal over time—and maintain that humans have little or no effect on how hot the Earth is. Consequently, rules to reduce carbon emissions are a waste of effort, and will only raise prices for industry. Thus, observes Rep. Michelle Bachmann: "Carbon dioxide is portrayed as harmful. But there isn't even one study that can be produced that shows that carbon dioxide is a harmful gas."

GUN CONTROL: Progressives—including progressive gun owners, like me—don't think citizens have a "right" to bear arms. Registering guns, and making them a lot harder to acquire, is simply smart public policy. It makes everyone safer. Gun control laws are favoured by victims and by police agencies: they know best, generally, and we should listen to them. Cons feel otherwise. They have a libidinal fixation with guns, and have convinced themselves that they possess a constitutional right to purchase machine guns for hunting ducks and/or self-protection from non-existent threats. They despise gun control. They reiterate ad nauseam that guns don't kill people; people kill people. In the immortal words of a speaker at the 1995 convention of the U.S. Taxpayers Party: "This Christmas, I want you to do the most loving thing and I want you to buy each of your children an SKS rifle and five hundred rounds of ammunition!"

IMMIGRATION: Legal immigration is good, we on the Left think, and it is essential for the society we hope to build. Immigrants should have the rights of other citizens, and it is wrong to malign or penalize immigrants and bona fide refugees. But conservatives think we need to seal off our borders, and kick out (or jail) anyone they deem to be here illegally.

A lot of conservatives also favour only permitting entry to those who look and sound like them, so as to not to alter—as no less than Canadian Prime Minister Stephen Harper once delicately put it in a policy statement—our "ethnic makeup." Describing his fellow citizens in the 2008 presidential race, here's former U.S. Senator Fred Thompson: "Twelve million illegal immigrants later, we are now living in a nation that is beset by people who are suicidal maniacs and want to kill countless innocent men, women and children around the world."

PROPERTY: In the U.S. they call it "eminent domain"; in the Commonwealth, expropriation, compulsory purchase or acquisition. Whatever you call it, the basic idea is the same, and it's one that we liberals generally support: governments should be able to use the law, sparingly and fairly, to acquire property to build things like roads, bridges, hospitals, schools and so on. Conservatives claim to oppose expropriation, saying that an individual's property rights should come before the greater good. (When in government, however, they seem to observe this one more in spirit than in practice.) Revealingly, here is far-Right kook author Ayn Rand on land claims by Aboriginal peoples: "They had no right to a country merely because they were born here and then acted like savages."

RELIGION: We progressives support the separation of church and state—even church-going progressives, like me. We don't think religious expressions have any place in anything that government does. Nor should governments involve themselves in anything that religious organizations do. That means no prayer in the classroom, no prayer in the legislature and no state funding for any religious institution. Conservatives, who were the target of a non-hostile takeover by sectarian lobbyists a couple decades ago, are now wholly in the sway of far-right religionists. Theirs is the Party of God. Per their relentless harridan, Ann Coulter: "Go forth, be fruitful, multiply, and rape the planet—it's yours."

SAME-SEX MARRIAGE: Marriage, we liberals think, is the union of two adults who love each other. It doesn't matter if you're straight, gay, lesbian, bisexual or transgendered: if you're of legal age, we think you should be able to get married if you want to. Period. Conservatives, meanwhile, think marriage should be available only to straight folks. They claim their position is validated by Christian, Jewish and Muslim law (see "Religion," above). Here's subtle conservative televangelist Jerry Falwell: "AIDS is the wrath of a just God against homosexuals. To oppose it would be like an Israelite jumping in the Red Sea to save one of Pharaoh's charioteers. . . . AIDS is not just God's punishment for homosexuals; it is God's punishment for the society that tolerates homosexuals."

SOCIAL SECURITY: There's all sorts of names for the concept— national pension plans, national insurance, security, what have you—but the basic idea is the same: a safety net for a nation's elderly, poor and needy. Liberals believe our social safety net needs to be protected. Conservatives, however, think it all costs too much and it isn't "viable" anymore. As with many things, conservatives want to privatize government pension plans and let individuals manage their own savings. When that doesn't happen, they kvetch about the system being ripe with "fraud," even when it isn't. Former Republican presidential nomination challenger Rick Perry on this: "[Social Security] is a Ponzi scheme. . . . Anybody that's for the status quo with Social Security today is involved with a monstrous lie to our kids, and it's not right."

TAXES: Progressives don't hate taxes; they consider them necessary, albeit hard to love. Taxes pay for the things that government needs to do. And for the most part, liberals believe those who *have* more should *pay* a bit more. As billionaire Warren Buffet put it, it doesn't make sense that the billionaire pays tax at a lower rate than his secretary does. Conservatives, of course, are horrified by the suggestion that taxation rates should be fairer and that billionaires should pay a fairer share. And more than anything else, they always, always think tax cuts are the way to go: if businesses pay less tax, they say, then they'll hire more people, and people will spend more. A quote for the ages, from George H. W. Bush in 1988: "The Congress will push me to raise taxes, and I'll say no, and they'll push, and I'll say no; they'll push again and I'll say to them, read my lips, no new taxes." (And then, er, he did.)

UNITED NATIONS: Progressives feel we need the United Nations, despite its occasional flaws: it promotes peace and human rights, and it provides a forum for nations to debate and decide important stuff. Moreover, it attempts to act as a useful counterbalance to so-called superpowers that often run roughshod over the less powerful. Conservatives, on the other hand, despise the U.N. In their view, the U.N. is a forum for despots and tyrants, a waste of money, and the precursor to One World Government, statism and all that sort of thing. A lot of them favour withdrawing from the world body entirely. Their preference: war. "The only way to reduce the number of nuclear weapons is to use them," says the former drug addict and radio personality Rush Limbaugh.

WAR ON TERROR: To not a few of us progressives, the euphemistic "war on terror" has become little more than a war on civil liberties, tolerance and the rule of law. Western governments, in particular, have used the terrible crimes of September 11, 2001, as a pretext for militarism and a greatly expanded police state. Internationally, the war on terror has been used as justification for wars that were illegal (as in Iraq) or unwinnable (as in Afghanistan). Conservatives, however, believe terrorism is the number one threat facing the West, and that peace with Islam is impossible. They favour prosecuting the terrorists they capture in military courts, not civilian ones. Meanwhile, conservatives delight in using the war on terror to swing at the dusky-skinned folks who don't share their faith. Sarah Palin, their muse, speaking on Twitter to Ground Zero mosque opponents: "Doesn't it stab you in the heart, as it does ours throughout the heartland? Peaceful Muslims, pls refudiate." Um, *refudiate?*

WELFARE: Progressives support it—because it's a safety net for the poor, and because it quite literally keeps many disadvantaged folks from living on the street, even starving. Conservatives are of the view that welfare robs people of their incentive to work and is subject to widespread abuse and fraud. It is more "compassionate," they insist, to let people be self-reliant. Conservative extremists like the Ontario Landowners Association—two of whose leaders are now Conservative members of the Ontario legislature—ardently oppose welfare, and also its equivalents, which they call "Native, Arts, Homosexual, Urban and Multi cultures."

You could add many more issues to the list, but the ones above are the biggies—the debates that take place, just about daily, in every legislature and newspaper, TV or radio broadcast. The thread woven through all of the above-noted conservative points of view, if you reflect on it, is the notion that humans are intrinsically *bad*. That, collectively, people cannot be trusted to do good. And that it is only individuals—conservative individuals—who possess the moral compass to lead us all to a better society. This, more than any other idea, is central to every true conservative's world view. We are born bad, they believe, and it is only through rigid adherence to certain time-tested conservative principles that we can lift ourselves out of the liberal darkness, and come to possess a big car, a big house and a big stock portfolio.

Let me explain. Or, again, let my friend George explain.

☆ ☆ ☆

Born bad?

George Lakoff, professor and smart guy, quickly agrees. I've just asked him about the theory that, to Thomas Hobbes and Niccolò Machiavelli and like-minded conservatives, human beings are mostly "born bad." In effect, that they are stink-o, right from the get-go.

"Well," he says, sounding amused by that, "conservatives have a hard line. They believe that liberals are people who just don't have any morality. That is, they are called 'feel-good liberals' because they simply do what feels good—just like a baby does what feels good. And their view of babies, of course, is that babies have to be disciplined when they're bad."

He continues, attempting to make sense of what, to a sane person, sounds completely insane. "In fact," he says of conservatives, "[they believe] the only way babies can become moral beings is for them to be punished when they are bad. So whether they are born bad—or they are just born to do what feels good, which is not moral—they have to be *made* moral in that way. So their view of the liberals is like that. Liberals are not moral. They haven't learned proper morals, because they haven't been properly disciplined."

Now, Lakoff wouldn't be the first scientist to suggest that the way in which we are raised determines what we are to become—per the Jesuits, who taught guys like me, "Give us the child until he is seven, and we will give you the man." But what distinguishes Lakoff from his peers (and the Jesuits) is that he is prepared to say things that others simply can't, or won't. (That, and he is unashamed of being branded a progressive in a country that, increasingly, is going the other way.) In his bestseller *The Political Mind*, he expanded on this "born bad" notion, memorably noting: "In conservative thought, people are born bad—greedy and unscrupulous. To maximize their self-interest, they need to learn discipline, to follow the rules and obey laws. . . . [The system] rewards those who acquire such discipline and punishes those who do not."

That notion is at the very centre of every conservative's solipsistic universe, Lakoff says: conservatives learn the importance of rules and laws at their father's knees—ideally, a strict father's knee. Conservatives obdurately cling to the notion that the best family is the most traditional one. A father who protects and provides for the wife and children, a wife who raises the kids and takes care of the homestead, and children who unthinkingly obey the parents—and Dad in particular. To conservatives, this sort of discipline breeds character and success. Lakoff acknowledges that love and empathy are arguably found in conservative-style families, but those sorts of things can "never outweigh parental authority."

And why is authority so important? Well, let Rudy Giuliani, deep-thinking conservative philosopher, answer that one: "Freedom is *about* authority." If that sounds rather oxymoronic to you, chances are pretty good that you are a liberal, like me. How can one ever achieve "freedom" in an environment where "authority" is paramount? Isn't that, well, a bit contradictory? Isn't freedom the *absence* of authority?

Lakoff explains that, in the Strict Father Club to which all true conservatives belong, the things that are most important are associated with moral strength. Self-control and self-discipline, he says, are important, because they help to conquer evil from within and without. Also important: respect for authority, obedience and behavioural norms. Only when those sorts of things are observed, conservatives believe, is anyone then free to pursue their own self-interest. When society's rules are obeyed, everyone benefits. To wit, you can't achieve freedom without first having achieved authority.

Liberals, Lakoff patiently explains, believe in family, too—but they have a radically different take on the subject. Liberal families nurture, Lakoff says, and "nurturance requires empathy for others, and the helping of those who need help." Conservatives despise "empathy," it turns out—both the word, and the concept. They regard it as weakness, says Lakoff. When asked about empathy, and its relationship to conservatives and their politics, Lakoff will provide you with an exhaustive and detailed explanation of how neuron systems and the prefrontal cortex operate. But when describing the conservative approach to empathy, he's pretty straightforward. Conservatives "misrepresent empathy. The misrepresentation is that empathy is like sympathy, which is very different. They believe that, if you have empathy, you have to be in favour of the person who is in front of you, even if it goes against your better judgment. That's their characterization of empathy, and it's utterly false."

Empathy, and what it means, has been mooted quite a bit by progressives and conservatives in recent years. That's because it is a word that neatly delineates the progressive and the conservative world views. No less than Barack Obama has spoken about the principle of empathy many times, in speeches and interviews. In one 2008 media encounter, for example, the presidential candidate was asked what was the best thing his mother—a single mom—ever taught him. Said Obama: "Empathy. Making sure you can see the world through someone else's eyes, stand in their shoes. I think that's the basis for kindness and compassion." But that's not all it is, of course. In an interview around the same time with CNN's Anderson Cooper, Obama returned to the subject and explicitly linked empathy to patriotism. "The core of patriotism," he said, "is, are we caring for each other? Are we willing to sacrifice on behalf of future generations?"

Obama's conception of empathy—that it is kind, that it is compassionate, that it even relates to patriotism and your relationship to your country—was central to a speech he gave for Father's Day in that same year, 2008. There, Obama identified nurturing, loving families as the source of one's empathic impulses, and not, apparently, strict and authoritarian families. "The thing we need to do, as fathers, is pass along the value of empathy to our children," Obama, then still a senator, told his hometown Chicago audience. "Not sympathy, but empathy— the ability to stand in somebody else's shoes; to look at the world through their eyes. Sometimes it's so easy to get caught up in 'us,' that we forget about our obligations to one another. There's a culture in our society that says remembering these obligations is somehow soft—that we can't show weakness, and so therefore we can't show kindness.

"But our young boys and girls see that. They see when you are ignoring or mistreating your wife. They see when you are inconsiderate at home; or when you are distant; or when you are thinking only of yourself. And so it's no surprise when we see that behavior in our schools or on our streets. That's why we pass on the values of empathy and kindness to our children by living them. We need to show our kids that you're not strong by putting other people down—you're strong by lifting them up. That's our responsibility as fathers."

And not, it goes without saying, just fathers. It's the responsibility of *every* member of society, if that society is to succeed.

True progressives know and understand that empathy and kindness are not weakness. They are strength. When all are lifted up, so, too, will be the society they create. And that is why empathy is central to a functioning, flourishing democracy.

Questioned about that, Lakoff provides one of the most useful explanations for how conservatives and liberals are fundamentally different. "You can have empathy for people who have lost their jobs. You can have empathy for people who have been injured. You can have empathy for veterans who have come back from the war with post-traumatic stress syndrome, and so on. You can have general empathy, in general cases, and not just for the person who is in front of you.

"That's what empathy is about. That's what Obama talks about in his speeches. And what Obama has correctly pointed out is that democracy is really based on empathy. Democracy has to do with citizens caring about other citizens. It has to do with having a government that protects and empowers everybody equally. That is what the public is. That's what empathy is."

Individuals, conservatives would have us believe, are the source of all greatness. But if you think about that, you know that it just isn't so. No one individual, Lakoff observes, is responsible for the roads and the bridges the businessperson uses to get to work, or the airport that allows them to go to meetings and make money and generate wealth. It is citizens, working *together*—along with government, protecting and empowering folks—who make those things, and thereby foster success. Coming together (as the public, for lack of a better word), we achieve greater things than we can on our own. That's not all: we are, indeed, our brother's and sister's keeper, and greatness can only be realized, suggests Lakoff, if we accept that and act upon it. Says Lakoff: "You can't make it in America, or any Western democracy, without the public."

George Lakoff pauses, as the music at the café is heard again.

He sighs. Liberals and progressives, he says, don't think about these things nearly enough. They don't do enough about these things—like basing a political campaign on them, for example. Conversely, Lakoff says, conservatives understand all too well how to talk about family, and values, and the importance of "authority." They do it all the time. And that, more than any other reason, is why the strict father stuff is now seen at work across Western democracy. Conservatives rule, and conservatives are putting their stamp on government.

☆ ☆ ☆

They're wily, these conservatives. They're good at masking their intentions. They pacify and they pander, using focus-grouped TV ads (paid for by taxpayers) and soothing talking points expertly prepared by conservative propagandists (ditto). It's hard to pin them down; it's hard to see who they truly are. They're veritable conservative chameleons, most days.

Unless you have a camera, that is.

In the fall of 2009, a young University of Toronto law student, Justin Tetreault, was invited to a Conservative Party rally at the Canadian Bushplane Heritage Centre in Sault Ste. Marie. Tetreault is an energetic young Liberal, and the organizers knew that, but they invited him anyway. Tetreault brought along his Canon PowerShot, and he wore a name tag that clearly identified who he was. Stephen Harper was there, too, to talk to his fellow Conservatives—and, presumably, Tetreault—about how conservatives can win.

As Harper may have been contemplating that fall, winning elections was something the Liberal Party of Canada used to be quite good at. Federal Liberals had held power for sixty-nine years in the last century, making the party the most successful political entity in the developed world. It was, truly, the natural governing party. The Liberal Party saw its principal opponent, the Conservatives, as a disputatious, mutinous, self-destructive bunch of losers, unfit for government. They didn't seem to believe in anything, or at least in anything coherent.

Around 2009 or so, the parties' respective roles in the Canadian political psychodrama started to change. Around the time that Justin Tetreault was powering up his Canon PowerShot, it was the Conservatives—with their iron communications discipline and their relentlessly strategic leader—who were starting to seem unbeatable. And it was the Liberals—still not fully recovered from a decade-long tribal war, and on their fifth leader in eight years—who were falling behind. The losers.

The Canadian Cons were starting to dominate the Canadian Grits on every political criteria that counts: fundraising, popular support, and (since 2006) elections. While not invincible, they certainly looked like winners. There were many reasons for this. Harper's social conservatism had been curbed, however temporarily, by the exigencies of minority government, and Canada still had abortion, gay marriage and a separation of church and state. On the economy, too, circumstances were obliging Harper to eschew his Reform Party roots. The great global recession of 2008–2009 saw the Conservative leader—the one-time president of the National Citizens Coalition, no less—transformed into a conventional pork-barrelling pol, merrily dishing out billions on hockey rinks and road paving. Meanwhile, all the dark warnings about health care, human rights and other government programs largely seemed to come to naught. Without a clear majority in the House of Commons, Harper would have been foolhardy to start remaking the country in his party's image. So he waited. He didn't stop being a hard-core conservative— he just became a *patient* hard-core conservative.

For a decade and a bit, Liberals had kept Harper and his acolytes far from power by publicizing every boneheaded and bigoted utterance by members of the Reform Party, and depicting its leaders as Albertacentric rageaholics. Harper therefore purged most of the homophobic, xenophobic red-necked mouth-breathers—and cultivated a phony but effective Tim Hortons Everyman populism, reminding everyone who would listen that he grew up in suburban Toronto, not conservative Calgary.

As much as he tried, by necessity, to seem moderate and reasonable and centrist—to show that he had become, in the immortal phrasing of Bush Sr., a kinder, gentler conservative—Canadian voters were still wary of Harper. As much as the Conservative leader tried to persuade Canadians that he could be trusted with a majority, they declined his advances.

By 2009, however, the Conservatives looked increasingly like a party preparing itself for an election campaign. Their protestations to the contrary, they were clearly sniffing about for an excuse to drop the election writ. I couldn't really blame them: there was well-founded concern that the global recession was going to get worse—and that newly minted Liberal leader Michael Ignatieff was going to get more popular. The Conservative election machine could be seen warming up at events all over the country, like the one in Sault Ste. Marie attended by Justin Tetreault.

At that time, I was the head of the federal Liberal Party's war room, and—as such—I had occasion to communicate with Justin. He wasn't a member of the team, but I knew him and I admired his energetic liberalism. He was smart, he was creative, and he was prepared to do what it takes to defeat Stephen Harper. Not surprisingly, I liked him. So, as Harper started to speak on September 2, 2009—perhaps unaware or perhaps not caring that a young Liberal had been invited to listen in—Justin Tetreault captured his words.

"Let me be clear about this," said Harper on the tape. "We need to win a majority in the next election campaign. I am not just saying that because we need a few more seats. We saw what happened last year. Do not be fooled for a moment. If we do not get a majority, the Liberals, the NDP and the Bloc Québécois will combine and they will form a government. They will deny this until they're blue in the face in an election campaign, but I guarantee it. If we do not win a majority, this country will have a Liberal government propped up by the socialists and the separatists."

He continued, his index finger jabbing away:"This country cannot afford a government like that. If they force us to the polls, if they get together and force us to the polls, we have to teach them a lesson and get back there with a majority to make sure their little coalition never happens . . . And, friends, I believe that government is within reach."

He went on like that for a while, as Tetreault happily collected the evidence. A Liberal government propped up by "the socialists and separatists," hissed Harper, as the assembled Conservatives presumably reeled in horror. "Imagine how many left-wing ideologues they would be putting in the courts, federal institutions, agencies, the Senate. I should say, how many *more* they would be putting in." Harper ranted on, declaring that a Liberal government would also create a "bloated bureaucracy" to run a national daycare program, institute a "carbon tax" and raise other taxes, peddle "soft on crime" policies, and—this was my favourite part—provide support for "left-wing fringe groups" to mount court challenges. By "left-wing fringe groups," he meant *women's* groups. (To emphasize the point, one Parliament Hill Liberal staffer, my friend Lisa Kirbie, established a robust online feminist presence to draw attention to Harper's words, called Not a Left-Wing Fringe Group.)

So give me a majority, Harper said. A majority would "teach them a lesson."

Well, lessons would be taught, all right, but not necessarily to Liberals. A few hours after Harper's speech, Tetreault reached me in Ottawa, where I was staying for part of every week in preparation for an election campaign that could come at any time. "I've got something big," he said, sounding a bit nervous. He certainly did.

Tetreault recalls: "I knew immediately when I was listening to [Harper's] speech that I had something big. He was discussing topics that were usually off-limits and talking about them in a way I had never heard him talk about them before. At first when he started talking about how the Court Challenges Program had been used by 'left-wing fringe groups,' I thought the tape could be useful and decided that I should send it to the [Liberal Party], but then Harper kept going: the need to cancel the gun registry, how the Liberals had filled the Senate and courts with left-wing ideologues, and finally his plea for a majority to prevent Canada from a Liberal government propped up by the 'socialists' and 'separatists.'"

The political significance of Harper's mistake was immediately apparent, Tetreault says. "I knew right away that Harper was making a big mistake. He had spent so much time recrafting his image as the sweater-wearing, kitten-loving, non-hidden-agenda-having prime minister and this speech was a return to the angry and spiteful Stephen Harper that Canadians didn't like. I mean, he literally said that if the opposition parties forced Canadians to the polls, the Conservatives would have to make them pay."

The tape was a bombshell, blowing to smithereens the compassionate conservatism Harper had been putting on display since winning a minority in 2006. I got in touch with Terry Milewski of CBC News and told him about the tape. A day later (much to the chagrin of other media outlets), CBC blasted what we called the "hidden agenda tape" all over the place. It dominated the news for days, and soon Stephen Harper could be seen furiously backpedalling away from the rumoured election call. On cue, conservative commentators chimed in, suddenly agreeing that the fall of 2009 was no time for an election. The election that had seemed inevitable wasn't all that inevitable anymore. In an election campaign TV spot, Justin Tetreault's little tape would have been devastating, and the Conservative cabal knew it. So they backed off.

But beyond its potential in an election campaign, Tetreault's tape was noteworthy for this reason: it provided a glimpse into the innermost soul of Stephen Harper and his fellow Conservatives. It showed them as they truly were: antigovernment, anticourts, anti–public servants, anti-environment, antichildren, antiwomen, anti-just-about-everything. It was revealing, and it was all right there on film.

In every election campaign these days, political operatives can been seen quietly doing what young Justin Tetreault did. Intent on capturing an opponent's misstep, they are ever more turning to technology to capture mistakes made when the mainstream news media aren't present—as Shekar Ramanuja Sidarth did with the Republican golden boy, George Allen.

George Allen's tale goes back to 2006, when he was seeking re-election to the U.S. Senate as the Republican standard-bearer. The former president of Young Virginians for Ronald Reagan was facing off against two opponents, but his main opponent was the Democrats' nominee, former secretary of the navy James H. Webb. Allen was widely seen as a possible future presidential candidate, and he assiduously sought the support of so-called cultural conservatives—that is, those traditional folks who want to preserve "one culture for one nation." Meaning, they're not fussy about foreigners, particularly foreigners who don't look like them. Allen was their (white, Christian) man.

One young man who didn't look like Allen, but who knew a great deal about him, was Shekar Ramanuja Sidarth. At the time, Sidarth—who also answers to Sid—was a straight-A senior at the University of Virginia. He was Virginia-born and -raised, and a Hindu. Though he was studying engineering, politics was what interested him the most. He'd volunteered on a few Democratic campaigns and by 2006 he was devoting himself to James Webb's Senate battle. His role was to be what I call a "road warrior": following around Webb's opponent with a camcorder like the one Justin Tetreault would use. He'd capture misstatements or mistakes, and then relay them back to the central campaign in Arlington. This went on for a few weeks, and while Allen's people didn't particularly like Sidarth following them around, they didn't do anything to stop him, and mostly treated him courteously.

Early in August, however, at a Friday afternoon event in a park near the Kentucky border, Allen did something he hadn't done before: he singled Sidarth out. He pointed at him. "This fellow here, over here with the yellow shirt, *macaca* or whatever his name is, he's with my opponent," said Allen, who had been raised in California. "So welcome, let's give a welcome to *macaca* here! Welcome to America and the real world of Virginia!" The crowd cheered, even though some of them knew, or suspected, that George Allen had just used a disgusting slur. "Macaca" means "monkey," and it has also been infamously used to describe African immigrants. Sidarth, who knew what the word meant, was shocked. On the resulting footage, you could see that his hand was shaking. He later said that he felt humiliated.

As with most such things in politics these days, the clip of Allen calling Sidarth a dark-skinned monkey eventually ended up on YouTube. Sidarth didn't upload it himself, but he wasn't upset about what would happen next. "This event," he said, "reflected on Allen's character."

It indisputably did, and it would also indisputably destroy Allen's political career. A few hours after the event, Sidarth called the Webb campaign's headquarters in Arlington to tell them what he had, and they sat on it over the weekend. A *Washington Post* reporter, who wasn't sure it was news, wrote a short item about the "macaca" statement, and with a news media pretext thus provided, the Webb campaign then uploaded the video to YouTube. Within hours the story went supernova. Very soon, many other stories were written, alleging yet more bigoted statements or behaviour by Webb. The conservative Great White Hope denied it all, of course, but he started to lose his double-digit lead in the polls, and he never regained his footing. In November 2006, Allen lost to Webb by nearly 10,000 votes, his once-unstoppable multi-million-dollar campaign effectively felled by a quiet young man with a camcorder. Even in the old Confederate-era stronghold of Dickenson County, where Allen had made his racist remark, Webb picked up more votes.

It was an important progressive victory because Allen's loss literally changed the face of U.S. politics. It shifted control of the Senate and, two years later, the same Virginians would help elect Barack Obama to the presidency. Recalling that day, Sidarth says Allen's actions "stood out because they were not representative of how I was treated while travelling around the state. Everywhere I went, though I was identifiably working on behalf of Allen's opponent, people treated me with dignity, respect and kindness." Republicans were among those who treated him in a neighbourly fashion, Sidarth recalled, sometimes even sharing food with him at rallies. But after Allen's comments, Sidarth's background became more of a focus than ever before. "After Allen's remarks, my heritage suddenly became a matter of widespread interest. I am proud to be a second-generation Indian American and a practising Hindu.

My parents were born and raised in India and immigrated here more than twenty-five years ago; I have known no home other than Northern Virginia.

"The fact that Allen believed I was an immigrant, when in fact I am a native Virginian, underlines the problems our society still faces. Then again, Webb's victory last week gives me hope that Virginia will not tolerate playing the race card," says Sidarth, now a law student. "The politics of division just don't work anymore. Nothing made me happier on election night than finding out the results from Dickenson County, where Allen and I had our encounter.

"Webb won there, in what I can only hope was a vote to deal the race card out of American politics once and for all."

☆ ☆ ☆

Defining conservatism, and identifying conservatives, is—as noted—no simple task. Conservatives, then, might be best defined by what they are *against* (taxes, and government, and human rights). Or, maybe, by what they are *for* (more religion, more guns, more privatization of things like health care). Or perhaps some of them should be judged for what they say about young people like Awish Aslam or Shekar Ramanuja Sidarth—or what they say when they think no one outside the fold is listening, and when young people like Justin Tetreault are there to capture their words. Any way you slice it, the picture that emerges isn't a particularly flattering one.

Are they amoral, as the conservative Jonah Goldberg contends? Do they regard happiness as a trick, as Greg Lyle told me? Are they better defined by their stance on the issues of the day, the ones about which they (maddeningly) never waver? Do they actually believe we are all born bad, as George Lakoff suggests, and do they wholly lack empathy for others? Good questions, all. If you were undecided about your political bent and you've got this far in this book, you now have a pretty good sense if you are a conservative or not.

And if you're a liberal, like me, you want to know how to beat 'em.

2

HOW A CONSERVATIVE THINKS
(OR DOESN'T)

Conservative behavioural patterns—the things
conservatives do, over and over.
Conservatives are creatures of habit. While they may profess to
embrace change, and while some may even call themselves
"progressives," the reality is that they are resolutely in favour
of only the conservative status quo. They squash progressive change,
and differences, whenever they manifest themselves.
An examination, herein, of the principal conservative behaviour,
and how it assists one in classifying their species.

———

C onservatives don't like *differences.*

You know: ideas that are different. Policies that are different. And in particular, conservatives dislike people who are different—from themselves, from what they consider to be "normal." Conservatives don't like those kinds of people at all. Perhaps the truest expression of the conservative zeitgeist is that they abhor anyone and anything that is different from them, and from what they consider to be the familiar and the ordinary.

Now, as I said a few pages back, their philosophy is often difficult to pin down. It wiggles like a loose tooth. But their antipathy to differences—different people, different cultures, different ways of doing things—is clear. They dislike differences. They fear differences. If homogeneity was a political party, they'd vote for it.

Let me give you a couple of important examples, which I witnessed up close, as bookends to the fiercely contested Ontario provincial election campaign of 2011. They are revealing little tales about how conservatives, and Conservatives, regard and react to those who are different from them.

Here's the first sad tale: in the Liberal platform we had a sentence on page 25 that became a great big raging controversy, attracting media attention from all over. Here's what it said: "We'll create a tax credit for business to give our highly skilled newcomers the Canadian work experience they need." That's it. Nineteen well-intentioned words, and that's all it said. Immigration is good for a modern society, we Liberals figured, and we therefore need to make sure our newest citizens gain the experience they need to succeed. From our perspective, qualified accountants and lawyers shouldn't be driving cabs or flipping burgers. They should instead be given the opportunity to beef up their language skills so they can be productive citizens, pay their taxes, and get ahead. The program, a tax credit for employers, would cost a few million bucks and help a few hundred new Canadian citizens yearly. No biggie.

We announced this in the first week of September, just as the 2011 campaign was getting underway. We didn't think the idea was a terribly controversial one, seeing as how our main opponent, the Progressive Conservatives, had pushed for a very similar program the year before. But the day after our platform made its debut, the Conservatives went nuts.

The Conservative leader, Tim Hudak, sneered that the program was rigged to favour "foreign workers." Within hours of our platform launch, he and his minions had issued a Republican-style ad on YouTube and unveiled a slick website, both falsely claiming that the idea would see ten thousand dollars handed to "foreign workers" while "YOU GET THE BILL." His candidates cheerfully picked up the refrain. One, Andrea Mandel-Campbell (running in Toronto) claimed that the whole thing was a "foreign worker subsidy." Another right-winger, Alan Wilson, declared: "[We should] be focusing on our own people here getting jobs." When questioned by the media, an Ottawa-area Conservative standard-bearer, Randall Denley, conceded that the "foreigners" his party was targeting were "people who come from other countries." And one of the so-called star Conservative candidates, Jane McKenna, actually said: "When did we become for immigrants?"

It was worse than disgusting; it was sick, in fact. These Conservatives were calling Canadian citizens—not refugees, *citizens*—foreigners. They didn't openly define foreigners as people who were black, brown or yellow, but they didn't need to. Everyone knew what they meant. That kind of xenophobia— that kind of racism, frankly—hadn't been observed in a Canadian election campaign in a long, long time. Even guys like me, who intensely detested the Hudak Conservatives, could not believe they would sink so low. But they had.

Liberals, naturally, didn't like what the Conservatives were saying. Neither did the few remaining liberal media outlets following the campaign. But what was surprising (and encouraging, even) was that a few pundits working at *conservative* papers were pretty unimpressed, too. Some reacted with amazement to Hudak's racist pandering. In the *National Post*—ground zero for most Canadian conservatives—one columnist called

Hudak's ploy "foreign worker nonsense," and suggested the Conservatives need to provide clarity on "exactly how long must someone born outside of Canada, but now a citizen, spend in the province before they stop being a foreigner and start being Ontarian?" Another *Post* columnist, John Ivison, wrote that Hudak's "foreigner" attacks "distort not only the facts but the scale of the program," adding that it showed the Cons were "not ready for prime time." Across town, a writer in the *Globe and Mail*—another right-leaning paper—suggested that Hudak came off as "glib and snarly, like a caricature of an opposition politician" who uses "carnival-style props [and] a striking degree of negativity." Up the highway, in the pages of the right-wing *Ottawa Citizen*—where the Cons had even recruited a columnist to run as one of their star candidates— another respected opinion-maker, Dan Gardner, said this episode revealed the Conservatives' racialist stance: "Tim Hudak is the sort of politician who searches for the inchoate fears and hatreds that lie, unspoken, just below the surface of consciousness. When he finds them, he drags them up and waves them for all to see, hoping that ugly emotions will serve his political purposes." Ouch: Gardner had, at one time, worked as a provincial Conservative staffer.

To everyone's surprise, some of Hudak's predecessors—true *progressives* who had been mostly driven out by far-right elements in their party—publicly expressed their opposition to the ugliness that completely hijacked the early days of the election campaign. The last sitting Progressive Conservative Premier, Ernie Eves, suggested that Hudak's rightward lurch had fostered a "Tea Party version of Ontario politics." Meanwhile, Hudak's immediate predecessor, John Tory, also condemned the Conservative race-baiting strategy, saying it was "pandering to the worst emotions of envy, jealousy and insecurity about so-called foreigners." Unsurprisingly, we

Liberals made sure that as many people as possible heard what these atypical progressive conservatives had said.

The far-right Hudak Conservatives, however, were undeterred. Day after day, they gleefully hammered away at foreigners and bald-facedly lied about what the Liberal program would mean. In their advertising, in their daily messaging, in every speech at every campaign stop, Hudak and his detestable crew of advisors stubbornly stuck to the chauvinistic script. Only when polling showed that the Conservatives were obliterating whatever chances they had in urban centres, where there was a lot of ethnic diversity, did they abandon their vile tactic. But they weren't done with bigotry, not by a long shot. They still had a few things to say about people who were different from them.

On the final weekend of the month-long ordeal, Conservative campaigners started to quietly distribute leaflets that suggested the race-baiting hadn't been inadvertent. The leaflets made clear that Conservatives were aggressively pursuing a strategy designed to stir up feelings of ill-will against just about anyone who looked, or acted, different. One of the flyers was lifted entirely from an advertisement an evangelical Christian group placed in two conservative-tilting newspapers, featuring a wide-eyed child under the banner: "Please! Don't confuse me." It falsely stated that the provincial sexual education curriculum taught children how to be "transsexual, transgendered, intersexed or two-spirited." After the ad ran, the *National Post*, to its credit, apologized "unreservedly," saying "the ad exceeded the bounds of civil discourse" through its manipulative use of imagery and "in the suggestion that such teaching 'corrupts' children." The paper declared that it would donate the money it received for the ad to a lesbian, gay or transgendered cause. (The newspaper chain I write a column for, Sun Media, ran a variation of the same ad, but sadly didn't apologize. The *Sun* defended the ad as an expression of free speech, which was wholly unconvincing to me—the chain frequently refused to run all kinds of advertising in the past, for all kinds of reasons. As a result, I donated what I received from the *Sun* that week to an LGBT advocacy group, and in a column that was published nationally, decried the decision to run the despicable ad.)

But back to the campaign and the nastiness. Despite the controversy (or perhaps because of it), the gay-hating ad was reproduced in its entirety by one Conservative candidate in a Toronto-area riding, complete with a statement indicating that the pamphlet had been officially authorized by the Ontario Progressive Conservative campaign. Two other PC campaigns—both in the Toronto area—used the ad as the basis of an even slicker looking antigay leaflet that was packed with lies. For example, it claimed that the sex-ed curriculum encouraged "cross-dressing" for six-year-olds. This leaflet also indicated that it had been "authorized by Chief Financial Officer of the Ontario PC Party." For the most part, the leaflets had been quietly distributed to evangelical churches, where socially conservative messages have a wide appeal. When one of our campaign workers intercepted a copy after watching a federal cabinet minister personally examine it and express his wholehearted approval—their blunt antigay message ignited a storm on the Internet and in the media, resulting in condemnations on editorial pages and on the airwaves.

One Liberal-hating shock-jock, Jim Richards, excoriated the Conservatives on air: "If you believe that this is the curriculum, you're too stupid for me to vote for you. You are absolutely too stupid for me to vote for you. You know that that's not the curriculum; you know that that is not the curriculum. How am I supposed to vote for someone that is that dumb? How am I supposed to vote for someone who is that stupid? You want to run this province? And you're that much of an ignoramus?"

At the *Globe and Mail,* a columnist wrote: "There have been some ugly moments in this campaign. But making up stuff about curriculum to try to stir up homophobia is right up there." The CBC, for its part, did a fact-check on the homophobic Conservative leaflet, and concluded: "The flyer includes one quote from the document—'cross-dressing for six-year olds'—that can't be found anywhere in the document." Gerry Nicholls, former head of the right-wing National Citizens Coalition, agreed that the gay-hating Conservative leaflets seemed "pretty desperate."

The provincial Conservatives had gone into the election leading the incumbent Liberals by up to 20 percent, depending on the pollster. By the final week, because of their despicable dog-whistle politicking, they were in a free fall. Tim Hudak was bombarded with media questions about why his party had made homophobia one of its key policies. Hudak—who seems as shallow as a puddle, and about as interesting—said the homophobic propaganda was simply a response to the Liberal leader's "out-of-the-mainstream" policy ideas. He declined to say what those might be, choosing instead to talk about how it was his daughter's fourth birthday. (Honest.) After his party was shut out in every major city in the province, Hudak continued to refuse to apologize for the lies and hate contained in the leaflets—even when Ontario's biggest school board formally asked him to do so.

Now, elections are emotional affairs. They can get ugly. Passions flare, objectionable things get said. But to direct fear and loathing at foreigners or gays and lesbians is wholly unethical and plainly wrong. It may be "speech," but it isn't the sort of speech we need. Fully half of the 2011 Ontario election campaign was dominated by expressions of bigotry, rather than ideas and debate about how to move the province forward.

The Conservatives could have legitimately attacked a liberalized immigration and refugee policy. That wouldn't be racist. People of good faith can disapprove of policies that are aimed at boosting the numbers of immigrants and refugees in a country. In fact, it's well known among political veterans that one of the demographics often most hostile to increased numbers of new immigrants is established immigrants. As one seasoned campaign pro—a Liberal—once said to me: "Lots of immigrants get here, and then they want to slam the door behind them on other immigrants."

Don't get me wrong: I'm no political Pollyanna. I love rough-and-tumble politics and bench-clearing brawls. During modern election campaigns, nastiness abounds. But from one corner of the Americas to another, it's been an endless election season of late, and it's been mean and mean-spirited, too. Americans and Canadians have been buffeted by all manner of malice and malevolence, as politicians jockeyed for position and scrambled for votes. Our politics are no longer governed by the Marquess of Queensberry rules (if they ever were). It's nasty out there, on all sides.

But it's conservatives who excel at being shitheads.

The moral of the tale? It's okay to have differences of *opinion*, in any election campaign or any debate. But to pander to the prejudiced—and to gleefully target people who are different by virtue of their creed or colour or sexual orientation—is disgraceful. It's shameful. And in the end, the majority of voters in Canada's biggest province came to see the Conservatives' campaign against those who were different for what it was.

Hate.

☆ ☆ ☆

Don't just take my admittedly partisan word for it: conservatives dislike anything—policies, programs, people—at odds with what they consider to be normal. It's not conjecture, either. It's a scientific fact! A bunch of studies have been done on this, and they're a lot of fun to read, although possibly not if you're a conservative.

The conservative disdain for differences goes back to the cradle. One celebrated American study, for example, found that whiny, insecure kids—you know, the ones who thought (accurately) that all of their classmates hated them, and were continually complaining (inaccurately) about how everyone was mean to them—tended to be conservatives. The voluminous study, which was published in something called the *Journal of Research Into Personality*, tracked a bunch of Berkeley, California-area kids going back to the sixties. Two married Berkeley psychology professors, Jack and Jeanne Block, carefully tracked the development of more than a hundred nursery school kids, relying upon the insights of the teachers and assistants who knew them the best.

The Blocks weren't interested in political orientation, just personality traits. The three- and four-year-olds were rated according to how they behaved, and the Blocks dutifully maintained and weighed the data. The kids were surveyed at regular intervals—at age 4, 5, 7, 11, 14, 18, 23 and, finally, 32. As the youngsters got older, the Blocks kept at it, and eventually published the results. What the Blocks found validated the suspicions of every tax-raising, latte-drinking, sushi-eating, Volvo-driving, *New York Times*–reading, body-piercing, left-wing freak-show type (like me).

The whiny, paranoid little kids grew up to become conservatives! They were rigid, they were thin-skinned, they didn't like ambiguity and they devotedly stuck to traditional gender roles. They looked to authority and tradition a lot more, and were highly uncomfortable when it was absent. The more confident kids, meanwhile, mainly grew up to be liberals.

They were nonconformists with diverse interests, and were more self-reliant and energetic, too.

"The whiny kids tended to grow up conservative," said Professor Jack Block, who passed away in 2010. "Knew it," said us liberals.

But that's not all. The Block Study, as it's become known, isn't without other studies that validate its conclusions. One, published in the journal *Nature Neuroscience,* brought together decades of previous research showing that political orientation is indeed linked to personality traits. So, said the neuroscientists, conservatives were way more rigid and closed-minded than liberals, and way less tolerant of ambiguity and new experiences. The traits associated with conservatives, the study found, were fear, aggression and a marked tolerance for *in*tolerance.

But that's not all! (I'm on a roll here.) A more recent survey of the psyches of more than three hundred individuals, conducted by experts at Ohio State University, examined whether partisans had a sense of humour. Result: conservatives don't! And there's more: a New York University study found that liberals had workspaces that were stylish, modern and colourful. Conservative desktops? "Less cluttered," said the professors. "More conventional and ordinary." Aha!

A psychologist at the National Institute on Aging, at the U.S. National Institutes of Health, is unsurprised by all of this. Robert McCrae, who has written libraries full of studies on personality, declares: "Open people, everywhere, tend to have more liberal values." Conservatives, meanwhile, are found to be less open, less exploratory, and less in need of change. Chris Mooney, in his wonderful book *The Republican Brain: The Science of Why They Deny Science—and Reality*, isn't all that surprised by all of this, either. Mooney concludes that liberals want to try new things, like new music, books, restaurants and vacation spots. Conservatives resist change, he says, and he's right.

I'm not making this stuff up. One May 2012 study in the U.K. by the University College London looked at the MRI scans of a bunch of young adults. The research team found that "greater conservatism was associated with increased volume of the right amygdala." If you are wondering what that is, as I was, the amygdala is a brain structure that is activated during states of fear and anxiety. Liberal brains, meanwhile, were found to have more grey matter in the parts that manage complexity. All of this validated a University of Nebraska–Lincoln study a few months earlier, which found that conservatives have stronger reactions to negative images—they "looked much more quickly at negative or threatening images, and [then] spent more time fixating on them." Certainly explains conservatives' preoccupation with negative ads, doesn't it?

Now, if you're a conservative, and you've made it this far, the chances are excellent that you agree with a study published this year by the University College London. Conservatives, found the British scientists, were much more prone to "disgust." See, conservatives? It's all scientific! You may be whiny, paranoid, intolerant, humourless neat-freaks, but recent political studies also find something else.

Unfortunately, there's a lot more of *you* than there are of *me*. (For now.)

☆ ☆ ☆

The most successful conservative movement in living memory—in fact, the most successful *political* movement in living memory—is the Tea Party. In February 2009, meetings of the populist conservative movement were attracting only a few dozen older Americans, barely enough to fill a room. Three years later, the Tea Party effectively drives the GOP's agenda on almost every issue.

The Tea Partiers—who ostensibly took their name from an on-air rant by a conservative financial-news demagogue, Rick Santelli, on the floor of the Chicago Mercantile Exchange—are, more than anything else, populists. Dictionaries define "populism" as "a political philosophy supporting the rights and power of the people in their struggle against the privileged elite," which sounds about right. The Tea Party started as a bottom-up kind of thing: a movement that railed against the power brokers and the privileged East. It especially hated big government.

On February 19, 2009, Santelli was apparently upset over the Obama administration's plan to provide limited mortgage relief for Americans facing the loss of their homes. So, while a CNBC camera was pointed in his direction, Santelli started what has become known as The Rant. "The government is promoting bad behaviour," Santelli began. "This is America! How many of you people want to pay for your neighbour's mortgage that has an extra bathroom and can't pay their bills?" Some of the traders around him cheered and whistled their approval. The government, Santelli hollered, was helping "the losers" while others are being asked to pay for it.

"We're thinking of having a Chicago Tea Party in July," he bellowed, coining a name for the movement. Within hours, Santelli's rant had attracted hundreds of thousands of hits on YouTube, and other far-right kooks, like Glenn Beck and Sean Hannity, were promoting it on air. Within days, Tea Party groups were organizing themselves across the United States. Almost uniformly white and elderly, they disliked abortion, gay marriage and Obama's $787 billion economic stimulus package. But what they disliked the most—what they hated, in fact—was Obama himself.

They're populists, the Tea Party folks, so if you're trying to understand the beliefs that lie at the centre of the movement, you need to take a close look at the things that preoccupy the very people who created it in the first place. In the early days, as now, Tea Partiers could be seen at rallies across America, wearing tricorne hats like the ones favoured by the Minutemen militia around the time of the American Revolution. They also liked the yellow DON'T TREAD ON ME Gadsden flag carried by the U.S. Marines into their first-ever battle.

And signs. Lots and lots of signs and placards. The Tea Partiers loved those, and they loved to see them on Fox News, their favoured broadcast outlet. The signs tell you quite a bit about what the Tea Party thinks.

"OBAMA'S PLAN," one professionally produced sign states, equals "WHITE SLAVERY." Another one reads: "THE AMERICAN TAXPAYERS ARE THE JEWS FOR OBAMA'S OVENS." Quite a few depict Obama as Hitler, or Osama bin Laden, or a monkey or a dog. Another proclaims, "SPEAK FOR YOURSELF OBAMA: WE ARE A CHRISTIAN NATION." (And, naturally, many signs still falsely claim that Obama is really an African, and not an American.)

At the Tea Party rallies, Confederate flags can be seen in abundance. One infamous sign, spotted in Texas, called Obama a "NIGGAR." (Sic. That sign caused enough of a stir that Tea Party activists later tried to Photoshop it into something less offensive, "WORK 4 U.") And "SAVE WHITE AMERICA." And "WE NEED A CHRISTIAN PRESIDENT." And Obama is "YOUR MUSLIM PRESIDENT" and "THE ANTI-CHRIST" and "OBAMA TERRORIST." And "THE NEW FACE OF HITLER." And "IMPEACH THE MUSLIM MARXIST" and "IMPEACH THE KENYAN."

The Tea Party movement does not disguise its connections to organized bigotry and extremism. Instead, it promotes them. The John Birch Society, for instance, is a far-right white supremacist breeding ground that has been in existence in the U.S. since the 1950s. It opposes laws designed to foster racial equality, which it has called "mongrelization." The Anti-Defamation

League of the B'nai Brith, for its part, has written that the society has long been "a repository for anti-Semites and racists." The Tea Party has been chummy with the John Birch Society from the very beginning. Society members have set up booths at innumerable Tea Party events and town halls, while Tea Party organizations promote Bircher events online. In fact, one report by the Institute for Research and Education and Human Rights found that the Tea Party had actively promoted the John Birch Society on a regular basis, and advertised Bircher events in California, Florida, Idaho, New Jersey, New York, Ohio, Oklahoma, Pennsylvania and Texas.

The connections, unfortunately, don't end there. Ron Paul—the libertarian Tea Party icon who sought the Republican presidential nomination and ended up doing better than anyone expected—spoke at the fiftieth anniversary dinner of the John Birch Society. Fittingly, the event was held in Joseph McCarthy's hometown of Appleton, Wisconsin. In his speech, Paul declared that the society was "a great patriotic organization featuring an educational program solidly based on constitutional principles." At other times, Paul has said, "The beneficial, educational impact of the John Birch Society over the past four decades would be hard to overestimate. It is certainly far more than most people realize. Anyone who has been in the trenches over the years battling on any of the major issues—whether it's pro-life, gun rights, property rights, taxes, government spending, [government] regulation, national security, privacy, national sovereignty, the United Nations, foreign aid—knows that members of the John Birch Society are always in there doing the heavy lifting."

As his popularity grew in late 2011, Paul's long-time association with racist ideology became an issue in the Republican presidential nomination race. The *New York Times* revealed that Paul had published several newsletters in the eighties and nineties containing avowedly racist and anti-Semitic material. For example, Paul's newsletters had proclaimed that 95 percent of Washington's black males are criminals; that the holiday bearing Martin Luther King's name was "Hate Whitey Day"; that the "white majority" was disappearing in America; that Mossad, the Israeli intelligence service, was responsible for the 1993 World Trade Center bombing; that gay men with AIDS were deliberately spreading the disease, "perhaps out of a pathological hatred"; that there existed a "federal-homosexual cover-up" to suppress evidence of AIDS's impact; and that there was "a coming race war in our big cities." And, finally, the newsletters offered praise to David Duke, the neo-Nazi and former leader of the Knights of the Ku Klux Klan.

Paul's extremism predictably attracted the attention of neo-Nazis and white supremacists, many of whom started to breathlessly campaign for the Tea Party's sibyl in the Republican primaries. One group, calling itself the Tea Party Americans Coalition (TPAC), described itself as "a working group for serious White racialist ACTIVISTS who want to effectively coordinate our efforts and intervene for effect in Tea Party-type events." It was overtly anti-Semitic, racist, and avowedly anti-immigrant. Among its members: Don Black, a former leader of the Knights of the Ku Klux Klan, and John Ubele, an activist with the neo-Nazi National Alliance—the group that provided the principal inspiration for the Oklahoma City bombing of April 1995.

The bigotry and prejudice that characterized Ron Paul's campaign wasn't unique. Other Tea Party Republican conservatives openly trafficked in intolerance as well. At a March 2010 Tea Party demonstration in Washington—convened to protest the passage of Obama's health-care reform bill—yet more hatred was on display. Groups of activists gathered outside the offices of legislators who had not yet indicated how they would vote.

They filled the hallways, while others actually held candlelight vigils outside. John Lewis—a Georgia congressman and a civil rights movement activist who had once been nearly beaten to death for opposing racism—was greeted by a chorus of Tea Party followers chanting "nigger" as he exited a legislative building. Another congressman, Maryland's Emanuel Cleaver, was spat upon as he walked behind Lewis (the assailant was arrested but Cleaver chose not to press charges). Massachusetts's Barney Frank, meanwhile, was targeted by antigay slurs.

It's fair to ask: are these sorts of repellent views—the racist signs, the dalliances with bigots like those found in the John Birch Society—representative of the majority of those within the Tea Party movement? Its members deny it and frequently claim that the movement has minority supporters. Perhaps. But a *New York Times*/CBS poll found that fully one-third of Tea Partiers are "birthers." That is, they believe Obama was born in Africa, and is therefore constitutionally barred from becoming president. Another *Times* poll found that up to 60 percent felt that "too much" had been made of the problems facing blacks and the poor. Meanwhile, those revealing signs continue to pop up at Tea Party rallies: "ZIONISTS CONTROL WALL STREET" and "OBAMA TAKES HIS ORDERS FROM THE ROTHSCHILDS," and one calling Obama's health reforms "NATIONAL SOCIALIST HEALTHCARE—DACHAU, GERMANY 1945" and depicting the bodies of Jews murdered in the Holocaust. Tea Party congresswoman and future presidential candidate Michele Bachmann was at the November 2009 Capitol Hill rally featuring that sign—and ignored calls (from Elie Wiesel, among others) to denounce it.

Is any of this significant? Every populist conservative movement has early flirtations with a minority of kooks, doesn't it?

Maybe. But most of the Republican presidential candidates claimed to support, and *had* the support, of the Tea Party.

Many of them, like Ron Paul and Michele Bachmann, owe their very political careers to the Tea Party. The Tea Party—with all that it believes—has become synonymous with the Republican Party.

The two are virtually indistinguishable, in fact.

☆ ☆ ☆

Mike McCurry, head of Public Strategies Washington, Inc., is arguably the best political communications guy in modern history. Among other things, for four years he was the twenty-first White House press secretary, representing President Bill Clinton to the national news media. He was also the fellow whose boss was the target of an impeachment effort—and who assisted said boss in remaining both popular and in office. To political folks of all stripes, McCurry is a communications wizard and a bit of a legend.

McCurry looks out his fourth-floor office window onto Pennsylvania Avenue. Outside, some of the antigovernment, antibanker, anti-elite Occupy Movement protestors can be heard chanting. I've just asked him about another newsworthy protest movement—the antigovernment, antibanker, anti-elite Tea Party—and the irony doesn't escape McCurry's nimble mind.

He smiles. "They're similar," he says. "But they're different."

McCurry explains: "Culturally, I think there has been a great exaltation of the individual in this country, the person who gets ahead economically. We kind of worshipped the hedge fund manager—but I get the sense that that is turning. That's interesting, because the Tea Party is hostile towards large corporate interests and they don't like large institutions, and they don't like big government and they don't like big business, they don't like big media . . ." He laughs. "They don't like *big* things!"

Mike McCurry is a big man himself, with an extra-large handshake. In his office, there are photographs of McCurry with lots of international leaders, along with pictures of his wife and three children. He's an easygoing guy, with an Irishman's facility for storytelling. It's why, one assumes, his acclaim as the White House spokesman is without equal. In 1998, when he packed it in, the accolades weren't in short supply. "You leave with your honour intact," said ABC's Sam Donaldson. "You've done a good job, Mike, under the circumstances," said Helen Thomas, the longest-serving member of the presidential press corps. He had "an agile wit," the ascetic *New York Times* wrote upon learning of his departure, and he "maintained cordial, respectful relations with the press." Said his former boss, Bill Clinton: "[McCurry is] the standard by which future White House press secretaries will be judged." And that, certainly, was true: Mike McCurry has indeed become the standard for the post.

Listening to the protestors make their case down on Pennsylvania Avenue, McCurry muses, "The Occupiers will not be willingly co-opted by Obama or the Democratic Party. The Occupiers would instead love to co-opt Obama, to turn things around, and bring him inside their movement," he says. "But I think the Tea Party is totally different. They spawned a movement, and then those they elected in this last midterm were licking their chops to come down here [to Washington] and get into the middle of the establishment as quick as they could."

The conservative outsiders, therefore, have become the conservative insiders. But they haven't shed all of their radicalism, nor have they lost all of the extremist tendencies that characterized the earliest Tea Party rallies. In particular, they haven't lost their detestation for those who are different from them: like seasoned political spinners, they've simply become more adept at disguising it. But just below the surface, the old Tea Party anger is still there to be seen. Shortly before McCurry received me, in fact, a Republican presidential debate—sponsored by the Tea Party Express at the Florida State fairgrounds—made clear that in the Tea Party–controlled Republican Party, loathing the Other is incontestably part of the catechism. When CNN moderator Wolf Blitzer asked Ron Paul whether a hypothetical uninsured thirty-year-old working man in a coma should be treated, Paul replied—straight-faced—that the man in the coma should "assume responsibility for himself." After the resulting cheers had died down, Blitzer asked, "Congressman, are you saying that society should just let him die?" To which a number of card-carrying Tea Party and Republican attendees yelled out: "Yeah!" *Let him die.*

McCurry winces at the memory. "The Tea Party—" he says, shaking his head "—the Tea Party is a reflection of a deep-seated anger. About the economy, about a fundamental economic truth, which is, there's been no real growth in wage income for Americans at the middle of the spectrum. The resentments of the Tea Party are fuelled by the notion that there is an economy, here in America, that is not functioning anymore. And the anger also comes about because of the destruction of the standard formulation of the American dream—you know, you work hard, play by the rules and you're going to have lots of opportunity. You're going to be able to pass on a better life for your kids.

"We're at a point where a lot of Americans don't believe that anymore. And that's bound to fuel rage and anger. And when that bubbles up in the American political equation, it comes out as really hostile xenophobia or nationalism—or, even worse, outright racism."

On the speakers' circuit, where McCurry remains a big draw, he is asked often if the Tea Party, with its campaign of

anger, has staying power. If it had remained leaderless, particularly at the national level, McCurry has said, the Tea Party
would have likely slipped beneath the waves of history. But its
alliance with the Republicans—who were initially as wary of
the Tea Party as the Democrats had been—suggests that the
Tea Party may be a factor in U.S. politics for many years to
come. With its relationship with the GOP looking less and less
like a one-night stand, McCurry says, the Tea Partiers have
become "a legitimate political force." They've become a success, more than even they had ever considered possible.

But all of that political success could be lost if the Tea Party—
and by extension, the Republican Party, which has willingly
provided it with a home—continues to be synonymous with
racism and bigotry. In politics, anger can certainly be a motivating force. But it can also be destructive and self-defeating.
Witness the extremism on display through the interminable
Republican presidential nomination race: by the time it ground
to a blessed halt at a stadium in Tampa, Florida, in August 2012,
the Tea Party–style hate that had characterized the contest had
turned off plenty of registered American voters. Republicans, as
McCurry noted, had attempted to contain the Tea Party's radicalism. In the bargain, all they did was convince independents
that the GOP *itself* had become radical. Says McCurry: "What's
interesting about the Right is that they can sometimes take that
anger and hostility, and they can organize it effectively, and use
it [to achieve] substantial political power. That was the out-
growth of Goldwater in 1964, for example. And that's been the
pattern ever since within the conservative movement. It's been
conscious effort, and it's been successful."

The Conservative Party of Canada co-opted the Reform
Party; the Republican Party co-opted the Tea Party. In recent
years, mainstream conservatives have indeed absorbed their
brethren found on the further right. But there can be a cost

to that, and for the wounded GOP, there unquestionably has been. "People who are the Right politically have been organized and disciplined about taking these very conservative views [within movements like the Tea Party] to a place where they can have some real political impact," McCurry says. "I think the Tea Party is an example of that. But will the Tea Party last? Maybe so. Maybe it will be around for a while. But remember this: when you get below the age fifty bracket, below the baby boom demographic, there is much less tolerance for that kind of angry conservative message. Right now, we're caught in a time warp, in a very polarizing moment. But I think we are going to have a slightly more generous approach, an approach to benefit the common good . . ."

He pauses. "I hope."

☆ ☆ ☆

Conservatives' antipathy to differences—to things, people or ideas they consider to be outside the norm—is pretty well documented. Most often, this disdain for differences manifests itself in racial- or gender-related small-mindedness, but there are other ways in which it can reveal itself.

Feelings of superiority, for instance. In late 2011, the Pew Research Center surveyed attitudes in a number of Western democracies, polling more than five thousand people at length. In three of the most conservative countries, the U.S., Britain and Germany, about half of respondents agreed with the statement "Our people are not perfect, but our *culture* is superior to others." In countries with a more dominant progressive tradition—Spain, France and so on—only about one in five respondents claimed that they were "culturally superior." Back in 2002, Pew found that a surprising 60 percent of Americans felt they were superior to others. Unsurprisingly, after confirming political affiliation, the vast majority were conservatives.

These condescending conservatives tend to get worse as they get older. In a number of polls conducted over the years, the Pew Center folks found "older Americans remain far more inclined than younger ones to believe that their culture is better than others. Six-in-ten Americans ages 50 or older share this view . . . those younger than 30 hold the opposite view, with just 37 per cent saying American culture is superior." This conservative superiority complex manifests itself most clearly in the way Western conservatives regard those who are unlike themselves. The Pew Center concluded, "Far more Western Europeans than Americans say homosexuality should be accepted by society." Older American conservatives were significantly opposed to equality measures for gays. As the Pew studies found, conservatives are less tolerant of others and far more likely to see themselves as superior to those who are unlike them.

At this point, American conservatives will typically point out—not unfairly—that this assertion is itself unfair. They're not bigots, they'll say. They'll frequently point out that the first and greatest Republican president, Abraham Lincoln, signed the Emancipation Proclamation, which effectively freed the slaves—and which hurt Lincoln's party's fortunes in the mainly Republican South, alienating South from North. That single courageous act, they will argue, demonstrates that conservatives are unafraid of historic, momentous change, and proves that conservatives are no less tolerant than liberals.

Perhaps. But Lincoln's pursuit of liberty and equality was not the act of a conservative Republican, per se. From the perspective that history gives us, in fact, his actions were clearly the conservative exception, not the conservative rule. Were Lincoln to return to the present-day United States—and were he to eyeball a seething, screeching Tea Party rally, up close—the greatest American president would undoubtedly thereafter be scrambling to register as a Democrat. Case in point: the speech that won Lincoln the White House and established him as one of the greatest Americans. One snowy evening in February 1860, the lanky Illinois politician visited New York City to make a passionate plea for racial egalitarianism. In his Cooper Institute address before fifteen hundred people, most of them Republicans, Lincoln declared, "You say you are conservative—eminently conservative—while we are revolutionary, destructive, or something of the sort. What is conservatism? Is it not adherence to the old and tried, against the new and untried?"

Lincoln went on, all fire and brimstone, excoriating those conservatives who clung to "the old and the tried" conservative way: "[You] spit upon that old policy [of the founding fathers], and insist upon substituting something new. True, you disagree among yourselves as to what that substitute shall be. You are divided on new propositions and plans, but you are unanimous in rejecting and denouncing the old policy of the fathers. Some of you are for reviving the foreign slave trade; some for a Congressional Slave Code for the Territories; some for Congress forbidding the Territories to prohibit Slavery within their limits; some for maintaining Slavery in the Territories through the judiciary; some for the 'great principle' that if one man would enslave another, no third man should object . . . but never a man among you is in favor of federal prohibition of slavery in federal territories. . . . Consider, then, whether your claim of conservatism for yourselves, and your charge or destructiveness against us, are based on the most clear and stable foundations."

He went on: "Again, you say we have made the slavery question more prominent than it formerly was. We deny it. We admit that it is more prominent, but we deny that we made it so. It was not we, but you, who discarded the old policy of the [founding] fathers. We resisted, and still resist!"

It was not the sort of speech one is likely to hear emanating from the modern Republican Party, and certainly not from the ugly nativism of Tea Party adherents. On the central question of his age (and of many subsequent ages, too), Abraham Lincoln explicitly associated conservatives with slavery, which is possibly the purest expression of bigotry. Simultaneously, he made clear that he was no conservative. Slavery, and the foul racism it embodies, was then the status quo. And it was Lincoln who opposed it and changed it. That wasn't just progressive—it was a truly *revolutionary* act.

Forget about Lincoln, then, a conservative might say. What about Martin Luther King? He was a Republican, too, they sometimes claim (though not as often as they claim lineage with Lincoln). Indeed, they insist, his own niece has said that King was a lifelong registered Republican. How can any sensible person, then, seriously claim that conservatives' aversion to differences and change aligns them with racial hatred? It's absurd, they'd say. King would not have been Republican, if that had been so.

If that is true, it's an entirely fair argument to make—but only *if* it's true, which is a point to be addressed shortly. Accepting, for the sake of debate, that Martin Luther King was indeed a Republican, he would have been a Republican only in the likeness of Abraham Lincoln—solely *because* of Lincoln. In those days, many black Americans gravitated towards the party due to Abraham Lincoln's historic role in championing the abolition of slavery, and because the South was then mainly Democrat (and, sadly, too often racist). In the days of segregation, some Democrats were "Dixiecrats": George Wallace, Robert Byrd and other Democrats were determined in their support of segregation and in their opposition to civil rights.

But John F. Kennedy came to champion civil rights, as did his successor, Lyndon B. Johnson. They did so at great political cost to their party in the South. Meanwhile, the Republicans abandoned whatever vestiges remained of Lincoln's greatest achievement in the early 1960s, with the divisive, race-baiting Southern Strategy, deliberately fashioned by Richard Nixon and his acolytes to attract the votes of white Americans frightened by the implications of the civil rights movement. After observing the saturnalian proceedings at the 1964 Republican national convention in a San Francisco arena—wherein Barry Goldwater's far-right dogma dominated, and wherein the Arizona Senator hollered that "extremism" was acceptable, even virtuous—King wrote in his autobiography: "The Republican Party geared its appeal and program to racism, reaction, and extremism." It was, he said, "the frenzied wedding at the Cow Palace of the KKK with the radical right." He thereafter had nothing to do with the GOP, and frequently denounced the extremism that Goldwater had exhorted the party to embrace.

Conservatives still claim that King's niece, herself a conservative, has said that her uncle had been a registered Republican. But the niece, Alveda King, says that isn't true. "I have never said Martin Luther King Jr. was a Republican," says Alveda King. "I never saw his registration card . . . [he] was not a Republican or Democrat. But everybody uses Martin Luther King's name for their own benefit." Especially, it seems, conservatives.

They do this—with Lincoln, with King, and with the few non-whites who align themselves with the conservative movement and whom they trot out whenever a camera is pointed in their direction—because they know, in their puny conservative hearts, that they have a problem. They are associated, far too often, with racism and racists.

That aside, it would be inaccurate to suggest that all, or even most, conservatives are bigots. When racists are found to be in their midst, mainstream conservatives will expel them— eventually. But the question they haven't asked of themselves is this: *If we're not bigots, why is it that so many bigots always want to join with us?*

That, too, is a fair question.

☆ ☆ ☆

When conservatives are criticized for pandering to intolerance—and their various political campaigns continue to provide plenty of reason to criticize—they will hurriedly offer talking points about the likes of Lincoln, or their historical opposition to slavery, or whatever is at hand. It's unfair to associate them with haters, they'll insist. But the fact is that haters are disproportionately represented on the conservative side of the ideological spectrum.

Stark evidence of this is found in one fairly recent, and truly horrific, crime. It was a crime that presented a tremendous dilemma for the oracles of the global conservative movement, because it was a crime committed by a blond-haired, blue-eyed, card-carrying conservative.

Most still remember that terrible day: in July 2011, a lone gunman named Anders Breivik killed seventy-seven people in Norway, most of them young people at the ruling Labour Party's youth camp, some of them as young as fourteen. His mass murder was a crime that shook Norway and the world. To target and murder children, as Breivik did, was sick, inhuman and profoundly evil. But some right-wing commentators were completely indifferent to that. Variously, these commentators actually seemed to suggest that the victims deserved to die, or the killer wasn't entirely bad, or Breivik—who had views about Muslims and immigrants eerily similar to their own—wasn't in fact motivated by those views. When he clearly *was*.

Here is a sampling:

- Glenn Beck, the U.S. conservative conspiracy theorist, said the young people at the Utoya Island camp targeted by Breivik were "like Hitler youth."

- Former GOP presidential candidate and Nixonian gadfly Pat Buchanan took a different tack—and expressed approval about the killer's ravings. He said Breivik's writings "reveal a knowledge of the history, culture and politics of Europe." He went on to make approving noises about Breivik's opposition to multiculturalism.

- Canadian broadcaster Michael Coren, in a blog post titled "Leftist syndrome," pointed out some of the youngsters at the Utoya Island camp had been critical of Israel's treatment of Palestinians—and, therefore, their murders were "ironic." The posting even seemed to suggest the Norwegian youth may have had it coming, since they had "showed no empathy at all for Jewish suffering."

- U.S.-based columnist Mark Steyn—who has achieved fame for his error-filled anti-Muslim screeds and who was referred to approvingly in Breivik's fifteen-hundred-page manifesto—scrambled to minimize clear evidence that Breivik hated Muslims. He insisted that, because both Breivik and his victims were "blonde-haired, blue-eyed Aryans," he could not have been in any way motivated by anti-Muslim hate.

These statements were more than deplorable and irresponsible; they didn't reflect the true facts about Breivik. The facts, as reported by the *New York Times*, the *Wall Street Journal* and the like, are quite different. The *Times* reported Breivik was "a right-wing fundamentalist Christian, a gun-loving Norwegian obsessed with what he saw as the threat of multiculturalism and Muslim immigration to the cultural and patriotic values of his country." The *Journal,* not usually a hotbed of leftist sentiment, also quoted Norwegian police authorities, who described Breivik as "a Norwegian gun enthusiast with a history of voicing nationalist, anti-immigration views," adding that Breivik "frequently agitated online against European policies too accommodating of multiculturalism and what he saw as the growing threat of radical Islam." Even Fox News reported that Breivik was "a right-winger with anti-Muslim views."

Those are the *facts.* Why, then, did Beck, Buchanan and Steyn, in particular, feel compelled to offer up such hateful rationalizations? Because, simply, Breivik represents a profound threat to the message the Right wants to communicate. Their message isn't difficult to identify, most days; they're not subtle, these conservatives. To them, all of Western, Christian, white society faces destruction at the hands of the Other: the Other, who looks different, and thinks differently and worships a different god. Islamophobia is the new anti-Semitism, and conservative commentators practise it with a vengeance.

They detest Muslims, despite the fact that Muslims are—overwhelmingly—good citizens. A 2006 Council on American-Islamic Relations (CAIR) survey of American Muslim voters showed that American Muslim voters are young, highly educated, mostly professional, and religiously diverse—with a third saying they attend a mosque once a week and a third saying they never attend at all. The survey results clearly showed that American Muslims are fully integrated into the broader American society: nearly 90 percent said they voted regularly and just as many said they celebrated the Fourth of July, most flew the U.S. flag at their home, and so on. They were pretty mainstream in attitude, as well: close to 90 percent said Muslims should strongly emphasize shared values with Christians and

Jews, and about 80 percent said Muslims worship the same God as Christians and Jews do.

Despite evidence showing Muslims are indistinguishable from any other citizen found in a modern democracy, there's been a big rise in anti-Muslim sentiment in politically conservative democracies like the U.S. The crimes of 9/11 are one reason, obviously—but another reason is the proliferation of Islamophobia by conservatives. In 2004, another Pew poll found that about as many Americans have an unfavourable view of Islam as don't have an unfavourable view. About half believed that Islam is more likely than other religions to "encourage violence" among its followers. A more recent CAIR survey found that one in ten Americans said that Muslims "believe in a moon god." Many favoured the authorities spying on Muslim groups or, where feasible, infiltrating them. All of this leads, naturally, to discrimination, exclusion and (sometimes) violence. In 2005, CAIR processed a total of 1,972 civil rights complaints, a 30 percent increase in anti-Muslim harassment, violence and discriminatory treatment from the year before.

Since 9/11, sadly, this sort of Islamophobia has been growing. Various surveys, by CAIR and Pew and others, found that between one-fourth and one-third of Americans now hold negative views of Islam and Muslims. Conservative opinion leaders, like Franklin Graham, Jerry Falwell and Pat Robertson, have enthusiastically pandered to this segment, doing their utmost to make a bad situation worse. They've called Islam "a wicked religion," the Prophet "a terrorist," and Muslims "worse than Nazis." Like Beck, Buchanan, Steyn and the "religious" propagandists, Anders Breivik was a white, conservative Christian. He hated Muslims and "leftists" like the children found at the camp. He and his ilk pay close attention to these leading conservative voices, buying their books, attending their lectures and cheering them on the Internet.

When you are a conservative oracle who seeks to demonize Islam—and non-white immigration, and non-white refugees and so on—the actions of madmen like Breivik tend to raise unhelpful questions. The Right's frantic spinning cannot obscure the gritty reality, however. Namely, that Anders Breivik hated those who were *different* from him.

And he acted on it.

✩ ✩ ✩

John Wright is a rarity: a pollster whose research is trusted by governments and political parties of every stripe. He is also unique because he polls on a global scale, and his Ipsos firm surveys public opinion regularly in dozens of countries. In the cloistered environs of the polling industry, Ipsos is a giant: billions in annual sales, offices in fifty-five countries with nearly twenty thousand employees.

Wright, a small-town Canadian boy, has been Ipsos's face for more than two decades. In recent years, he and the Ipsos team have been paying close attention to the shifting attitudes within the Right, and particularly within the North American Right. His firm has conducted dozens of surveys of the ranks of card-carrying conservatives and of the broader public. He believes the Tea Party element isn't anything new. It's just another name for a divisive and destructive constituency that has always existed within mainstream conservative political parties.

"The rise of the Tea Party in the United States may seem to be a reaction to the times," says Wright. "But, actually, it's a core segment of the Republican right that has always been there. Except that, right now, they have a label and rallying cry that makes them easy to identify." By choosing the iconic Boston Tea Party as their inspiration, he says, the Tea Partiers are invoking a key metaphor. "[They're] not just tossing tea overboard

to rail against taxes. [They're doing it] to symbolize their defi-
ance of governments that tell them what they can or can't do."

They are more than just libertarians, says Wright. They
despise government, certainly, and much of government's preoccupation with equality and fairness. Regulations and rules
related to concepts like equality, he says, are things they
"rebuke and defy." They're "God-fearing, puritan, capitalist
and free-willed," Wright says, and they want to wrench the
country back to the simple—perhaps, simplistic—values
ostensibly seen at its beginning.

As impossible as that may seem to achieve, Wright says,
the Tea Party–style conservatives are a force to be reckoned
with. He estimates they represent 30 percent of the American
voting population. "That may not sound like much, but that
is huge." Since the Civil War, Wright says, Americans have
pretty much split right down the middle in a two-party
system. Essentially, Democrats and Republicans can capture
about 49 percent each. Says Wright: "It's 2 percent who
decide who will be president."

The problem for the American Right, he says—echoing
Mike McCurry—is that they have moved too far to the hard
right, too fast. While the surging Tea Party constituency has
reinvigorated the Republicans, it has simultaneously alienated
anyone who happens to be in some way different from them.
Wright slides a poll across his desk. "Look at this," he says.

On one slide, a surprising 75 percent of Republicans say they
identify with the Tea Party. Wright produces two more slides: on
one, 37 percent of registered voters say they don't identify, at all,
with the Tea Party elements within the Republican Party. And,
among all Americans, even more feel that way. "Republicans
must decide," he says. "A candidate they really like, or a candidate who can beat Obama. Hard-right politics alienate independent voters. It makes Republicans less electable on a national

scale." While Wright agrees that conservatives are ascendant pretty much everywhere, he doesn't agree that the politics of the United States are transportable anywhere else. In fact, he says, "tea partying in Canada is probably more like a coffee klatch."

Wright explains: "There is no party called the Tea Party in Canada. In the United States, the term 'tea party' has a much deeper historical base. It touches on the fundamental philosophy which founded the very country—get taxes and government out of our lives, and let us be free to live and make choices on our own. The Boston Tea Party was its epicentre, something that [didn't] happen in Canada ... In fact, it pretty much went the other way, with the British colony growing under the banner of 'peace, order and good government.'"

America embraced individualism and populism, and developed a two-party system where Republicans tended to be on the Right and the far right. Canadians, he notes, formed many other parties that were allowed to flourish over time—including those that wanted to destroy the country through separation.

Smart political operatives—and the conservative movement has plenty of them—aren't nearly as preoccupied with these sorts of distinctions, Wright adds. "What they see is a virtual sea of voters, some who are hardliners attached to a party, the ones who are the fundamentalists. Whereas others are movable ... the hard fundamentalists may be guided by a philosophical belief, but the reality is that most voters aren't." That's the danger to conservatives who highlight differences between people instead of trying to bring people together, he says. "Voters can move back and forth between parties because they simply can't stomach the alternative. While they may like to have voted against an incumbent government, many voters will decide to stick with what they have rather than embrace an unpalatable choice. [That] was the case in Ontario where the Conservatives were leading by [at least] ten points at the outset of a campaign against the incumbent Liberals—and the Liberals then won the election by ten points."

And therein lies the danger to conservatives, Wright says. The very thing that motivates them, and gives them their identity and their ideology—their fear of differences—is also their weakness. The risk inherent in continually railing against the Other is that voters may get turned off and start aligning themselves with the Other, and not with conservatives. "That's what was so striking about [the Ontario] Conservative campaign," Wright says. "It could probably have worked better against the Democrats in the United States, rather than the Liberals in Ontario. Many of the messages that the Ontario [Conservative] campaign ran on have resonance with Tea Party or fundamentalist conservatives in the United States. But by demonizing taxes, promoting chain gangs, attacking immigrant workers, [distributing a] homophobic pamphlet, all surrounded by a tone of pessimism—all of which was scripted ad nauseam—the Conservative campaign alienated more than it motivated."

Wright shakes his head. "Swing voters, or switchers, took a look at the choices they were being given, and decided to stay with the government that they had rather than take a chance on something that was advocating radical right-wing change. The Conservative campaign alienated many of those voters— especially in cities who shared different values than those in other parts of the province—and it failed to offer anything to bring people together. It failed to create a coalition.

"The best political operatives look for coalitions of voters. That's how you win: you make sure that you don't disenfranchise your fundamentalists, while trying to make it palatable for less dogmatic voters to join your party at the polls."

But will conservatives ever learn that lesson? I ask him. Will they ever understand that it's better to bring people together than to drive them apart?

John Wright raises an eyebrow, but says nothing. He doesn't need to.

☆ ☆ ☆

Conservatives can't define conservatism, most days, so it's no sin that liberals mostly can't, either. What a conservative is, and how conservatism is to be defined, is a difficult task, perhaps even an impossible one. Even conservative leaders, and the so-called philosophers of their movement, are unable to come up with a serviceable explanation for what they are.

That's why it's fair to try and find a meaning in the main behaviour all conservatives share: their unambiguous opposition to just about anything and anyone who isn't "normal." Or what a conservative, at least, considers to be normal.

It need not be expressed in racist terms (as with the Tea Party), or as something homophobic (as with the Ontario Conservative Party), or as something hateful. It can be as simple, and as mundane, as opposition to accommodating disabled people so that they can work in society. When the aforementioned conservative pundit Mark Steyn wrote about the early days of 9/11, for example, he actually insinuated that people in wheelchairs shouldn't have been in the Twin Towers in the first place. Left unsaid was the notion that the disabled, you know, kind of deserved what they got. Because, if they hadn't pushed for a more equal society, they wouldn't be dead.

Conservatives will holler, naturally, that they don't oppose all societal change. In a way, that is true. (When progressives have changed something, conservatives will typically want to change it back to what it was.) But their mission is to wrench everything and everyone back to a simpler time that, of course, did not ever exist. In this way, William F. Buckley Jr.'s aphorism is best: to Buckley and those like him, conservatives are seen planted in the soil, leaning against the times, trying to stop the movement of history. Among other things, it's a wonderfully colourful metaphor.

And, when one considers conservatives' undeniable antipathy to things, and people, that are different, it's pretty accurate, too.

3

HOW CONSERVATIVES STOLE VALUES

The dangers conservatives represent to modern society are myriad.
They are clever, they are conniving and they are crafty.
A detailed analysis of how conservatives have purloined values
and morals to defeat progressives, who are good and just. How, in
particular, they deploy cunning and conniving value-laden messages
to frame and dominate the debate.
Also: an exposition of conservative word games, in which they delight.

———

E verywhere you look these days, conservatives are on the march.

Across the Americas and Europe, previously progressive strongholds have been falling to the conservative barbarians. The barbarians aren't just at the gates, either. They've crossed the moat, battered down the walls, and have been happily pillaging the treasury and the wine cellar for quite some time now. They're running things, in fact. Their former progressive overlords, to extend the metaphor, are now up in the hills, running around wearing animal skins, eking out a meagre living and longing for the good old days.

How did it happen? Lots of reasons. Progressive forces rested on their proverbial laurels. They made dumb mistakes. They underestimated their rivals. They got cocky. They assumed, for instance, that their opponents would never get their act together. They therefore allowed themselves to be split into warring tribes—as in Canada, for example, where federal Liberals and New Democrats endlessly battle for the same vote, while the Conservatives cheerfully sail up the middle to register big wins, with fewer votes.

And most of all, we progressives lost the values war.

Yes, *values*. After every electoral loss, progressives everywhere confuse "values" with "messaging." But they shouldn't. They're not the same thing. The challenges facing progressives extend to more than mere linguistics. Values are the ineffable, keenly felt issues that hit folks at a primordial level. Not the stuff we think about—the stuff we feel. The stuff that attracts the attention of hearts, not heads. Values: in political terms, that means morals.

"The entire moral vocabulary is now a wholly owned language of the religious right," writes the progressive author and newspaper columnist Ellen Goodman. Progressives, she says, are typically "tongue-tied talking about values." These days, agrees Democratic muse George Lakoff, millions of people "vote their moral identity and values, often at the expense of their economic interests." Even a guy named Barack Obama, back when he was only a senator, complained that progressives needed "a new narrative" if they were ever going to win again. (He got one—"Yes, we can"—and won the presidency.)

It's more than just narrative, however. You can't slip into a political backroom without hearing someone lamenting the need for a narrative. Admittedly, it's true: having a simple, compelling story to tell voters is important. Progressives have great stories to tell, too—about health care and peace and the environment, for instance. And while polls consistently show voters agreeing that all that stuff is important, those self-same voters will repeatedly vote against their interests and for conservatives—the partisans who, mostly, don't give a rat's ass about health care, peace or the environment. How come?

Values, morals. In short, conservatives have them, and progressives don't—or at least, that's what an increasing number of voters believe.

Conservatives started to steal the values-and-morals construct from liberals back in the sixties. That black-hearted old villain, Richard Nixon, is—improbably—the guy who did it. Nixon successfully equated antiwar protests with anti-Americanism; he got blue-collar whites to believe "civil rights" was synonymous with lawlessness and preferential hiring for blacks; and he manipulated many into thinking that feminism was a plot to undermine the authority of fathers, and therefore, the nation's moral structure. Conservatives who came after him learned from that and built on it.

Conservatives, now, *own* "values" and "morals." The likes of Stephen Harper and George W. Bush pepper their speeches with the words liberally, so to speak. They know that most folks couldn't define either word if their lives depended on it. But they also know that's entirely beside the point. You don't need to articulate values and morals. You just feel them, deep down, in your gut.

And conservatives have become the gut-level political champs. Until progressives understand their need to compete at the same level, they'll remain up in the hills, wearing animal skins and longing for the good old days.

☆ ☆ ☆

Whenever we are beaten to a pulp by the aforementioned barbarians, and whenever we are engaged in one of those seemingly interminable "what went wrong" postelection self-flagellation sessions that progressives simply adore, lefties like me will invariably curl up into a fetal ball and whimper: "It's not our fault. We just didn't communicate well." With the greatest of respect to my fellow fruit-juice-drinking, sandal-wearing, sex-maniac nudist pacifist feminists (to paraphrase no less than George Orwell's wonderful characterization in *The Road to Wigan Pier*), that's bullshit! What we have here, to appropriate a famous phrase, is not just a failure to communicate. It's way worse than that.

Former *Atlantic* editor and writer Josh Green nails it. Progressives, Green once observed, are in an "Olympian state of denial." They haven't glimpsed the outlines of "a truth that ought to be perfectly clear: rather than being misunderstood, they were understood all too well."

And therein lies the rub. Advertising execs know it as a platitude: a smart slogan or a catchy tagline can persuade the uncommitted to pay attention for a little bit, but it won't mask the absence of a soul. A catchy jingle won't make your fellow citizens forget that you lack an ethical centre. It won't hide your lack of morals. Progressives lack morals, and voters know it. Or, at least, suspect it.

Now, it's not as if we progressives aren't sadly aware we have a values gap. We are. One smart Democrat, Geraldine Ferraro, placed the values conundrum at the centre of her vice-presidential nomination acceptance speech back in 1984: "To those concerned about the strength of American and family values, as I am, I say: We are going to restore those values—love, caring, partnership—by including, and not excluding, those whose beliefs differ from our own. Because our own faith is strong, we will fight to preserve the freedom of faith for others."

Love and partnership, by the by, aren't values. They're a Hallmark card line. But Ferraro, at least, was trying. Like her, the majority of progressives and liberals are keenly aware that we are still seen as having a moral deficit. So we keep trying to fix it. Almost a quarter-century after Ferraro's stirring pledge, the party of Barack Obama could be seen attempting to grasp at the values-and-morals brass ring. "Ultimately," a campaigning Obama observed in 2007, "what I think voters will be looking for is not so much a litmus test on faith, as an assurance that a candidate has a value system."

True enough. No debate here. But polls show that, most of the time, voters aren't reassured by what we say or, more accurately, try to say. They think progressives don't have a value system—or, if they do, it doesn't adequately correspond with their own. Stanley B. Greenberg, a U.S. pollster who is married to a Democratic congresswoman, suggests that everywhere "voters are generally turning to conservative and right-wing political parties, most notably in Europe and in Canada." Why? Says Greenberg: "Oddly, many voters prefer the *policies* of Democrats to the policies of Republicans. They just don't trust the Democrats to carry out those promises." After conducting multiple focus groups, Greenberg concluded that voters are "fairly cynical" about a Democratic politician's honesty, as opposed to a Republican politician's. For progressives, this finding may be as surprising as it is depressing: voters aren't necessarily attracted to the morality of the Right. What they find attractive, apparently, is their belief that the Right *has* morality. "A crisis of government legitimacy is a crisis of liberalism. It doesn't hurt Republicans," says Greenberg. "Government operates by the wrong values and rules, for the wrong people and purposes, the [people] I've surveyed believe. Government rushes to help the irresponsible and does little for the responsible. Wall Street lobbyists govern, not Main Street voters." Progressives, Greenberg says, need to be seen as operating with "the right values." Right now, we aren't.

Part of the attraction to the morality of conservatives may be traced to a stereotypical conservative behavioural trait: their rigidity. Voters, it seems, associate inflexibility with moral uprightness—and not just conservative voters, either. To them, mind-bogglingly, being a stubborn sonofabitch is more of a virtue than a vice. As a massive 2011 Pew Research Center survey found: "Core [Republican] groups largely prefer elected officials who stick to their positions rather than those who compromise. Solid liberals overwhelmingly prefer officials who compromise, but . . . other Democratic[s] do not."

For example: near the end of the recession in the early nineties—which ended in the U.S. around 1992 and in Canada around 1995—American voters were asked what mattered most to them, values or economics. In one NBC/ *Wall Street Journal* poll, 54 percent said "moral values" mattered most. Only 34 percent said "financial pressures" did. *Newsweek* did another poll, around the same time, which concluded that "moral decline" was a bigger cause of voter dissatisfaction than the president, Congress, or the news media. When pressed, they indicated that conservative politicians contributed less to their feelings of dissatisfaction than the liberal ones did.

Now, some progressives might protest, conducting polls about voter satisfaction in recessionary times—and at presidential midterms—is perhaps unfair to incumbents. People are *always* unhappy after a particular political party has been in government for a couple of years, and they vote accordingly. But another U.S. national poll, conducted by the *L.A. Times* on election day in 1996, found that voters believed the Republican choice (Bob Dole) was four times more likely to "have values like mine" than the Democratic choice (Bill Clinton). Clinton won that election, of course. But he won because he was seen as having a better understanding of the pocketbook issues that mattered most to voters, and because he had experience as president—not, obviously, because he had cornered the market on morality (think "bimbo eruptions").

If morality and values are the ballot question, conservatives have always beaten progressives. George W. Bush, whatever his intellectual failings, knew this better than most. "Whenever I go to the heartland," said Bush to a gathering of boy scouts (natch) in 2000, "I am reminded of the values that build strong families, strong communities and strong character, the values that make our people unique." See that? Dubya didn't even identify what one of these "values" is, not once, but it didn't matter. He won that election, and the election that came after it. Values, more than even Dick Cheney, were his running mate.

☆ ☆ ☆

So, um, what's a "value"?

Beats me. I don't know for sure, and neither does anybody else, it seems. A value can be whatever a politician makes it out to be, most days. One fun open-ended online poll conducted by City-Data, an Illinois social networking firm, produced some hilarious results about values. The values of ordinary people, the firm found, are best represented by pickup trucks (14 percent), white picket fences (16 percent) and small-town diners (32 percent). Among other things, this explains politicians' fondness for driving to and from small-town diners in pickup trucks at election time. And where possible, leaning against—but not necessarily sitting upon—picket fences. (Ask Mitt Romney: sitting on the fence is unhelpful to one's political fortunes).

Another poll, at once funny but mostly not, was conducted by Research 2000 for the progressive folks at the Daily Kos community blog. It zeroes in on the values of conservatives in the U.S. While it doesn't assist us much in properly defining values, it tells us quite a bit about what conservatives think their values are these days. And it's not a pretty picture, presented in reverse order of total lunacy, as it was in the *New Yorker* and elsewhere:

- 36 percent don't believe Obama was born in the United States, and 22 percent aren't sure.

- Only 36 percent say that Obama doesn't hate white people.

- Only 7 percent support same-sex marriage.

- 68 percent don't think gay couples should receive *any* state or federal benefits, while 21 per cent are not sure.

- 39 percent believe Obama should be impeached.

- 23 percent want their state to secede from the U.S.

- 24 percent say that Obama "wants the terrorists to win," while 33 percent are not sure.

- Only 24 percent say they *definitely* don't believe that Association of Community Organizations for Reform Now (ACORN) stole the election in some Left-wing conspiracy.

- 31 percent think contraception should be outlawed.

- 73 percent believe that openly gay men or women should be prohibited from teaching in public schools, and 19 percent aren't sure.

Like I said: sort of funny, but generally unfunny. There's a reason why guys like me consider conservatives so dreadful, you know.

A definition for "values," however, stubbornly remains elusive. Pollsters, pundits and political scientists talk a lot about values, but none of them ever seems to be able to offer a working definition. In particular, those on the progressive side of the spectrum don't seem to understand that "loving, caring, partnership" or "environment" or "child care" aren't values—or at least not in the way that voters identify values. If a value is easily reduced to words, chances are it isn't one. It's known, it's felt, but a value isn't easily described. One of the best guys to ask about this wooly concept is Geoffrey Nunberg, the acclaimed and affable author of *Talking Right.*

A linguist by training, Nunberg teaches at the University of California at Berkeley and is regularly called upon to dissect the mischievous—and, intermittently, plainly evil—ways in which conservatives maul language to win. Though an acclaimed academic, Nunberg is also refreshingly plain-spoken and candid. So when the billionaire birther Donald Trump was musing about seeking the Republican presidential nomination, Nunberg could only shake his head in disbelief. "It's like the asshole of the month club," he says of the Republicans, marvelling. "And they really are assholes. They were talking about *Trump.* So, when he was thinking about announcing [his candidacy], he went right to the top of the Republican polls."

Nunberg pauses. "Jesus Christ! These people are crazy! And I think that they're making themselves look very crazy to independent voters, too."

I *like* this kind of academic! We press on.

"The Right is better at values," says Nunberg, who is taking a break from writing his next book at his San Francisco home to talk with me. "The Right has a natural advantage in the modern context, because a lot of the issues they are promoting are emotional issues—cultural prejudices that are easier to work with, linguistically, than some of the issues that Canadian Liberals and American Democrats are concerned with."

In *Talking Right*, Nunberg writes that progressives have "a certain semantic cluelessness." Conversely, the values proposition works for the Right, he notes, because it validates the phony populist narratives that millionaires like George W. Bush, John McCain and Mitt Romney are continually spinning: hard work, just plain folks, pull-oneself-up-by-the-bootstraps, blah blah blah. (None of which these men have done, incidentally— all having been fortunate enough to be born the sons of millionaires, politicians and/or four-star generals.) Values, in the conservative context, Nunberg writes, don't simply mean being principled. They mean upholding the morals of so-called ordinary people who "have been mocked and traduced by out-of-touch elite liberals." The conservative approach to values, he adds, is charged with righteous anger and class-based resentments that the Right has been preoccupied with for decades.

So, are values the same things as morals? Nunberg muses. "Yeah, but I think morals is a tricky word," he says. "As a linguist, I'm interested in those words that have a double meaning—words that live close to each other, and nobody really notices that. Values can mean 'morals' on one side, and 'mores' on the other."

Conservatives delight in values-related debate, because they know that surveys consistently show that voters believe that conservatives *have* values, and liberals don't. Citizens don't always agree with conservatives' sets of values—but they are reassured, often, by the fact that conservatives endeavour to acquire them in the first place. Says Nunberg, agreeing: "For example, my values and your values are different. That's one way [of looking at it]. The other way is this: I have values—and you don't. That's the moral side of it. And the trick is getting people in different parts of the country, with different cultures, to associate values with moral differences. And conservatives have been able to do this. [Rick] Santorum was saying just the other night that these liberals do have a religion, but it's a religion of the self. 'While we conservatives,' he said, 'have a religion of God.' They have been able to convince people—how many people, I don't know—that values are a moral question."

How many people? Clearly: enough to matter. Enough to get elected in circumstances where, historically, progressive points of view were supposed to constitute the majority. Nunberg, among many others, says that it's become a truism to observe that people tend vote their values more than their self-interest. U.S. election-year exit polls in 2004, for instance, found that "moral values" were the single most important issue in the campaign that resulted in George W. Bush being re-elected. Progressive giants like Nicholas Kristof in the *New York Times* despaired of this, writing at the time: "[Democrats] should be feeling wretched about the millions of farmers, factory workers, and waitresses who ended up voting—utterly against their own interests—for Republican candidates." Kristof may be overstating things, Nunberg says, but his main point is a truism. "And this," he observes, "helps Republicans more often than it does Democrats."

Why? Because, frankly, progressives are too often observed fussing over minutiae. Because they are proponents of nanny statism and social engineering, whether they realize it or not. Because they're policy fuss-budgets. Conservatives, meanwhile, are more concerned with what Garance Franke-Ruta, the online politics editor of the *Atlantic,* calls "the fundamental stuff of life." They're all big picture, the conservatives. Progressives, meanwhile, are all about the little things: laundry lists of pica-yune political promises; minor tactical tweaks; everything that is vertical, in policy terms, but little that is horizontal. Voters know it. Or, more accurately, they feel it.

"Basically," Nunberg continues, "the Right has had a political program. And I don't just mean a [political] platform. It's a set of issues, and they've been able to link those values to a narrative about the nature of political life and the relationship of ordinary people to politics. Their idea about 'big government,' for example, is a rhetorical steamroller. In its modern form, it took shape in the time of Ronald Reagan—who was more responsible for advancing that idea more than anybody before him. And liberals, Democrats, have responded to that defensively, which is always a mistake. The Right has always been very good at playing to resentments, and particularly class resentments of the white working class. That was Nixon's great achievement, if you want to call it an achievement: in the late sixties and the early seventies, he moved the South into the Republican column with racism and a set of connected social issues [which he knew white voters would warm to]. I mean, white males without college degrees are 75 percent conservative!"

He pauses. "It's just gotten so fucking crazy. It's *weird.*"

☆ ☆ ☆

While the inability of progressives to take back "values" from conservatives isn't just a communications problem, there's no doubt that communications are a big part of the problem. Frank Luntz understands this better than most.

Luntz is a baby-faced Republican consultant who, perhaps more than any other unelected person, has radically revised the lexicon of the Right. Like all communication consultants, he has done this to soften the edges of some pretty hard political issues and thereby assist his clients. That's part of the job, and unfortunately he does it well. But Luntz has become famous, and rich, for another reason: he has figured out how to manipulate language in such a way that it is conservatives— at least the ones who listen to him—who are now winning the communications war. With a marketer's ear finely tuned to public opinion and clever turns of phrase, Luntz has dramatically improved the fortunes of ambitious conservatives everywhere. In particular, he's helped the Right peddle its wares much more effectively to the emblematic "middle class" and "working families" that every campaign strategist covets, and whose votes every campaign needs to win. When you consider that it is conservatives who are most closely aligned with millionaires and management—*against* the interests of ordinary folks and labour—that is no inconsiderable achievement.

"Frank is a marketing guy," says Geoffrey Nunberg, who, like me, is no fan of Luntz. "He knows how this stuff works. Luntz is very skilled. He sees these issues, he gets these issues, and he's been successful in making these little linguistic shifts that move the discourse a little bit, in a way that helps the Right."

Luntz's formula is straightforward, and it's no state secret. "It's not what you say," he has proclaimed, so many times that it has become his firm's slogan. "It's what people *hear*." It may sound bumper-stickerish, but it is no less true for that.

In one of his much-read newsletters—on the environment, but it's the same sort of advice he gives in respect of just about any issue—Luntz writes: "The first (and most important) step to neutralizing the problem and eventually bringing the public around to your point of view . . . is to convince them of your *sincerity and concern*. Any discussion . . . has to be grounded in an effort to reassure a skeptical public that you care—that your intentions are strictly honorable." Luntz emphasizes those two words—sincerity, concern—so his point is not lost: whatever your message is, whatever you are attempting to promote, you need to exude authenticity and attentiveness. Whether a voter or consumer agrees with you is, at least initially, irrelevant. They need to feel that you are authentic. This, more than any other reason, is why conservatives have heeded Luntz's advice so often and why so many of them have sought to promote values that resonate at the level of one's heart, and not one's head.

Thus, as Frank Luntz tells rapt conservative audiences (including George W. Bush's verbally maladroit father, George Bush Sr.), don't say cutbacks—say "common-sense solutions." Don't say deregulation—say "balanced approaches." Don't say global warming—say (when obliged to) "climate change." In one much-quoted memorandum circulated to his clients, modestly titled "The New American Lexicon," Luntz writes: "Sometimes it is not what you say that matters but what you don't say. Other times a single word or phrase can undermine or destroy the credibility of a paragraph or entire presentation. This memo was originally prepared exclusively for congressional spouses because they are your eyes and ears, a one-person reality check and truth squad combined. However, by popular demand, I have included and expanded that document because effectively communicating the *New American Lexicon* requires you to *stop* saying words and phrases that undermine your ability to educate the American people. So from today forward, *you* are the language police. From today forward, these are the words never to say again."

It's hokey as hell, it's simplistic, but evidently it works. Luntz went on: "Never say government—instead say Washington. Never say tax reform—say tax simplification. Never say inheritance or estate tax—say death tax. Never say a global economy, or globalization or capitalism—say a free market economy. Never say undocumented workers—say illegal aliens. Never say foreign trade—say international trade. Never say drilling for oil—say exploring for energy. Never say health-care choice— say the right to choose."

Luntz provides chirpy rationales for each of these linguistic sleights of hand. In every case, he cites public opinion research (most often, his own), and recommends that conservatives choose the words and phrases that are shown to be the most agreeable to the potential audience. In particular, Luntz is keenly interested in alleviating anxiety with voters and consumers, and in not coming across as phony (when conservatives so often are).

Luntz is a bit of a self-promoter and he's preoccupied with expanding his firm's bottom line. In fairness to him, he wouldn't be the first political consultant to do either; he works in a highly competitive field, after all. He's entitled to make a buck, and Luntz, by his own admission, makes plenty.

What makes Frank Luntz unique isn't that he has helped to convert millions of voters to the conservative cause. It is, as Nunberg notes wryly, that Luntz helps conservatives "by allaying public concerns about their insensitivity to [certain] issues, so that people can go ahead and vote for them . . . on moral values." In effect, Luntz and his disciples use language to alleviate voter anxieties about a conservative's real purpose. That's what George W. Bush's infamous invocation of "compassionate conservatism" was in 2000: a phony but effective bit of ad-speak, a hoax, designed to persuade voters to suspend their doubts, however briefly, and inscribe an X in the right box. As things turned out, compassionate conservatism was quite a bit of the latter to the near-total exclusion of the former. But the phrase worked. And Luntzisms continue to work, unfortunately, because we have a collective memory in the Americas of about seven minutes.

Not long ago, Luntz popped up to Canada for a chummy meeting with Conservative Prime Minister Stephen Harper, and to give a speech to a secretive far-right organization, Civitas. His talk was titled "Massaging the Conservative Message for Voters," and it was enthusiastically received by Harper's chief of staff, Ian Brodie, his campaign manager, Tom Flanagan, and National Citizens Coalition vice-president, Gerry Nicholls, who had earlier worked with Harper at the government-loathing conservative lobby group. Said Luntz: "Start and end with accountability. It matters most . . . Talk about opportunity. [Progressives] have their fair share of communicators who can rally [the middle class] by appeals to fairness. Remove that capability and you will hold a majority for a decade . . ." Fairness is not a notion regular folks often associate with conservatives, Luntz correctly implied.

As Luntz told the powerful Canadian conservatives, "It is perfectly acceptable, if not imperative, that you address the values debate. And yes, it is *family values* that [voters] want and expect to see in you and your policies. Language is your base. Symbols knock it out of the park. [And] our research has shown us precisely those that work."

Conservative wordsmith Frank Luntz: he isn't always modest, but he isn't entirely wrong, either.

☆ ☆ ☆

It wasn't a very big sample size, but it was an interesting experiment, nonetheless: in and around the final days of the 2004 U.S. election, a team of psychologists decided to try and learn a bit more about how the brain—specifically, the political brain—works. Led by Drew Westen, the team hand-picked a group of fifteen Democrats and fifteen Republicans, and wired up their heads to monitor brain activity as they received different kinds of political information. What they found was published by Westen in his much-discussed book, *The Political Brain: The Role of Emotion in Deciding the Fate of the Nation.* Concluded Westen and his team: "The political brain is an emotional brain." They found that most unaligned voters—that is, so-called swing voters—"think with their guts, too."

No news there, perhaps. Conservatives have been merrily profiting from voter emotion for years. Liberals too often figure it's enough to wordily moot the issues and then let voters decide, as in some idyllic Athenian democracy. Westen and team concluded that, well, those liberals tend to *lose*. Voters make choices mainly based on "feelings" about candidates, campaigns or causes, not words. In effect, Westen's team declared, voter decisions are made within an emotional marketplace that is crowded with morality and value judgments. Logic only "plays a supporting role."

So, while progressives are currently lousy at competing in the marketplace of emotion, conservatives positively excel at it. Conservatives have "a monopoly" in this putative emotional marketplace, Westen observed. They are undisputed champs at connecting with the feelings of voters. Progressives, meanwhile, too often insist on antiseptically, and rationally, discussing "the issues."

George Lakoff, Geoffrey Nunberg, Frank Luntz and plenty of others have noted that voters agree more with progressive policies, but they vote more for conservative politicians. All agree it is because voters consider morals, values and identity politics—as emotionally charged as they may be—to be of far greater importance than antiseptic debates about policy choices. Progressives find this maddening: to us, reason should always precede passion. Most progressives find the raw emotional appeals of the type that conservatives favour appalling. (It also explains why we so often fall into the trap of calling our conservative opponents "dumb.") What, then, is a progressive to do? If values and morality dominate the discourse (and they do), and if conservatives rule in a political environment that is suffused with emotion (and they do), how can a frustrated liberal get in on the action?

We can do it by understanding, for starters, that unsolvable moral dilemmas are exactly that: unsolvable. Progressives, observes Oklahoma Democrat Brad Carson, need to "move away from any hope of bringing peace to irreconcilable moral disputes." For example: barring dramatic changes in human behaviour, abortion is likely to be an issue for many years to come. People are going to keep debating it, incessantly, and everyone knows the possibility of pro-life folks changing the minds of pro-choice folks—or vice-versa—is somewhere between slim to none. Paradoxically, the Right doesn't ever win the abortion debate on the ground: polls consistently show that most voters, particularly the female ones, over-whelmingly favour reproductive choice. But in respect of issues like abortion, the Right is successful in another way: its side is seen as more passionate and much less conflicted on the issue. Whether you favour abortion or not, you know where conservatives stand on it. Progressives, not so much. Therein lies the win: conservatives, on the values-and-morals stuff, are transparent, even when they're repellant. Clarity, and authenticity, matter more to the voters than one's actual policies.

To progressives, as noted, the Right's take on complex issues of morality often seems simplistic. Some days, in fact, the Right seems *stupid* to the Left. Nunberg, among many other progressive thinkers, cautions liberals to stop underestimating our opponents. "It's precisely the vagueness and super-ficiality of the Right's cultural stereotypes that make them so useful," Nunberg explained in *Talking Right*. "They create an illusion of shared experience among people whose actual commonalities don't extend to much more than the products on their shelves and a general sense of grievance."

The Right loves it when the Left calls them dumb. They are dizzy with pleasure when an effete liberal elitist calls them stupid. Consider, for instance, American conservative Laura Ingraham. She's a product of the reviled East Coast Ivy League establishment, but you'd never know it; like too many conservative hucksters, she excels at phony populist appeals. Here's how she kicks off her book *Shut Up and Sing*, writing about liberal elitists:"They think we're stupid.They think our patriotism is stupid. They think our churchgoing is stupid. They think having more than two children is stupid. They think where we live—anywhere but near or in a few major cities—is stupid.They think our SUVs are stupid.They think owning a gun is stupid."And so on.What isn't stupid, of course, is how Ingraham and her ilk shrewdly align themselves with millions of voters who consider themselves anything but elites; the millions, in effect, who make up the Occupiers' 99 percent. So when a liberal condescends to a conservative, it can backfire dramatically. Among other things, it allows conservatives to align themselves with the ordinary folks and working families whose votes they covet.

I'm like you, they say, over and over. *And see those liberal elitists? They think our values, and our way of life, is stupid. But we know better, don't we?*

☆ ☆ ☆

Brad Woodhouse scans the ceiling.

I've just asked him if the politics of the United States of America, which he knows rather well, are becoming way more conservative. As in, perhaps, *batshit crazy* conservative. Because to a liberal from another country, it sure as hell looks that way.

"Well . . ." he says, in his broad North Carolina twang. He laughs. "Well . . ."

If you're looking to take the temperature of political America, Brad Woodhouse should be one of the folks at the top of your list. His title is Communications Director to the Democratic National Committee, and as such, he's the guy charged with messaging (and massaging) everything that the Democratic Party has to say. But on the street, he's also widely regarded as a pretty sharp political operator, one who knows how to fashion progressive wins in an environment that, these days, looks distinctly inhospitable to liberals.

Growing up, he was always a liberal. Not everyone around the kitchen table at home in Raleigh, North Carolina, was, however. His brother Dallas, for instance, is the head of something called Americans for Prosperity and is a card-carrying Republican, no less. Their relationship, or lack of one, has attracted quite a bit of attention.

One time, the two brothers were invited on CNN to debate Obama's health-care reforms. Said Dallas to the CNN anchor, former Canadian TV personality John Roberts: "It's simple that the president is losing this debate. You know he's losing this debate when people like my brother and the White House start attacking hard-working, tax-paying citizens as mobsters." Said Brad to CNN: "You cannot have an honest debate with folks like my brother on this issue." While their mother doesn't like all this nastiness one bit, the two Woodhouse boys continue to duke it out, on-air and off. Dallas says his brother "is a professional reputation destroyer" who engages in a lot of "twisting and spinning." Brad, meanwhile, doesn't retreat from the field of familial battle. Dallas, he says, peddles "lies, innuendo and conspiracy theories." Also, "he's a right-wing nut-job." Yikes!

Conservatives hate Brad, which, from this liberal's perspective, is always a good sign. When President Obama won the Nobel Peace Prize in October 2009, the Republican Party went bananas, huffing that the president didn't deserve the award. Hamas and the Taliban felt likewise, a useful fact that did not escape the notice of Brad Woodhouse: "The Republican Party has thrown in its lot with the terrorists . . . in criticizing the president for receiving the Nobel Peace Prize—an award he did not seek but that is nonetheless an honour in which every American can take great pride. Unless, of course, you are the Republican Party. The 2009 version of the Republican Party has no boundaries, has no shame, and has proved that they will put politics above patriotism at every turn. It's no wonder only 20 percent of Americans admit to being Republicans anymore." Sputtering with rage, the apoplectic Republicans declared that Woodhouse's rhetoric was "shameful." It achieved the desired purpose, however: it showed that Democrats everywhere were no longer going to accept Republican smears with equanimity or silence. Hit back, hard. Leave no charge unanswered. In a media environment dominated by conservatives, it's the only way. And it works.

Brad Woodhouse, therefore, knows how to fight and beat conservatives. He's good at it. He's also smart, he's sharp-witted and he's one of the most effective liberal voices in the United States today. Right out of university, he busied himself toiling on assorted Democratic senatorial campaigns. After that, he did stints consulting, and was the head communications guy at an organization preoccupied with saving social security. In 2008, he starting working for the Democratic National Committee full-time and, by 2009, took on his present role. He wasn't with Obama early on, he says. In fact, he came to toil at the DNC, in his current role, only after Obama was inaugurated as the forty-fourth president.

Woodhouse muses about how—in the midst of a lousy economy, and against a revitalized Republican Party—Obama can win again. And how that can be done when American voters (as noted) seem more and more conservative.

"I think Republicans have been very successful in the past thirty years. This isn't a new thing," he says, hands laced behind his head, feet up a chair at the shiny and secure DNC headquarters in Washington, D.C. "They demonize government. And I think they've been very successful at demonizing about taxes. But that's their problem. That's where they look totally hypocritical."

He leans forward and regards his Canadian guest. "The entire time that Bush was in office, there were Republicans demonizing government. And then they would take [government money] for government projects in their districts. And while they were demonizing government, they were still making sure there were government contracts for defence, and buildings and bridges in their districts. And you know, it was Republicans who ran up the deficit. And then they let Wall Street write its own rules."

They're no-good, stinkin' hypocrites, in other words, but he's too polite to say so, so his guest says it for him. Woodhouse, laughing, agrees. But it can't be denied—as George Lakoff, Geoffrey Nunberg and others have opined—that conservatives have been much more effective communicators in recent years. They used to be lousy at it. But not so much anymore. Says Woodhouse, who has squared off against more than his fair share of conservative causes, candidates and campaigns: "Being a Democrat, you have lots of priorities. Clean air, clean water, health, education, and so on. Republicans have very few. They have a single-minded focus, you know. Cut taxes. Downsize government. Have a strong defence. If you say those things in a Republican district, over and over, you can get elected to office. You don't have to say much else."

A vocabulary of simplicity "will be of service throughout your life," the conservative named Winston Churchill said. Churchill, among others, knew that one need not talk about priorities; if you are doing your job right, priorities reveal themselves in action. Conservatives generally and Republicans specifically have been winning because they have learned the crucial importance of staying on message. In circumstances where citizens are extraordinarily busy, and where fewer and fewer of them are paying attention to government and public institutions, the message that captures the largest number of eyes and ears is the message that is simplest. It is the message that is seen, and not just heard.

The best kind of communications—"comms," as politicos call it—is the comms that reaches the largest possible audience. To achieve that challenging task, the words and phrases a communicator employs should have meaning to as many people as possible. Their advocacy needs to be understood by the greatest number. And complexity, as noted (and as conservatives know best), is the enemy of understanding. On the values-and-morals front—on the frontlines of what former Republican presidential aspirant Pat Buchanan infamously called the "culture war"—conservatives will always gravitate towards themes that are straightforward and easy to understand. Liberals, however, typically favour complexity. As with doctors, lawyers and engineers, jargon gives us comfort.

"Sure. I think that's something that the Democratic Party has been grappling with for many, many decades," Brad Woodhouse says, agreeing. "Now, I think presidents are confronted with so many different things, it is almost impossible to stick to just one, you know? With this president, would he have wanted to deal with the BP oil spill for sixty to ninety days? No. Would this president have chosen to have this big fight with Republicans over the debt ceiling? No. And I think Republicans did that so the president would have difficulty getting any other message out. Presidents don't have the luxury of concentrating on just one thing, but that's all that the opposition does.

"Conservatives have had to simplify their marketing strategy in the past thirty years," he says. "They have talked about values. They talk about the values of free enterprise, and protecting your family from the reach of government and all that kind of stuff. They talk about it in ways that are devoid of policy. Their rhetoric is all about values, all the time." And a lot of the time, it's helped them win, too.

☆ ☆ ☆

George W. Bush: he taunts us still.

Bush—along with two-term Republican president Ronald Reagan—was one of the greatest conservative communicators to ever lend his name to a ballot. Sure, he could sound dumb (personal favourite: "Rarely is the question asked: Is our children learning?"). Sure, he could be inarticulate (personal favourite: "I promise you I will listen to what has been said here, even though I wasn't here."). Sure, he could make verbal gaffes (personal favourite: "I know how hard it is for you to put food on your family."). Sure, he was sometimes completely and totally incomprehensible (personal favourite: "I know what I believe. I will continue to articulate what I believe and what I believe—I believe what I believe is right.").

But when his presidency is examined from the perspective of hindsight and history, Dubya was well and truly understood when it counted. Not by the so-called liberal elites he maligned on a regular basis, of course: them, he didn't care about. But he was understood by the *people*. When he talked about values and morals, they knew exactly what he meant. Even if they disagreed with him—and on not a few issues, they did—no one could accuse Bush of being misunderstood. He kept his message simple. (Which is why he was so regularly pilloried by progressives for being simplistic.)

Many of us snobby, pointy-headed liberals followed the former U.S. president on the talk-show circuit as he flogged his autobiography, *Decision Points*. For those of us who still cling to the centre-left, Bush-watching is a fundamentally unsettling experience. It's not unlike running into a former spouse in the airport bookstore: it's awkward, and it brings back plenty of bad memories, but for the life of you, you can't turn away. Mostly, you find it impossible to dislike him as much as you once did.

There he was, on Oprah, sort-of suggesting he didn't have the authority to send in the troops after Hurricane Katrina levelled New Orleans in 2005—while, inexplicably, insisting that he had the authority to send in the same troops to invade Iraq two years earlier. Or there he was on another channel, telling Matt Lauer he had no regrets about permitting terror suspects to be waterboarded—which, the dictionaries remind us, is "a form of torture" wherein drowning is simulated. "Damn right," Dubya tells Lauer. He then goes on to say his feelings were "hurt" when Kanye West called him a racist for failing to help the predominantly black population of New Orleans in the wake of Katrina. Got that? Torture—damn right, it's A-okay. Being called a racist by a musician a lot of people don't look to for political insight—that hurts.

All over the dial on his book tour, Bush skilfully rebuffed assorted inquisitors, insisting he didn't want to get drawn back into "the swamp" of politics. And then, in that engaging, laconic Texan dialect, he proceeded to recount all kinds of stories about politics.

Bush was president while we Canadians went through three different prime ministers. One day, I asked one of them, Jean Chrétien, what he thought of the younger Bush. "He's a nice guy," Chrétien said. "I always got along with him." The conservative commentariat were forever suggesting the opposite, of course. They were in full spit-flecked apoplexy when Chrétien declined to follow Bush into the quagmire that would become Iraq. As noted, Conservative leader Stephen

Harper even called Chrétien a "coward" over it. While Bush was surprised Canada wouldn't participate, it didn't affect the bilateral relationship, Chrétien recalled.

So, are we liberals going soft on Bush, the fellow quite a few of us thought made the planet measurably less safe, clean and prosperous? Nope; we still blame him for all of those things. But, like I say, he's a hard guy to hate. I attribute this to the one characteristic that values-obsessed conservative politicians generally possess in much greater quantities than Liberal politicians: HOAG.

That is, Bush was a *Hell of a Guy*. As the political cliché goes, you can picture yourself at a tailgate party with Dubya, swigging Buds, telling lies about the ones that got away. With John Kerry or Al Gore, you just can't. Eating quiche and sipping spritzers at a rich debutante's coming-out party at Harvard, maybe. But are they HOAGS? Nope.

This is not to suggest that Liberals are incapable of HOAG-ism. Chrétien was eating at Tim Hortons long before focus groups persuaded Stephen Harper to do likewise. Bill Clinton, too, was always a HOAG. Watching him hoover a Big Mac, you wouldn't ever guess he was once a Rhodes Scholar. But Bush—despite being the son of a New England multimillionaire, despite his pricey Yale education and his connections to American aristocracy—was a true-blue HOAG. He was the ultimate HOAG, in fact. He made his inability to string a few words together work *for* him. Moreover, when he talked about "values"—which, Google informs us, he did literally hundreds of times during his presidency—he could light up a conservative audience like a Christmas tree.

He was upfront about it, too. In one of his campaign ads in the summer of 2000, Bush said this: "This is a moment in history when we have a chance to focus on tough problems. It's not always popular to say . . . we have a deficit in *values*. But those are the right things to say. And the right way to make America better for everyone is to be bold and decisive, to unite instead of divide. Now is the time to do the hard things." On values and morality plays, Bush made his HOAGism work for him. And when Bush's presidency came to its constitutionally mandated end, as he defiantly told a crowd at the inauguration of the George W. Bush Presidential Center, "I came home to Texas with my values intact."

And that, I think, is why we effete lefties couldn't stop watching him as he peddled his book hither and yon: on values, he spoke to our suppressed inner HOAGs.

(Now, where's that plate of quiche?)

☆ ☆ ☆

The values that conservatives favour the most—the values they seek to champion all the time—are family values.

They name conservative think tanks and foundations after family values. They make innumerable fundraising appeals in the name of family values. In every campaign speech, in every press release, in every focus-grouped talking point, conservatives are desperate to be seen as champions of family values. Why?

George Lakoff, the most famous progressive cognitive linguist on the planet (possibly, the only one), regards "family values" as the very epicentre of the conservative values crusade. "I had asked myself why conservatives were talking so much about family values," Lakoff wrote in his seminal book on how values frame the political debate, *Don't Think of an Elephant!* "And why did certain 'family values' count while others did not? Why would anyone in a presidential campaign, in congressional campaigns, and so on, when the future of the world is being threatened by nuclear proliferation and global warming, constantly talk about family values?"

Because, as Lakoff and quite a few others have concluded, the "family" in the family values construct is an idealized one. It doesn't really exist anymore. The conservative family is from another time: Dad works, Mom doesn't. Mom and kids always respect and obey Father, who is the boss of all things. Dad provides, Mom runs the house; both provide authority, which the kids are expected to obey without question. As Lakoff writes: "God above man, man above nature, adults above children, Western culture over non-Western culture." It's *Leave It to Beaver*, without the laughs. Preserving and extending the conservative conception of family values is, he says, "the highest priority" to conservatives.

There's a problem, however. It's fictional; it's false. For instance: the realm where this illusory family resides is opposed to letting Mom work outside the family home—and it particularly opposes Dad staying home to raise the kids while Mom works. It doesn't contemplate, let alone permit, one dad to marry another dad, or be with one. (Ditto a family with two moms.) It wouldn't *ever* allow two dads to raise children without a mom in the picture. It's a family where contraception is unnecessary because nobody ever has sex outside marriage—and naturally, marriage is forever. It's a family where the kids unquestioningly do what they're told, never resisting corporal punishment, rulings about personal appearance or the military draft. Everyone knows who they are and what role they play in the conservative "family values" type of family.

This kind of family, of course, doesn't exist and probably never did. It resides in conservative dreams but nowhere else. Just a few statistics testify to how fully the conservative family values lobby has lost the war. More than 75 percent of mothers in North America now work full- or part-time. More than a million same-sex couples are estimated to live in the U.S. Nearly fifty thousand children have been adopted by same-sex couples in the U.S. In Canada, the Supreme Court outlawed school corporal punishment in 2004, and in the U.S. the majority of states have banned it for almost as long. Conservatives keep uttering the siren call of family values, however, because voters are listening. And voters, as we have seen, are motivated by what conservatives have to say, however obtuse progressives may consider it to be.

Voters vote their values—and their morality and their self-identity—before they vote their economic self-interests. Voters are quite comfortable supporting an illusion that is consistent with their own values, even if it's at odds with their own lives. Even if they intuitively know it has never existed and likely never will. How else to explain the millions of trade unionists who voted for Ronald Reagan? How else to understand the millions of crime-hating Canadians who voted for Stephen Harper, who scrapped gun safety laws over the overwhelming opposition of police chiefs and crime victims? In the politics of values, there isn't much room for rationality.

James Carville, testify.

☆ ☆ ☆

The Ragin' Cajun, as he's known, is the political operative who helped get Bill Clinton the keys to the White House. James Carville is bald, he's bombastic and—to progressives and liberals everywhere—he's the *best*. He's the campaign guy that every campaign guy wants to be. During the 1993 federal election campaign, in which Jean Chrétien won a massive majority government and his Conservative opponents were reduced to two seats, we put a picture of Carville on the Liberal war room wall. Below it, I wrote "God."

God's achievements were the stuff of legend. Most notably, in 1991, when serial bimbo eruptions had resulted in the

Arkansas governor being written off by pundits and politicos, Carville refused to give up, deflecting scandals and building Clinton's campaign around the notion that "It's the economy, stupid." With the U.S. still mired in a bruising recession, there was no question that the state of the economy was the presidential ballot question. But not nearly as much attention is paid to how Carville assisted Clinton in outmanoeuvring George Bush Sr. on the front lines of the morals-and-values battlefield. Carville has plenty to say on the subject, too.

Way back in February 2008, I was asked to introduce Carville at a meeting of a dinner club in Toronto. The event was held at crowded Italian restaurant on Yonge Street, during a raging snowstorm that had effectively shut down Canada's largest city. Many of us thought Carville wouldn't make it, as the roads were impassable and his plane to Toronto had been cancelled. But the Louisiana native simply commandeered a rented car and pointed it north. He arrived on time, slightly frazzled, but in one piece.

At that point, Carville was deeply involved in advising Hillary Clinton's campaign against Barack Obama for the Democratic presidential nomination. He fielded a few questions about who was likely to secure the presidential nomination. Carville favoured Hillary, and said so.

I asked him about whether values—which had been at the centre of Bush Jr.'s presidency—would figure in the 2008 election campaign in the way that the economy had in 1992. Right away, he became animated, his big hands gesturing all over the place, his eyes flashing.

"Fuck, yeah," he said. "And it's got me worried. The Republicans have become wizards at that stuff. And they're better at it than we [Democrats] are."

For decades, Carville explained, conservatives generally and Republicans specifically have been waging a war to seize the hearts and minds of middle-class and lower-middle-class voters. Their favoured approach, he said, has been to whip up anger and resentment about values—what was dubbed the culture war in the Nixon era—and leverage the resulting votes to advance their political agenda. Race, abortion, gun control, school prayer and other such moral issues have been deployed expertly by conservatives, Carville said, to drive a wedge between voting blocs and win seats. Hands in full flight, he said that, once they win power, the true conservative agenda always reveals itself. "Their *real* values," Carville growled, are tax cuts for the rich, or chipping away at hard-won union bargaining rights, or empowering judges who turn back the clock on everything from child labour to worker safety. Carville shook his impressively bald head. "These country-club elitists have won over the country-music crowd," he said. It's a phrase I've heard him use before, but it was still funny as it was apt. "But we've gotta get those folks back."

When I suggest that Barack Obama looks squeaky clean, and will acquit himself well in the values debate, Carville looks unconvinced. "Too many of my fellow Americans, especially where I come from [in the South], still have racist beliefs. It's wrong, and it's terrible, and it's disgusting. But the Republicans have made race a proxy for sorts of values judgments. Shame on them, but they've done it."

I ask him if the progressives too often look down their noses at the country-music-playing, gun-loving, abortion-hating, beer-swilling, good-old-boy conservative crowd. "You know, the HOAGS," I ask.

"HOAG? What the fuck is that?" Carville says, laughing, looking at me like I'm crazy. I explain: Hell Of A Guy. With the exception of Bill Clinton and Jean Chrétien, conservatives have cornered the market on HOAGS. As a result, conservatives

seem closer to Main Street, not Wall Street. Even when, overwhelmingly, they're not.

He laughs again. "HOAGS. I like that. I'm gonna use that,"
he says. "For sure. It's a trap. All these attacks Democrats made
on Bush's intelligence just made him look like one of the
guys, you know? Liberals always need to feel like they're
smarter than conservatives, but we're not. And so it lets [con-
servatives] say we're liberal elitists."

Intellectual arrogance, as Carville has written in one of his
books with his friend and fellow Clinton Democrat Paul
Begala—a certifiable genius—is a luxury that progressives
can't afford. When progressives sneer at the family values that
conservatives like to talk about so much, they risk losing
votes. Lots of votes. Conservatives point to this liberal arrogance, Carville and Begala note, and they exaggerate it. They
use it to distract middle-class voters from the many ways in
which conservative economic policies will cause them real
and lasting pain. George Wallace, Carville continues, showed
conservatives in the sixties how to do it—with his constant
harangues against "pointy-headed intellectuals" who wanted
to impose their elitist social engineering schemes on down-
home regular folks—and they have stuck doggedly to their
message track ever since.

Abortion, Carville says, is a classic example of an issue that
progressives have too often mishandled. Most Americans, he
said, don't want to ban abortion. "But they don't *like* it, either,"
Carville says. "They want to restrict it in certain cases."

Statistics certainly support what Carville was saying. Around
85 percent favour abortion when a woman's life is in danger;
nearly 80 percent feel that way when her physical health is at
risk. So, too, when a pregnancy is caused by rape or incest—
nearly 80 percent of Americans support abortion then. And 60
percent support it in "all or most cases," Carville and Begala

point out. But there's a problem, and it's a problem progressives have created for themselves. In their desire to appear progressive, many have gone too far on abortion, Carville and Begala say. They put themselves on the fringe of the issue when they should be in the mainstream of the issue. For instance, in 2004, all eight Democratic presidential candidates went on the record to oppose every possible restriction on abortion, including partial-birth and late-term abortions. That's a mistake, Carville says, because 70 percent of Americans—including many of those who support abortion rights—favour a ban on partial-birth abortions. So, Carville says, "the Democratic Party has become viewed as a tool of the abortion rights groups" at the presidential level.

This is a dilemma for Democrats, he adds, because "abortion is a class issue." Highly educated people, with higher incomes and living on the coasts, are mostly pro-choice. Pro-lifers, meanwhile, generally have less education, less income, and are not found on either coast. Says Carville: "They resent what they believe is the snobbery, the elitism, the supposed intellectual superiority of the pro-choicers."

That resentment of overpaid, overeducated liberal elitists—in the view of James Carville, Paul Begala, George Lakoff, Brad Woodhouse and Geoffrey Nunberg—is a crucial consideration for liberals and progressives everywhere. Three points need to be remembered by progressives, Carville says.

One, for candidates to stress the role values and morals should play in political life isn't a sign that they are stupid. Family values, therefore, are legitimate points of view for citizens to have. In some cases, they are even defensible positions.

Two, black-hearted conservative strategists like Frank Luntz have used values and morality to win over constituencies that were, previously, in the Democratic or Liberal column. They have successfully persuaded these voters that liberal elites and pointy-headed intellectuals look down on them and theirs, and have contempt for their values and priorities. In so doing, Luntz and his conservative ilk have aligned themselves with voters who, in earlier circumstances, would have detested conservatives. Progressives need to pay attention to that and learn from it, Carville says, and take those voters back.

Three, it's not what we liberals and progressives are supposed to be like. We're supposed to be better than that. "We're supposed to be the ones who are open and understanding about other people, and other people's beliefs," says Carville, getting ready to give his speech. "*We're* supposed to be on the side of the little guy. Not those conservative assholes."

He points a finger at my chest: "Tell your liberal friends we need to capture voters' *hearts*, and not just their minds!"

Will do.

HOW CONSERVATIVES MESS WITH WORDS
(AND YOUR HEAD)

The sounds made by conservatives to attract the attention of
uncommitted voters are, to trained ears, highly disturbing.
To some, the conservative's trills and warbles are highly primitive and
coarse. However, when seeking the affection of voters who are not attached
to another political animal, their mating calls sound appealing.
But to those expert in the ways of the conservative species, the cry of
the conservative is to be feared and detested. In the political wilderness,
their sound is the sound of deceit.

———

Ian Davey, chief of staff to Liberal Party leader Michael Ignatieff, slumped into a chair in his modest Parliament Hill
office. "I tried," he said, looking grim. "He won't do it."

It was October 2009. For days, we had been attempting to
persuade Ignatieff that he desperately needs a winning ballot
question. His end-of-summer promise to defeat the Harper government and force a general election—for no stated reason—
had sent the Liberal Party into a tailspin. Whatever popularity
we'd enjoyed in the spring and summer was slipping away.

Simultaneously, Harper's defence minister had been equiv-
ocating in the House of Commons on ending Canada's military presence in Afghanistan by June 2011. Despite an all-party
resolution favouring the conclusion of our combat role, it was
clear that many within the hawkish Conservative government
wanted to stay. Davey—the son of the legendary Grit rainmaker, Keith Davey, and a friend who had brought me to
Ottawa to run the Liberal war room—agreed that an election
fought on the extension of the war could end badly for the
Conservatives. And it would banish a few ghosts, too.

Ignatieff had secured the Liberal leadership just a few months
earlier, but was still dogged by concerns about his writings, particularly from the progressive side of our party. The former
Harvard professor, who had reported on the conflict in the
former Yugoslavia, had been an enthusiastic proponent of the
war in Iraq, unambiguously pro-American and, seemingly, an
advocate of "coercive techniques" with terror suspects.

Canada, some of us agreed, had done its bit over nearly a
decade in Afghanistan, with too many Canadian lives lost. Like
most Liberals, we felt it was time to let some other Western
nations step up. In the election to come, Liberals would be the
ones offering an end to the war. Let the Conservative administration—with its bellicose military rhetoric and willingness
to give the generals whatever shiny new toy they desired—
become the party that favoured war with no end.

"We can banish the pro-American, pro-torture, pro–Iraq
war stuff in one move," I'd said to Davey and others in the
Office of the Leader of the Opposition. "We'd pick up a ton
of NDP and Bloc support. And Harper will be caught in the
quagmire like John McCain was. It's perfect."

But Ignatieff wouldn't do it. Not only would he not discuss
the notion, Davey said, he was angry that we had suggested it
to him in the first place.

"What did you say?" I asked Davey.

"I told him we just wanted him to, you know, win the fucking election. That's all."

☆ ☆ ☆

In the fall of 2009, beating the Conservatives in a campaign—*winning the fucking election*, as Davey aptly put it—shouldn't have been too difficult for those of us on the progressive side of the spectrum. The war in Afghanistan was dragging on and on with no end in sight; the Conservatives had badly botched their response to the outbreak of H1N1 swine flu (on one occasion, even sending body bags to a Manitoba First Nation instead of vaccines); and rumours swirled that federal infrastructure projects were rife with cronyism and favouritism, with the lion's share of contracts going to ridings represented by Conservatives. Most seriously, the economy had been mired in a deep recession for months, and hundreds of thousands of people had lost their jobs. As in the U.S., the global recession had brutally hammered Canada: according to some economists, it had been the longest and deepest recession of the postwar era. From coast to coast, Canadians were saddled with debt, massive unemployment and a nagging sense that the Conservative regime of Stephen Harper had been wholly unprepared for the bad times.

In fact, before the recession hit, Harper had strenuously denied it was coming. "This country will not go into recession [in 2009]," the Conservative leader huffed at the end of 2008. When a recession finally *did* hit a few months later, Harper and his gang tried to deny it, actually claiming it was a "technical recession," whatever that is. They looked like a bunch of political rookies, not the cautious economic managers they habitually claimed to be. They looked nervous—clueless, in fact.

On the other side of the political aisle, Canadian progressives were in comparatively better shape. Jack Layton, the best-
liked politician in the country, led the New Democrats. My
Liberal Party, meanwhile, had recently selected Ignatieff—an
acclaimed international human rights expert, and the most
popular Liberal leader in the province of Quebec since Pierre
Trudeau—to be its leader. Both the Dippers and the Grits
were well financed, election-ready and together supported by
as much as two-thirds of Canadian voters. If an election were
to be held, it seemed likely that the Liberals would win a
minority government, with the New Democrats providing
vote support when needed.

So in early October 2009, we Liberals finally decided we
would attempt to topple the Conservative government in a
vote in the House of Commons, with the principal reason
being the state of the economy. Ignatieff opened debate on
the motion by saying that hundreds of thousands of unemployed Canadians felt "totally abandoned" by the government.
As those of us who advised him looked on from the visitors'
galleries, Ignatieff declared: "How do I explain to these people
that I keep letting this government go on? And that is why in
my hearts of hearts, after much reflection, we've decided as a
party that we can't continue to give the government confidence in the House of Commons." The Conservative regime's
record was terrible, the Liberal leader rightly said, "and someone must stand up in this House and call it for what it is."

But the New Democrats—who, as social democrats, usually
professed to oppose everything the Conservatives stood for—
weren't standing up with us. In fact, they intended to keep
their behinds firmly planted in their cushy Commons seats,
despite earlier suggestions to the contrary. When it came time
for a vote, the New Democrats had decided to abstain. Pressed
by the media, Layton's party admitted that they had made a

backroom deal with the Conservatives to extend employment insurance benefits. As a result, the Harper Conservatives survived, defeating our motion 144 to 117. Up in the visitors' gallery, some of us made chicken sounds in the direction of the NDP members of Parliament, many of whom were showing a deep interest in whatever was on top of their desks.

But fair's fair: the failure to hold a destructive gang of conservatives to account wasn't solely the New Democrats' fault. Later that month, Ian Davey and I pressured Ignatieff to come out against the war. As he listened, stone-faced, we told him that the war in Afghanistan was looking increasingly like an unwinnable quagmire. It would form the basis for an important choice for voters in any election campaign, with our side being the side that favoured peace, and the Conservatives pushing for yet more war. But the Liberal leader angrily refused. Along with his former university chum and leadership rival Bob Rae, Ignatieff chose discretion over valour, and this time it was the Liberal Party that elected to keep propping up the Conservative minority government. The war went on. So did the Conservative-led government.

All of that—the NDP capitulating on the economy, and we Liberals capitulating on the war—amounted to big mistake number one. When progressives had conservatives on the proverbial ropes, we folded like a cheap suit. The economy started to improve and the war began to fade from the headlines. Our chief arguments for throwing out the right-wing bums slipped away. We progressives could have won an election that fall, but we chose instead to let the Conservatives continue to govern. They did not hesitate to take advantage of the opportunity we had given them.

Big mistake number two was one we lefties make all the time. It was not about the economy or the war; it concerned something else entirely. It is the kind of mistake that liberals and progressives routinely make these days, and all over, too. We get arrogant, and we start to believe that conservatives are lousy communicators. When, in truth, they've become better communicators than we are.

Take, for example, the Internet. On the web—and particularly in blogs—conservatives utterly dominate. Demographically, blog authors more often than not are white, Christian, college-educated conservative men (while Facebook, globally, is the realm of liberal women). As a lonely progressive voice in a sea of angry conservatives, I can testify to the fact that the Right rules supreme in the blogosphere. The Ipsos polling firm has estimated that nearly 70 percent of blogs are conservative. The kind of communications conservative generally favour, other polls tell us, are like them—*negative*. As the January 2012 University of Nebraska–Lincoln study found, conservatives tend to favour negative content.

Here, then, is an unassailable truth (and it's one that has had hefty consequences for innumerable progressive political campaigns): so-called negative conservative ad campaigns usually work. Indeed, if someone tells you that conservative political attack ads aren't effective, you are talking to either a liar or a fool. Few people will ever confess to having been influenced by such advertising, but they are. Voters remember negative ads more than any other type of advocacy ads. Conservatives—whether Harper's gang up here or the Tea Party–dominated Republicans down south—know this too well.

Let me give you an example. When I was younger, way back before the dawn of time, I was a University of Calgary law student. To keep myself in Kraft Dinner and beer, I toiled part-time as a police beat reporter at the *Calgary Herald*. Most weekends, I borrowed a desk in the newsroom and kept an ear cocked to the police radio. Whenever a big crime or car crash took place, I would leap into my battered old Gremlin and peel out onto Calgary's roadways to learn more. If the car crashes were sufficiently spectacular, I would write a story about them. Usually, my news editors would assign a photographer to take pictures. And when there wasn't very much else going on in the news world, we would run photos of the wreckage.

Whenever the paper did that, folks would threaten to cancel their subscriptions. Subscribers would call to tell us we were awful people, and all that we cared about was nasty, negative stuff. "Why can't your people print good news, for a change," I recall more than a few saying to me. But whenever I was out at those accident scenes, scribbling away in my notepad, I noticed that everyone making their way past the orange pylons and the traffic cops—*every single one of them*—would slow down to take a look. Sometimes, I'd see them reaching for a camera so they could take some pictures, too.

What is true of car crashes is true of political life, too. Whenever polled, voters will insist they hate it when political parties or newspapers promote negativity. They tell pollsters they oppose negativity generally and negative ads in particular. But, with the greatest of respect, as lawyers like to say, they're lying. When they think no one is looking, they slow down and take a look. And they remember what they see.

Conservative politicos know this best. Some of them will piously claim they don't like doing the tough stuff, but they do. And voters say they aren't influenced by tough stuff, but they are.

Because I've written a couple books that dealt extensively with political advertising, and because I'm a statistical anomaly—a liberal who doesn't ever mind "going neg" about an opponent's public record—Liberal Party leader Ignatieff was a bit wary of me. That was fine by me: I was wary of him, too. My mother, who is what I call my one-person focus group, is more liberal than deepest San Francisco. "I don't know, dear," she memorably said to me in one of our twice-daily calls. "I think he's a conservative."

So I kept my distance and got to work. From my perspective, no party leader should ever know everything that their war room is up to. In the spring and summer of 2009, my war room team in Ottawa and Toronto had been covertly producing a series of nasty anti-Conservative Internet ads under the pseud-onym Grit Girl. The idea was to give Harper's Reformatories, as I called them, a taste of their own medicine—and to do to Harper what his black-hearted ad men had done to Paul Martin and Stéphane Dion, Ignatieff's Liberal predecessors. The ads depicted Harper's party as confused, clumsy and corrupt. All of the ads were approved by Ian Davey or Paul Zed, but we kept them from Ignatieff.

One sunny day, Ignatieff spotted me outside his parliamentary offices, 409-S, talking to Davey in the hallway. Ignatieff put an arm around me and asked if we could talk. Sure, I said.

"This Grit Girl stuff," he said. "You're being careful, right?"

I nodded.

"I'm supposed to be the guy who does politics differently," he said, regarding me suspiciously. "I'm just not sure attack ads are the way to go."

I sighed. The Conservatives' multimillion-dollar attack-ad barrage hadn't started yet. My talkative Conservative contacts had told me they would target Ignatieff's main weakness: namely, that he had lived outside of Canada for so long and was only returning to the colonies to seize power. The imperious Ignatieff, the Conservative TV spots would devastatingly claim, was basically a tourist in Canada. Over and over, I was told, their ad campaign would question why Ignatieff had been away from Canada for thirty-four years—and along the way, it would suggest he was a poncey aristocrat, one who "wasn't in it for you, just for himself." The devastating TV spots would be called the "Just Visiting" ads, and they would reportedly cost the Tories more than three million dollars. As things turned out, they would be wildly successful, working beyond any conservative's expectations.

"Listen, sir," I said. "If we could put together some nice ads of children running through a field of daisies, with nice music playing in the background, we'd do that. If we could do nice stuff like that and win the election for you, we would. But these bastards are getting ready to rip your face off. So I want to rip their faces off first."

Ignatieff looked at me as one would look at a used-car salesman. As things turned out, he wasn't persuaded. He wanted to "do politics differently." Neither Zed nor Davey agreed with Ignatieff's directive. But Iggy, as Ian called him, was the leader of the Liberal Party of Canada, and we weren't. Reluctantly, we dialed down the Grit Girl stuff. Just a few weeks later, the Just Visiting spots did what they were designed to do. The Liberal leader's personal numbers became an unmitigated disaster; whatever honeymoon he'd enjoyed was over. Ignatieff, like Dion before him, had made the fatal error of letting his opponents define him first. His goose was cooked, pretty much.

Not long before I packed my bag to return home to Toronto, I ran into Ignatieff, who regarded me wearily and said, "I guess it's too late for me to tell you to go rip the Conservatives' faces off, now."

"Yep," I said. "It's too late."

☆ ☆ ☆

Define or be defined.

That is the truest political truism of them all. It is the principal reason Ignatieff was eviscerated in the election campaign, and it is why the once-great Liberal Party was reduced to a rump and third-party status in the House of Commons in

May 2011. Ignatieff let his Conservative opponents define him before he could define himself.

In politics, in communications, definition is something—it's everything. And the Conservatives know this best.

Consider the NDP race to replace the late Jack Layton. It felt like the New Democrats had more leadership candidates than they did caucus members. The race was boring as a dog's arse. Most of the contestants were nobodies, and that's putting it nicely. And all of them, to a one, lacked Layton's charisma. Why would anyone bother to pay a lot of attention?

Well, if you didn't, don't worry: the Conservative Research Group was happily paying attention on your behalf. The CRG consists of dozens of neatly barbered young Conservatives who toil in a government office building on Queen Street in downtown Ottawa, not far from Parliament Hill. They've been around since 2006, when Conservative boss Stephen Harper set up the office under the tutelage of his capable communications director-to-be, Sandra Buckler.

From the start, CRG apparatchiks did a really good job. They were swift, they were deadly, and they were relentless. Most notably, they made miserable the lives of various Liberal leaders—Stéphane Dion and Michael Ignatieff in particular. And after Jack Layton died, the CRG got to work on the many unknowns who were vying for the NDP leadership. Evidence of this was found, early on, in the much-read Parliament Hill weekly, the *Hill Times*. In a semiregular column, the Conservatives' Tim Powers, the New Democrats' Karl Bélanger or Brad Lavigne, and I go at each other. For years, the CRG's talking head, Tim Powers, naturally targeted my Liberals. In 2011, his focus necessarily changed, and he started to fling mud at the Official Opposition New Democrats. What Powers said in the *Hill Times* wasn't all that novel—he correctly pointed out that the willingness of the top Dipper leadership candidates to tax us more isn't much of a get-elected strategy. What was interesting, though, was how early the CRG started defining the next NDP leader, long before he could define himself.

A few weeks later, the Conservatives fired off another shot at the listing New Democrats. One of the front-runners in the quest for the party's leadership, Thomas Mulcair, was revealed to have dual Canadian and French citizenship. The CRG-led Conservatives had a great old time with that one, poking fun at Mulcair and pointing out that Harper's passport was all-Canadian—and would ever be thus. The New Democrats squirmed in embarrassment. (They should have: a few years earlier, Layton and his NDP had hypocritically lambasted Dion for possessing French citizenship.) It all followed a tried-and-true conservative methodology. For months, the CRG threw punches at the various contenders for the NDP leadership, but nothing lethal. Mostly, they just clipped and catalogued every word the candidates uttered (and fabricated more than a few that they didn't). And then, once Mulcair was selected as leader, they swung down on the NDP like a snarling pack of ravenous jackals. In June 2012, the Conservatives released tough attack ads, excoriating a sinister-looking Mulcair for his attacks on Canada's energy industry and his economic policies. Mulcair is "RISKY," the ads declared; he's "DANGEROUS." It followed a tried-and-true CRG approach.

It's their modus operandi. These conservatives are not especially subtle, they're not original, but they are convinced it works. And it does: it certainly worked against Ignatieff and Dion. By the time the Just Visiting ads had run their course, for instance, Canadians' attitudes towards Ignatieff had shifted dramatically. When he became leader in 2009, and for much of that year, Ignatieff's party polled ahead of the governing

Conservatives, and the former Harvard prof looked very much like a prime minister in waiting (which was why Ian Davey and I wanted to force an election). But Just Visiting would change all of that.

. One huge 2011 poll, done for the QMI Agency by Leger Marketing, showed that the Conservative attack ads had radically affected public opinion in a number of key Canadian election battlegrounds. In vote-rich Ontario, for example, where we Liberals needed to do well to have any hope of forming a government, 43 percent said it was "a bad thing" that Ignatieff had spent most of his working life outside of Canada. Only 9 percent said it was "a good thing." Ouch.

With Dion, it had been the same sad story. In December 2006, he came from behind to win the Liberal Party leadership at a convention in Montreal. He was cerebral, he was tough and he was a thoroughly decent man; after the chaotic fratricide of the Paul Martin era, things were looking promising. By April 2007, however, the CRG-led Conservatives had initiated a multimillion-dollar onslaught of anti-Dion attack ads under the slogan "Not a Leader." By the time the campaign had run its course, just about every living, breathing Canadian had viewed the Not a Leader ads innumerable times—and most of them could be seen agreeing with the Conservatives. Nine out of ten Canadians told the *Toronto Star*'s pollsters that they disapproved of, or at best were "not sure" about, Dion's performance as leader of the Liberals. That was the worst approval rating anyone had seen in decades, going way back to when former Liberal leader John Turner set a record with a puny 14 percent approval rating shortly after losing the 1988 federal election. It goes without saying that you can't win a national election campaign when only 10 percent of voters approve of the job you're doing. Effectively, you're toast.

So, did my party learn any of these lessons? Did we change our ways?

Not on your life.

☆ ☆ ☆

Fast-forward to 2012, which started off not badly for the forces of Canadian liberaldom. If the vitality of a political party can be measured by bums in seats, then the former natural governing party was regaining its health.

More than 3,300 Grits converged on the nation's capital for a policy convention in mid-January. That was remarkable because policy conventions tend to be pretty dull affairs. The Liberal turnout was remarkable for another reason: the weather. Couldn't any sensible person think of any other place they'd rather be than Ottawa—one of the coldest national capitals in the world—in the middle of January? Why would thousands risk life and limb to travel in the middle of a big winter storm to get there?

Many Liberals did just that. More than fifteen hundred delegates would have been a success. But more Grits turned out than the governing Conservatives and the official opposition New Democrats got at their earlier policy confabs combined. The Tories and Dippers present as observers looked shocked by that, and they should have been. It was an astonishing show of support for a political party that many had given up for dead the previous May, when Ignatieff led it to its worst election showing in its history. Peter C. Newman even wrote a bestselling book about Canadian liberalism's morbid state, suggesting the Liberals were fully deceased. But they weren't. More than 3,300 people, in Ottawa, in January! Not bad at all.

Now, as a rule, political success attracts political attacks. No one should have been surprised, therefore, that just as the Ottawa Liberal Party policy convention was getting underway, an anti-Liberal attack ad was released by the National Citizens Coalition. Everything about the Internet spot was familiar. It had the customary look and feel of political attack ads, targeting the NDP past of interim Liberal leader Bob Rae. It featured headlines ripped from newspapers, reminding viewers of Rae's tenure as Ontario premier in the early nineties, when the province was an economic basket case.

It had blurry footage of a younger Rae, plus a big unflattering photo. Rae killed jobs, raised taxes on everything and put a hundred thousand people out of work, the ad claimed. The tag line—"Don't let him do it again"—was familiar, too; it has been used many times on the campaign trail, most notably in some early 2012 anti–Newt Gingrich campaign bumph during the Republican presidential nomination race. If the soundtrack sounded familiar, too, it's because it was. As the *Huffington Post* noted, the NCC's anti-Rae spot borrowed the ominous background music from the movie *Inception*. The menacing melody, by Daft Punk, can also be heard in *Super Eight, Rise of the Planet of the Apes, Battle Los Angeles, Transformers: Dark of the Moon, The Girl with the Dragon Tattoo* and a bunch of other movies.

There was absolutely nothing new or creative about the NCC's broadside against the interim Grit boss. If there was any criticism that could be made of the ad, in fact, it was that it was thoroughly unoriginal. But that didn't stop New Democrat and Liberal MPs from screeching about the NCC's effrontery. Both parties immediately called for laws to be passed to stop third-party ads between election periods. Said NDP MP Joe Comartin: "It's just so wide open to abuse . . . I think we badly need to [pass a law prohibiting such advertising], it's just such a glaring, gaping hole in our system." Huffed Liberal MP Jim Karygiannis: "This is where we need legislation."

Actually, Canada doesn't. Comartin and Karygiannis were wrong. The legality of third-party political advertising has been litigated many times in Canada—and when he was the NCC's head, Harper initiated much of the litigation himself. Three times, the Supreme Court of Canada has found that third-party political ads are constitutionally protected speech. During elections, everybody's spending is regulated. But outside writ periods, people shouldn't be unduly restricted from expressing their points of view. Thus, a B.C. government attempt to curtail advertising outside elections was ruled unconstitutional. What Comartin and Karygiannis were proposing—a law that could see a union hauled into court for supporting them, say, even when an election isn't underway—was fundamentally the wrong strategy.

In politics, as noted, rule number one is *define or be defined.* Conservatives, small and large *c,* were doing precisely what some of us had warned they would do: unearthing unhelpful facts about Bob Rae's ruinous reign and publicizing them. They were doing to Rae what they'd done so successfully to Dion and Ignatieff. They were shaping impressions about him before he even got out of bed.

The best strategy wasn't to call for laws restricting legitimate political speech. The best strategy was to hit first and twice as hard. Be swift and brutal. Remind people about the Conservative record. Remind them that Harper, the man who said he could be trusted with Canada's economy, moved it from a structural surplus to a structural deficit. That he's a warmonger who favoured George W. Bush's war in Iraq, and called Canadians who disagreed "cowards." That he didn't see the recession coming. That he called Canada "second rate." That he wants to dismantle health care. That he leads a party that has been convicted of breaking election laws and is being investigated for widespread election fraud. That he has made Canada less safe by killing gun safety laws. That he favours Alberta over other provinces. That he has a far-right socon agenda that would target abortion, gay marriage and the wall between church and state.

Stéphane Dion and Michael Ignatieff complained about how mean Stephen Harper is, and it got them precisely nowhere. Their spinners sounded like wimps, frankly, when they whined that Harper was a "bully." The best response to nasty attack ads, then, is simple.

Make your own attack ads, fast, and make 'em *nastier*.

☆ ☆ ☆

The two victories the North American right probably prizes the most: George W. Bush's narrow win over Al Gore in 2000, and Stephen Harper's trouncing of Michael Ignatieff in 2011. In the epic battles between conservatives and liberals, those are the two that the Right cherishes. Against all odds, conservatives humiliated liberals in the latter and seized ultimate power from them in the former. For conservatives, 2000 and 2011 were historic years.

The Bush and Harper election conquests are alike in another way: both remain tainted by allegations of election fraud.

In 2000, as history records—but as perhaps too few of us now remember—Bush won the presidential race with 271 electoral college votes to Al Gore's 266. But in truth, Bush didn't really win at all. In the popular vote, Gore—at just under fifty-one million votes—received half a million more than Bush. However, Bush ended up winning because conservative jurists on the U.S. Supreme Court halted a crucial recount of ballots cast in Florida—thereby ensuring that all of the state's twenty-five electoral college votes were awarded to Bush, not Gore. There had been suspicious ballots, overvoting, and the infamous "hanging chads," which spoiled punch-card paper ballots. None of that mattered. Hundreds of thousands more Americans wanted Gore to be their president, but that didn't matter so much, either. The seven judges on the Supreme Court effectively chose to ignore that. Like Republican officials in Florida—which, coincidentally, was then governed by George W. Bush's brother, Jeb—the conservatives presiding over the highest U.S. court were disinterested in the popular will. They stopped the recount that many nonpartisan experts say would have seen Gore win the presidency.

In Canada a decade later, the methodologies were different, but the utter disregard for fairness and democracy was apparently the same. It is alleged that Conservatives cheated in dozens of ridings across Canada, using a consistent approach: they'd call up voters and ask them if they planned to vote for Harper's party. If the answer was no, the voters would subsequently receive calls—some automated, some not—directing them to the wrong polling station. The callers would falsely claim to be calling from Elections Canada.

Elections Canada and the Mounties are still investigating the so-called robocall scandal. No one has been charged yet, but the fraudulent misdirection calls are alleged to have taken place in more than two hundred ridings, in every single province. So far, no one has suggested that the campaign of election fraud could have affected the overall election result. However, the Elections Act contains tough new provisions for dealing with election fraud and punishing wrongdoers. If the outcomes in just a dozen or so ridings change, Canadian Conservatives could lose the prize they covet most of all—their parliamentary majority.

Now, conservatives regularly like to assert that their values are superior to those of liberals. They do it all the time. They have different appellations for these values, too. They will say that their values are those of the family, or law and order, or populism. There are libertarian conservatives, and fiscal conservatives, and religious conservatives, and constitutional conservatives and even progressive conservatives.

Differences aside, what unites conservatives is the belief that their values are superior to those of liberals—or, sometimes, that liberals don't even have values. Thus, as the folks at the Pew Research Center showed in their most recent study, the North American demographic that is most devotedly conservative— older white men—overwhelmingly tend to view their culture as superior. What George Lakoff has said about this bears repeating: "Conservatives have a hard line. They believe that liberals are people who just don't have any morality." Conservatives believe liberals have no *values*, Lakoff says.

When you believe that your ideology has a monopoly on morality, as conservatives often do, then cheating in elections isn't so hard to justify. When you believe that you are engaged in a divinely ordained struggle between good and evil, as many conservatives do, cutting a few ethical corners doesn't seem like such a big deal anymore. Breaking the accepted rules isn't a conservative value, per se, but it certainly seems to be an ongoing characteristic of conservatives. During democratic contests—as the Bush and Harper cases show—conservatives are far less hesitant to cheat. Conservatives are undeterred by all of that, because despite the media revelations about robocall— and about George W. Bush's victory in 2000—the Conservative and Republican parties weren't hurt at all. In the first full year of his presidency, 2001, Bush had the extraordinary approval rating of 90 percent. And in the wake of supposedly damaging revelations about election fraud in the 2011 Canadian general election, Stephen Harper's Conservative government sat atop, or near the top, of successive public opinion polls. But all of that misses the point.

The point is this: it's never the break-in, it's always the cover-up. In politics, that Watergate-era aphorism has come to describe the well-established principle that voters will often forgive the first sin. But they'll rarely forgive repeated lies about the sin. In Canada, the robocall scandal is a classic example. Had the Harper regime reacted to the first allegations of vote suppression with calm and clarity, they'd be in better shape right about now. They could have simply said, "We are very concerned about what the media is reporting, and we pledge to co-operate with Elections Canada on their independent investigation."

Instead, they adopted Paul Martin's approach, the "mad as hell" strategy. When Jean Chrétien left the prime ministerial residence at 24 Sussex, the sponsorship mess had been the subject of an RCMP probe for nearly two years, and the Liberal Party of Canada was polling above 50 percent. It wasn't a big deal yet. But when Martin assumed the post of prime minister, he started shrieking, coast to coast, about how he was "mad as hell" about sponsorship. Voters therefore got mad, too—at *him*. In one extraordinary week, the Liberal party lost 15 percent of its support, and it never recovered. Martin blamed "rogue bureaucrats" for the scandal. His craven, cowardly staff accused Chrétien of concealing criminal wrongdoing (off the record, of course). They blamed fellow Liberals. They blamed everyone for the mess—except themselves, naturally. History tells us what happened next. A big majority, to a minority, to successive losses, and—now—little more than a rump in the House of Commons.

After robocall broke, Stephen Harper and his minions passed the buck, too. In the days after the allegations of election fraud became known, Harper's gang closely resembled Martin's in their attempts to cover up. Harper stood in the House of Commons and falsely blamed the Liberals for vote suppression calls emanating out of call centres in the U.S. He hasn't yet apologized for that. His parliamentary secretary, Dean Del Mastro, told the CBC that the Conservatives didn't commit electoral fraud: they would "know" if they did. Around the same time, House leader Peter Van Loan said that when robocalls happened in Montreal, it was an exercise in "free speech."

Harper's former campaign manager, Doug Finley, said it either didn't happen or it was exaggerated, and implied that the media was to blame for the fuss. His campaign chairman, Guy Giorno, said there was no "proof" and tried to minimize the gravity of the situation, saying the federal campaign was not involved. The Minister of Defence, Peter MacKay, gamely attempted to pin the mess on a single departed Con staffer. One of Harper's MPs, Shelly Glover, said all parties do it, not just hers. Any one of these defences may have merit; no one still knows for certain. We do know what Harper himself used to say about Martin: when you have too many priorities, you don't have any. Equally, if you have too many excuses, you don't have one at all. The Cons made the election fraud controversy far worse than it needed to be. They needed to find a line and stick to it. They didn't.

Now, living north of the Queensway, as they all do, some members of the Ottawa commentariat stubbornly clung to the view that the burgeoning robocall scandal wasn't ever going to harm the Conservative regime. In the midst of the robocall mess, the *Toronto Star's* much-respected Chantal Hébert cited—with no apparent enthusiasm—two public opinion polls, by Ekos and Nanos, and declared the Conservative government's support "rock solid." Wrote she: "The bottom line is that the Conservative core vote is more solid than that of either of the other two main parties." She was right, as far as it went.

Acclaimed author and commentator Michael Harris, no fan of the Harper cabal, was similarly pessimistic. We will "never get to the bottom" of the scandal, a weary Harris wrote on the political website iPolitics. There were simply too many details for a beleaguered agency like Elections Canada to chase down. He was probably right about that, too.

Both Hébert and Harris were missing something crucial, though. When a scandal of the magnitude of robocall starts to metastasize, it takes months to register in the public's consciousness. Voters have heard too many baseless allegations of criminality, too many times, to take opposition scandal-mongering seriously from the outset. As a general rule, they will not pass judgment unless they see perps being led away in handcuffs and orange jumpsuits. Thus, when my former boss Jean Chrétien called in the RCMP in May 2002 to probe the then-nascent sponsorship file, the Liberal Party was sitting at more than 50 percent in national public opinion polls. It remained there for nearly two years, until Paul Martin's juvenile wrecking crew took over, energetically devoting themselves to shredding the Grit brand. Commencing in February 2004, the party went into a free-fall from which it never recovered.

So merely peering at a pair of early polls and concluding the public has already rendered a verdict is a case of premature evaluation. Political graves, I always tell the candidates I'm privileged to work for, are dug with tiny shovels. Robocall was no different. Harris's assertion that the sheer size of robocall would overwhelm Elections Canada and the RCMP, too, was premature. To be sure, more than thirty-one thousand complaints to elections watchdogs about voting irregularities and fraud is daunting. To some, the sheer number of complaints makes robocall too complex to ever be fully investigated. But in the case of the sponsorship scandal, only a handful of prosecutions have taken place, most of them related to the theft of a few thousand bucks. The Mounties and the Crown didn't need thirty-one thousand complaints, or billions of dollars missing, to blow the Liberal Party's reputation to smithereens.

In a democracy, stomping all over the rules in general elections—as happened indisputably in the U.S. in 2000, and allegedly in Canada in 2011—is no small offence. While conservatives claim to possess superior values, no "value" justifies election fraud. No "morality" validates immorality in democratic contests.

Al Gore made a historic error when he didn't insist on a recount in 2000. Canadian progressives should heed Gore's lesson, and tell the story—over and over—about how Stephen Harper didn't win fair and square. From sea to sea to sea, they need to remind Canadians that Harper didn't win the old-fashioned way.

☆ ☆ ☆

The suggestion that the Conservatives intended to define Michael Ignatieff before he could define himself wasn't particularly revolutionary. It was old news.

In December 2008, just as Ignatieff was about to become leader of the Liberal Party, I wrote an ultra-top-secret memo to Ian Davey, Don Guy, and a few other Grits who were going to run his office—and, ultimately, the Liberal Party's election campaign. In it, I talked about setting up an election war room right away, who I wanted in it, where it would be located and so on. There was, I explained, some urgency associated with being prepared. "We need to be ready as soon as possible because (a) the government could fall [soon] and (b) principally, because the Conservatives possess a very large budget which will be applied to defining our leader before he can positively define himself," I wrote. "This threat cannot be overestimated."

Everyone agreed. So we got to work on election readiness. But when the Conservatives' Just Visiting ads started to air in May, the Liberal Party did not respond in kind. (The Grits would finally get around to releasing some very tough ads of their own—on fighter jets and tax cuts—but they did so too late: they waited months, until the election campaign. By then,

Ignatieff's reputation had been shredded, and he could not possibly recover.)

One sunny spring day in 2009, I sat with Ignatieff in his wood-panelled House of Commons office. As Ian Davey, Paul Zed and legislative assistant Jim Pimblett moved in and out of the room, ensuring that the Liberal team was ready for the day's question period ritual, Ignatieff told me I had been right. "Those ads are everywhere," he said, sprawled in a chair, looking out the window in the direction of Wellington Street. "And it pisses me off. Are these guys actually saying that the million-plus Canadians who live and work abroad are somehow less Canadian? That we don't count?"

He looked at me, his expression fierce. "I love this country! I am *Canadian*!"

I waited a moment. "I know. You're right," I said, then pointed out the window. "But to the people out there, Just Visiting suggests that you didn't love it *enough* to stay here. Just Visiting brings to the surface a suspicion that you gave up on your citizenship. But that's actually not the worst thing about Harper's ads."

"What's worse? What could be worse than that?" Ignatieff demanded, looking understandably frustrated.

"What's worse is the footage," I said. "You're a TV guy. You've done TV for years. The shots they used—the waves, the shots of you on the escalator, looking down—were designed to make you look imperial and out of touch. Without doing it directly, they were trying to suggest that you've never used public transit, or worried about missing a mortgage payment, or actually know how to turn on a computer by yourself." I paused and waited to see if Ignatieff was going to slug me. He didn't, so I continued, "Their objective hasn't just been to suggest that you're from another country. Their objective has been to suggest that you come from another *planet*.

That you're just another out-of-touch liberal elitist who doesn't understand the daily existence of regular folks."

Later on, we continued the discussion with Davey, Zed and Ignatieff's amiable communications director, Jill Fairbrother. I urged them to examine how the Conservatives' communications strategy always came back a single theme: that our guy was out-of-touch and from Mars, while their guy was intimately familiar with the day-to-day reality of an average Canadian's life and was just like the guy next door. "Everything they do, every speech, every photo op, every avail, everything they do every single day: it's all aimed at making people feel Harper understands their life, and Iggy has never *lived* their life," I said.

For example, I said, look at the Conservative regime's laser-like focus on the cherished Canadian sport of hockey and the cherished coffee and doughnut franchise Tim Hortons. Harper seems to be obsessively preoccupied with both, even though he's been photographed furtively drinking Starbucks on the campaign trail and no can recall ever seeing a photo of him in a pair of skates. "They're political Everyman symbols," I said, "and he's brilliantly swiped both of them. He's an economist, for Chrissakes—he's just as much of an intellectual as our guy, but he's terrified of people finding that out. He wants our guy to be the brainy geek; he wants our guy to be the snob. So he goes after Joe and Jane Frontporch with hockey and Tims, and it works. Voters get Tim Hortons hockey dads. Harvard human rights professors, who don't do sports and who hang out with other pinheads, they don't get."

None of this was new or exceptionally insightful. As early as 2007, smart folks were noticing how Harper was fixated on political symbols like hockey. The progressive folks at Straight Goods, for instance, wrote back in 2007 that "hockey is an important part of the frame of Stephen Harper's Conservatives. Since [2004], Harper has strived to court for the vote of the urban working middle class—people earning under $50,000 in trades, service industries, small business or sales. Establishing himself as a hockey-loving tough guy is intended to play to this demographic." To that end, Harper is frequently photographed cradling a cup of Tim Hortons at hockey rinks, or chumming with National Hockey League all-stars. He's even let it be known that he's writing a book about hockey, even though nobody has seen it yet.

None of this happens by accident. It's all part of an intricate plan, I told the Ignatieff team: one that was mainly put together was someone I know quite well.

At the Toronto political consulting firm where I used to work, I related, one of our employees was a thoughtful young man named Patrick Muttart. An Ontario native, Muttart left the consulting firm around the same time I did—me to start my own, and Muttart to help elect the Conservatives under Stephen Harper. We had different political philosophies, but we became and remained friends. Muttart's a quiet, intense fellow, now living in Chicago with his young family and his pit bull, Jerome. From there, he assists conservatives in the U.S., the U.K. and Canada.

In 2006, Muttart came to visit me at my new offices in Toronto. I told him I didn't see a majority in the cards for his party any time soon. Too many women, young Canadians and new Canadians didn't like or trust his leader. And too many Quebecers, I said, were still in the sway of the separatist Bloc Québécois. Numerically, I told Muttart, a majority was impossible for the foreseeable future.

"You're right, to a point," Muttart said. But then he started to describe a five-year Conservative battle plan, one that he was still mapping out in his impressive brain. First, I was told, smart Conservatives accepted that Canada was still a mainly a liberal country. The Conservative vote was committed and highly motivated—but at 30 to 35 percent, it was still mad-deningly far from a majority.

Second, Muttart said, ethnic communities, which the Liberal Party had taken for granted for too long, were in a mood to be courted. On taxation, on crime, on social issues, on foreign policy, Conservatives believed that they could woo away so-called ethnic communities. Previously all-Liberal blocs (Jews, Chinese, Eastern Europeans) have moved allegiance to the Conservatives.

Third, he said, the Liberal Party no longer existed at the riding level; they had an immense organizational deficit. By his estimate, there were only five hundred or so experienced Liberal organizers left, and many of them (like me) had lost enthusiasm during Paul Martin's war of attrition against Jean Chrétien. Conservatives, meanwhile, were overwhelmingly united behind Harper. They were disciplined, and they didn't easily tolerate dissent. To get out the vote, moreover, the Cons had more money and more people.

On every count, Muttart was right. The Conservative coalition still wasn't as big as it needed to be, but almost every single Conservative loyalist could be counted to get out the vote. Liberals, on the other hand, still had problems identifying and motivating their larger share of the vote. How did Muttart and his conservative friends do it?

With research. The sort of research and the sort of polling that in the past only huge corporations have been able to undertake. Under Muttart's leadership, the federal Conservative Party has surveyed and established how much targeted voters earn, what they like and don't like, the toothpaste they use and the breakfast cereal they eat. Values, opinions, religious beliefs, you name it—everything there is to know about a voter, the Conservatives know.

Using very expensive advertising industry research tech-niques called geodemographics and psychographics, Muttart took everything he could learn about average Canadians—which, he noted, was a lot—and plugged it into something called CIMS, or the Constituent Information Management System. CIMS started in 2004, around the time Muttart arrived in Ottawa, and it contains data gathered through phone calls, online research, the census, private consumer data, mailings, fundraising and even door-to-door canvassing. With CIMS, Muttart and his Conservatives could make targeted messages aimed at particular ethnic or demographic groups, or even geographic areas as small as a suburban street. It identifies potential supporters, it creates voter profiles, it helps craft policies—like the Tim Hortons and hockey stuff—to win over key voting segments. And then Muttart's gang "narrowcast": they reach out to their targets using everything from email and phone calls to personal visits. Anything and everything.

In 2005, an enterprising reporter at the Canadian Press, Alex Panetta, asked Environics Analytics, which specializes in consumer profiling, to come up with some of the kinds of data available to guys like Patrick Muttart. So in the Ontario riding of Guelph, Panetta reported that 27.7 percent of households have children under the age of six, which made them eligible for a twelve-hundred-dollar Conservative tax credit. "About 6.4 per cent fall into the Blue-Collar Comfort category—one of dozens of character types identified by Environics," Panetta wrote. "Blue-Collar Comfort types generally have skilled, stable, working-class jobs, a high-school degree, earn average household incomes of $68,833, and enjoy power-boating, going to casinos and playing golf. [In the 2006 election], the Liberals held the riding by 5,000 votes—or 8 percent of the electorate." That meant, Panetta wrote, that the Blue-Collar Comfort group, on its own, "could have made the difference" and won the Conservatives the seat. They still haven't, however; happily, I can report that Liberal legend Frank Valeriote has beaten back every attempt to dislodge him in Guelph. (Not that the Conservatives have given up—early in 2012, Elections Canada and the RCMP started to investigate fraud by the Conservatives, targeting places like Guelph.)

Patrick Muttart's strategy has helped Harper's Conservatives be winners just about everywhere else in the country—winning in 2006, in 2008 and in 2011.

☆ ☆ ☆

It isn't infallible, but the strength of Muttart's research—as well as the conservative communications strategies that flow from it—is everywhere to be seen these days. Outside the cities, especially.

For instance, on the way up to my cabin during the 2008 election campaign, my kids and I drove through small Ontario towns like Belleville, Madoc, Cobourg and the like—those places where folks still listen to Shania Twain as they drive family vans with Support Our Troops ribbons on the back, don't read the *Globe and Mail*, and don't go to black-tie fundraisers. If the signs meant anything, the Conservatives had the countryside won, hands down. Outside the cities, folks were settled in. They were going for the guy they think is most like them, the guy who spoke to them, the guy with their values. They usually do.

Stephen Harper—hockey Dad, Leafs fan, middle-aged guy with a paunch (all of us middle-aged guys have a paunch, pretty much)—was winning. Outrider polls would pop up a few times until election day because a lot of pollsters get things wrong. But, mostly, Harper was somewhere between a big minority or a small majority. That was where he'd been for a while. How come?

By design or by accident, consciously or not, Harper had become the Canadian Everyman. He had let us know that early on, when he grinned and said that meeting Bono of U2 about world peace was his predecessor's shtick. Midcampaign, when he was photographed carrying his son's hockey bag to a game, the resulting photograph said to a few million Canadians: *He doesn't just understand my life. He is living my life.* To me, the day that photo was published was the day that he had won the election.

Whether he was faking it or not was immaterial, just as it didn't matter if Pierre Trudeau's pirouettes and dating of starlets and cosmopolitan airs were real or the product of rainmaker Keith Davey's genius. It was what people believed to be true about the guy.

Now, being the Everyman isn't some surefire, never-fail formula for electoral success. Your persona, real or not, has to seem authentic. And it has to be congruent with what CBC Radio hosts refer to as the zeitgeist: you have to fit the times. Trudeau did, coming as he did when Expo '67 had Canadians aspiring to worldliness. Harper fits his era, because he arrived at a difficult time when folks were looking for suburban simplicity, as Patrick Muttart's research indisputably shows.

At a time when unsupervised twenty-four-year-olds in red suspenders (to borrow the characterization of another Everyman, Jean Chrétien) have been wreaking havoc on the global economy, the Everyman has many attractions. When things are going to crap, people don't go looking for flamboyant visionaries to lead them out of the darkness. They go looking for guys with a flashlight. Guys like Stephen Harper or George W. Bush. That's what the psychographic research shows, too.

Liberal leader Stéphane Dion, the guy Harper was well on his way to clobbering in that election campaign, was actually sort of like an Everyman. He showed up in Ottawa carrying a book bag, and he actually took the bus to get there. He was upright and trustworthy, and he didn't seem to give a sweet damn about the elites and the chattering classes, either. Like Harper, he didn't go to society parties and he seemed awkward in large groups of people. He loved his country in an unashamed and unpretentious way and he didn't care whether *Le Devoir* approved or not.

But despite all of the characteristics he shared with Stephen Harper, Stéphane Dion was different in one crucial respect: he was really hard to understand. If politics is a daily campaign, and the daily campaign is a great big communications exercise (and it is), then Stéphane Dion was at a distinct disadvantage. He didn't communicate in one of the official languages as well as Stephen Harper; his English, in fact, was terrible. As a result, his goals—almost all of them thoughtful and praiseworthy—were susceptible to being characterized by the likes of Patrick Muttart as risky or unworthy. Which Muttart and co. did, big time.

Now, don't get me wrong. I don't want to overromanticize this suburban, Leafs-loving Everyman stuff. The time will come when voters will again go in search of an erudite, overachieving intellectual to lead them, and the Everyman will be discarded like last year's election pamphlets. But in that election year, the unremarkable was what voters wanted. And the voters are the bosses.

In that campaign, too many Liberals were running around like deranged street-corner prophets, screeching about Conservatives being evil or stupid, or both. As a member of the Alberta liberal diaspora, it still pisses me off that central Canadians perpetually associate Albertans, out loud or not, with Holocaust denier Jim Keegstra or hooded Klansmen. When they got impatient with persuasion and argument, and when they started to insinuate that Harper was a Nazi or a fool, they lost me and a few million other folks, too. Many progressives fundamentally disagreed with many of the man's policies, sure. But those progressives didn't feel the need to peddle facile bullshit to beat him on the campaign trail. *Tell the truth* about conservatives; don't exaggerate. That's how they can be beaten.

In 2008, Stephen Harper would win through more than the Tim Hortons Everyman versus Starbucks elitist frame that Patrick Muttart and others had originally conjured up for him two years earlier. It was a bit harder to make that case this time, because Harper had been in power for three years—and it's pretty difficult to depict as a populist someone who lives in a big mansion, has servants and hangs out with the president of the United States. Harper would win in 2008 because he had fully morphed into the Everyman, and that was what folks wanted right about then. They wanted someone *like* them. Next year, or maybe the year after that, they may want someone who isn't like them at all.

In this way, politics is like comedy. It isn't about the quality of the material, necessarily; it's mainly about good timing and good communications.

Stephen Harper's lucky. Who he is, how he is, fit the time. And his team communicated that.

☆ ☆ ☆

There's a reason the news media use battlefield analogies when writing about politics. It's because a lot of politics is like war. It's tough. It's nasty.

Still, it's pretty hard to regard Frank Luntz as warrior, which—one suspects—is what he wants. With his self-deprecating jokes about his weight, and his easygoing aw-shucks demeanour, it's not easy to regard the most infamous conservative communications strategist on the planet as someone who is engaged in a war against anyone. He genuinely seems like a nice guy. During the Republican primaries, he could be seen everywhere, bringing Newt Gingrich to tears with a question about his mother, or appearing on Fox News as an amiable

Republican talking head, or happily cajoling conservative crowds at rallies across America. Even when you talk to Democratic luminaries like George Lakoff and Geoffrey Nunberg—who discuss Luntz often in their writings—there is a grudging respect for the man.

Except there's this: too often Frank Luntz peddles hokum. He's in the bullshit business. He's made untold millions, in fact, advising conservatives how to market untruths more effectively. Spin, former Bill Clinton advisor George Stephanopoulos once unforgettably said, is "hopeful persuasion." It isn't lying. It's editorializing; it's providing a shiny gloss to one's candidate or campaign or cause. But "spin" doesn't entirely capture what Frank Luntz does. What Luntz does is help his well-heeled conservative clients occasionally mangle and shred language to cover up inconvenient truths. What he does, arguably, is get paid lots of money to help conservatives fib, or worse.

There's plenty of evidence to suggest that Frank Luntz can be a bit of a fibber himself. For example, in 1997, the American Association for Public Opinion Research reprimanded Luntz for the "polling" he did on behalf of the Republican Party's 1994 Contract with America effort. After a fourteen-month investigation, the nonpartisan AAPOR ruled that Luntz "repeatedly refused to make public essential facts about his research on public attitudes about the Republicans' 'Contract with America.' In particular, the AAPOR inquiry focused on Luntz's reporting, prior to the November [congressional] elections in 1994, that his research showed at least 60 percent of the public favored each of the elements in the GOP 'Contract.' When later asked to provide some basic facts about this research, Luntz refused. AAPOR holds that researchers must disclose, or make available for public disclosure, the wording of questions and other basic methodological details when poll findings are made public. This disclosure is important so that claims made on the basis of opinion research findings can be independently evaluated." At the time, Salon.com dryly described Luntz as "possibly the best example of what we could call the pollster pundit: someone who both purports to scientifically poll the opinions of the public, and then also interpret that data to support his own—in Luntz's case, conservative—point of view."

That's not all. The censure by AAPOR was followed by another in 2000, when Luntz was excoriated by the National Council on Public Polls for "allegedly mischaracterizing on MSNBC the results of focus groups he conducted during [that year's] Republican Convention." Then, four years later, the selfsame MSNBC dropped Luntz from its planned coverage of that year's presidential debate, following a letter from Media Matters that outlined Luntz's GOP ties and questionable polling methodology. Luntz has "questionable ethical standards," the media watchdog concluded. Then Luntz got hammered again, in 2010: in that year, he was awarded PolitiFact's Lie of the Year award for his use of the phrase "government takeover" to refer to health-care reform. "Takeovers are like coups," Luntz wrote in a chatty twenty-eight-page memo. "They both lead to dictators and a loss of freedom." That bald statement wasn't true, PolitiFact concluded.*

Journalist Joshua Marshall did more fact-checking on Luntz, too, specifically on a Luntz claim that "he's done no GOP work since 2001." That was a great big untruth, Marshall found, because Luntz was well known to the players on the House Republican Caucus, and long after 2001, as well. Wrote Marshall: "Luntz provides regular strategy briefings for Republicans and does it, not surprisingly, in part to troll for

---

* The above information regarding these criticisms has been freely available from Wikipedia and the organizations cited for some time.

work." Later on, Marshall found evidence that Luntz had been assisting Republicans at the state level—in places like California, where Luntz now lives—for hundreds of thousands of dollars. To claim that he doesn't do work for the Republican Party, as Luntz did, was to misrepresent, or worse.

Repeated attempts to reach Frank Luntz to respond to any or all of this are rebuffed. He's "too busy" to respond, claims his secretary at his Arlington, Virginia, consulting firm, Luntz Global, whose website modestly describes itself as "a power-house" in "the profession [sic] of message creation and image management." Boasts Luntz on his website: "We have coun-seled Presidents and Prime Ministers, Fortune 100 CEOs and Hollywood creative teams in harnessing the power of lan-guage and visuals to change hearts, change minds and change behaviors." While some of that is actually true, Luntz is appar-ently "too busy" to rebut criticisms by AAPOR, Media Matters and others that he may be little more than a New Age snake-oil salesman. A promised phone call by one of his staff never materializes.

"He's from the marketing world," says George Lakoff. "He has a very good ear."

Geoffrey Nunberg agrees. "He's a marketing guy, yes. He knows how this stuff works. Luntz is very skilled, he gets it. He's been successful in marketing himself, and marketing these little linguistic shifts that move the discourse a little bit. He has a consulting business on the side, and he does a lot of commercial consulting. And he's helped the Right get a certain narrative about political life and the relationship of people to political life."

Luntz has always been a conservative, of course, and has always had his snout in or near to the Republican establish-ment's trough. Early on, he worked for Ronald Reagan's poll-ster, among others. After that, he was retained by Ross Perot for his presidential run, and Luntz did his level best to ensure that everyone knew that he had provided the quixotic billionaire with budget and platform advice.

To no one's surprise, he was hired by Newt Gingrich after the Perot campaign, to provide communications advice about Gingrich's spectacularly dishonest Contract with America—the work that earned Luntz the AAPOR reprimand. Later on, he assisted Rudy Giuliani's New York City mayoral bids. He didn't always support conservative winners, but he had an unerring instinct for deep conservative pockets. What has made Frank Luntz famous, however—what has made him a millionaire a few times over, with a phalanx of fart-catchers following him across the hinterland, capturing all of his "words that work," as he calls them, and laughing at all of his jokes—are his oxymoronic "straight talk" memos. In conservative circles, the memoranda are somewhat difficult to get, and are therefore highly prized. They cover subjects like financial reform, health care, immigration, Israel—and, like the one we saw in the previous chapter, the environment. If you look hard enough, however, you can get your hands on them. One of the memos was about financial reform, and it actually sort of anticipated the Occupy movement.

Luntz, like a lot of conservatives, is afraid of the Occupy movement and what it represents. In fact, he told a late-2011 meeting of Republican governors in Florida that the Occupiers simply terrify him. "I'm so scared of this anti–Wall Street effort," Luntz said, in what some might say was a rare moment of candour. "I'm frightened to death." Why? Because, Luntz confessed, "they're having an impact on what the American people think of capitalism."

For Frank Luntz—for a big guy who makes big bucks gleefully assisting big polluters, big credit card companies, big mortgage brokers, big pharmaceutical companies, big bankers, and even one of the biggest of the big media magnates (phone hacker Rupert Murdoch)—this admission about the ragtag Occupiers was no small thing. Lots of people noticed. How could someone as powerful and as influential as Luntz, the self-described counsellor to presidents and prime ministers, be "frightened to death" of a bunch of kids camped out in city parks? A bunch of kids lacking a leader or a clear message, no less. For a "powerhouse" in the "profession of message creation," the Occupiers should be a pushover, no?

Apparently not. At the closed-door session with the Republican Governors Association, Luntz devoted much of his remarks to defeating the Occupier's main criticism: namely, that the rich were getting richer and everyone else was getting poorer. That it wasn't fair or right. And that things had to change. Thus, in his remarks, Luntz urged the assembled conservatives to stop saying "capitalism," a piece of advice that must have left their coiffed heads reeling. "Get that word removed!" said Luntz. "We're replacing it with either 'economic freedom' or 'free market.' The public still prefers capitalism to socialism, but they think capitalism is immoral. And if we're seen as defenders of, quote, Wall Street, end quote, we've got a problem." The same goes for the nomenclature describing "the rich," Luntz said to his GOP audience. The public like it when Occupiers—and others—talk about "raising taxes on the rich," Luntz cautioned. "If you talk about government 'taking' the money from 'hardworking Americans,' the public says no. Taxing, the public will say yes."

In a moment of candour, conservatives, Luntz continued, could no longer credibly claim to be representing the little guy. "We can say we defend the 'middle class,' and the public will say they're not sure about that [anymore]." The focus, he counselled, needed to be on protecting the interests of "hardworking taxpayers." Among other things, conservative politicians had allied themselves with the rich for too long. They are now increasingly seen as serving only the rich. In the same vein, Luntz said, that mainstay of capitalism, the entrepreneur, was decidedly out. Say "job creators" or "small business owners" instead. Also, he said, "government spending" wasn't nearly as bad, in these post-recessionary times, as Republicans would like. Say, instead, "waste." Said Luntz: "It's not about government spending. It's about waste. That's what makes people angry."

On the remarkable populist movement then grabbing headlines around the world? Luntz was clear: conservatives should not engage in a battle of words with the Occupiers, however much they'd like to. Because, mainly, the Occupiers would win. Said Luntz to the Republican faithful: "Here are three words for you all: *I get it*. I get that you are angry. I get that you've seen inequality. I get that you want to fix the system." Whatever conservatives do, said Luntz, they shouldn't attempt to deny the reality of the Occupy movement's criticisms. What the Occupiers were saying, to billions of people around the planet, was regarded as an undeniable truth. Capitalism, Luntz was admitting—at long last—was not nearly as popular as it had once been. People were mad, all over. And they liked the message that the Occupiers were offering, even if they didn't always agree with the way in which the Occupiers were doing it.

For millionaire Republican politicians, then, some of whom claim to be in regular conversation with God himself, the Occupiers presented a clear challenge to the established order. The reason for this could be summarized by tweaking a question, Luntz-like, that conservatives make recourse to all the time. Namely: *What would Jesus do?*

In November 2011, the very week Frank Luntz met with his Republican cronies, the question was quite relevant worldwide.

If Jesus was here, to see all that we have become—with the chasm dividing rich and poor growing ever wider, with governments bailing out bankers but never the masses, with average folks having to borrow just to keep food on the table—what would he do?

The question would have occurred to Luntz, perhaps, if he had popped into a Roman Catholic service a couple weeks earlier (as I did). The relevant gospel was a well-known one—the one about the attempt of the Pharisees to trap Jesus with a question about taxes (Matthew 22:15–22). "Give back to Caesar the things that are Caesar's," Christ said to them. "And to God what is God's." Doesn't sound much like a tax-fighter, does he?

The "what would Jesus do" question—WWJD, for short—is one of the great debates of this era, or any era. On the Right, assorted televangelists, conservative politicians and the likes of Frank Luntz will perhaps always have us believe that the Son of God would have been a fan of Reaganomics, travelling to megachurches in a Hummer, loudly playing Hank Williams tunes as he went. They are continually invoking his name to legitimize their noxious deeds. But the fact is this: if you really want to know WWJD, he wouldn't be, say, bailing out Wall Street bankers whose greed helped cause the 2008–2009 recession and who very nearly brought down the teetering walls of capitalism. As Jesus memorably told his disciples, after telling a rich man to give everything away: "How hard it is for the rich to enter the Kingdom of God!" (Mark 10:23). Frank Luntz, one suspects, knows this. That's why he's frightened of what Occupy represents.

Nor, for that matter, would Jesus Christ have been particularly pleased by the politicians who scrambled to bail out the bankers—and then turned their backs on the regular folks who lost their homes, their jobs and their futures to the recession. As in John 12:50, favouring the rich, the ones who wear finery, is "evil." God, said Jesus, chooses the poor because they are "rich in faith." They are the ones who deserve support. Not, one supposes, twenty-something millionaire bankers in their little red suspenders moving paper around on their big desks. Not millionaire conservative communications consultants, certainly, who are the unvarnished dictionary definition of Orwellian.

As the peaceful Occupy movement spread across North America in the fall of 2011, and as Frank Luntz prepared to speak to the Republican governors, the threat the Occupiers represented to the bankers—and the bankers' conservative allies and advisors—wasn't difficult to see. They were leaderless, as noted, and they lacked an agenda that a dismissive, cynical corporate media could summarize in a sound bite. But the Occupiers were the first truly populist, progressive movement to seize peoples' imaginations in a long, long time.

In this way—and this will anger some conservatives, but too bad—the Occupiers are a bit Christ-like. As noted most memorably in Matthew 25:31–46, when Judgment Day arrives, the ones who will be admitted into the Kingdom are the ones who have done the most for "the least" among us—the hungry, the sick, the poor. In fact, if you strive to know him (like some of us do), there can't be much doubt that the rabbi named Jesus was no capitalist. Nor is there any mystery about WWJD with the Occupiers that momentous fall.

He'd have been right down there with them, chanting against the bankers and the politicians who do the bankers' bidding.

And, perhaps, against conservative communications advisors like Frank Luntz.

HOW PROGRESSIVES CAN STEAL BACK VALUES

Heretofore, an intensive examination of the conservative species has shown that conservatives exhibit difficulty in expressing who they are and what they favour. However, it is clear what conservatives are against (to wit, most everything and everyone).
Notwithstanding this, the population of the conservative animal grows, due to its facility at manipulating "morals" and "values" as well as its ability to communicate in a highly duplicitous and deceiving manner.
Herewith, how progressives, who are right and good, can regain the moral high ground.

Take back values. That's what progressives need to do. But how?

As with many things, the answer might be right there in plain view. In a local city park, in fact.

Progressives and liberals are more than perplexed that conservatives have been able to seize the so-called moral high ground, and thereby win elections. They're angry. How, they ask, can we take back what is rightly ours? How can the forces of conservatism—who regularly favour the desires of the few over the needs of the many—be depicted as they largely are, namely, as selfish, greedy corporate shills? How can we reassert the truth: that progressive values are better for civilization than conservative values?

Geoffrey Nunberg has an answer. "Occupy," he says, without hesitation. "The Occupy movement may change things enormously in the coming election cycle." He pauses. "I think that 'the 99 percent' is the most important linguistic contribution for the Left in the last twenty years or more."

Earlier, during a discussion on National Public Radio, Nunberg declared that "occupy" was the Word of the Year for 2011. The Occupy movement, and the simple message at its core—the 1 percent versus the 99 percent—has gone global and truly viral. It is one of those rare instances, he says, where a word and a concept comes out of nowhere and "actually helps to create the very thing it names." As such, Nunberg continues, Occupy dramatically revived the notion of revolt and protest among young people who, previously, hadn't been all that interested in politics. It has been a true game-changer, and particularly for the simplicity of the morality it underlines: *too few possess too much.* When even world leaders and billionaires start musing out loud that "capitalism" needs a fundamental rethink (as they did at the World Economic Forum in Davos, Switzerland, in January 2012) then progressives need to pay heed.

"[Occupy] has already altered the political language with that slogan, 'We are the 99 percent,'" Nunberg said on NPR. "Economists have been talking about the top 1 percent for a long time, but it has suddenly become part of our national table talk. It's the most specific term for 'class' in American public life since the late nineteenth century, when social reformers warned about the undue power and influence of what they called 'the upper tenth.'"

Many weeks later and many hundreds of kilometres away—at the far corner of the continent from where Nunberg is, in fact—two of the last Occupiers in Canada, Jim Parsons and Mark Stacey, agree. "They've called it 'the vanishing middle class' up until now, I think," says Parsons, a writer himself. "The 99 percent is now that. And what happens when the middle class has all vanished? You'll get a very big proletariat, or working class, below a very small number of oligarchs." And that, says Parsons, is a situation that is unlikely to end well for the oligarchs who make up the 1 percent.

Stacey, a thoughtful computer science student at Memorial University, explains what Occupy aims to do. "The first step to fixing our society is to gather together and discuss what's wrong with it. The Occupy encampments serve as a place for political discussion and debate, a physical location where we could gather and propose potential problems and solutions. And that's exactly what Occupy has done," he says. "We've drawn attention to this blight upon our society. Solutions are a bit slower to materialize, but we try to come up [with some], at least locally here in Newfoundland."

The "blight," as Stacey puts it, is the huge gulf in income between the rich and the poor, or (to twist a Luntzism) the near-poor. It has become part of the global lexicon—as Nunberg and others note—because, Stacey says, "it's so easy to relate to. It's a concise description of the economic disparity in our society, and it frames it in such a way that draws attention to how we're all directly affected. The disparity between the 1 percent, with the highest income, versus the bottom 99 percent is higher than it ever has been, and people are starting to notice. It doesn't hurt that it's catchy, either."

At the moment, Parsons and Stacey are to be found in the last Occupy camp in Canada, and one of the last in North America. Near the end of 2011, cities across the United States

and Canada sent in police to remove Occupier encampments, in some cases forcibly. St. John's, Newfoundland—
wonderfully, surprisingly—wasn't one of them. The mayor of
St. John's, a sensible fellow named Dennis O'Keefe, said they
should be left alone. "They're not bothering anybody," O'Keefe
replied, matter-of-factly, when asked about the Occupiers
who had been tucked in a corner of a small city park, near the
ocean, since the middle of October. "They're not a danger to
themselves. They're not a danger to the public. They are there
because they want to express an opinion. We do not have an
issue with them."

Others, of course, did. Conservatives, to be precise. In the
fall of 2011, you could not turn the page of a newspaper, or
flip on a radio or TV broadcast, without hearing some hysteri-
cal conservative meat puppet hissing that the Occupiers were
untidy, unsightly and unsafe. They were accused of being drug
addicts, rapists and worse. "Shut the Occupy camps down,"
the rightist mouthpieces demanded, and most conservative-
controlled municipalities speedily obliged. By year's end, there
wasn't a single Occupy outpost left in all of Canada—except
on a seaside perch in St. John's, that is, where Jim Parsons and
a few others held out, undeterred by apathy and the weather.

"Holding on here is part of our way of thinking," says
Parsons, who is also a musician and a blogger. "We
[Newfoundlanders] live with a marine climate, and it gets
cold and fierce sometimes. But I didn't doubt for a second
that we would be ready for the worst weather. Contributions
from the community have been constant, in terms of food
and fuel. Many of us do chores at the camp, even if we don't
sleep there all the time."

The sky is clear as Parsons and Stacey respond to questions,
but not, Parsons says, unseasonably cold. It's all right, as they
say. For months, the St. John's Occupy camp has been little

more than a ramshackle collection of tents and tarps in a corner of the lovely Harbourside Park, just off Water Street. Some flimsy plywood walls have been propped up to try and keep out some of the cold Atlantic winds. Some citizens have donated a couple of space heaters. Behind the last Occupiers, a ship looms overhead and gulls swing by. Waves can be heard crashing up against the harbour walls. It's a beautiful spot, actually, in a beautiful city.

When asked about the conservatives who angrily railed against Occupy, Parsons—with a shaved head and what seems like a bemused expression—seems at ease. To him, the suggestion by conservatives to shut down Occupy, for good, is laughable. The conservatives and the media that do their bidding may have hoped to shut down Occupy, but they failed, he says. "The anti–Occupy movement people weren't successful, not in the slightest," he says. "[We] re-established in houses, abandoned buildings and side projects."

Stacey, the chattier of the two, agrees. To condemn Occupy for being an unsuccessful political movement, as conservatives delight in doing, is to fundamentally misunderstand what Occupy is all about. Says he: "[Their] criticism mostly stems from a misunderstanding about what Occupy is. We're unlike most other protest organizations the public is used to hear protesting, like unions and special interest groups. We're something different, an all-encompassing organization, structured to facilitate getting regular people more involved with politics. We advocate only for what we can all agree on, and we're open to literally every issue and every person.

"We may be the only encampment left in Canada—aside from one guy in a tent in Moncton!—but we're certainly not the last Occupiers. Occupy groups are still quite active all across [North America]. The encampments are very important, I think, for many reasons, but they're not essential to the cause . . . I'm not exactly sure why the mainstream media portrayed Occupy in such a negative light. Much of it, particularly Fox News and its conservative affiliates, seem to be anti-Occupy because they are owned by those that perpetuate the various problems we're fighting against. Other media organizations could be opposed for the same reason, but it's just as likely to be a case of lazy journalism. It's not that hard to figure out what Occupy is about, just attend a General Assembly. Or ask the people directly involved, as you have done."

When I suggest to Parsons and Stacey and their fellow Newfoundland and Labrador Occupiers that big-deal conservatives like Frank Luntz are actually afraid of them—and that the billionaires and world leaders gathered in Davos are a bit concerned, too—they're amused, but they're not surprised. The debate that Occupy has stirred up was always going to happen, they say.

"Look at how much is being hoarded by the few," he says. "How much their industries overproduce for the most rich, the top percentages. They cannot spend all they earn, ever, in fact."

Is it, Parsons is asked, the sort of message that *should* worry conservatives?

"Oh, yes," he says. "Oh, yes."

☆ ☆ ☆

The right-leaning Tea Party movement and the left-leaning Occupy movement are often compared. In a way, their respective philosophies—anti–Wall Street, antibanker, anti-elite, antipolitician—are similar, if not identical. To some, they are doppelgangers.

Both came into being around the same time, and both reflected the anger of those who had been left behind by the great global recession of the last decade. While bankers and multinationals received government bailouts, average folks—who lost their jobs, their homes and their futures—did not. Bankers went back to handing out obscene bonuses to themselves; average folks objected, but conservative politicians didn't care. Out of this grew rage and resentment—and the Tea Party and Occupy.

While few Americans said both groups had values that were identical to their own, a comprehensive end-of-2011 poll conducted by Washington's Public Religion Research Institute (PRRI) found that 23 percent said they identified with the Tea Party—and 23 percent said they identified with the Occupy movement, too. An even split.

But there was one crucial difference: the Tea Party protestors were absorbed, without resistance, by the Republican Party. They became part of the establishment; they became, in effect, what they had pledged to destroy. Occupy, on the other hand, still remains defiantly outside the establishment, huddling in tents in places like Harbourside Park—and neither the Democratic Party in the United States nor the Liberal or New Democratic parties in Canada have yet brought it into the fold. Progressive political parties, however, have repeatedly tried to harness the Occupiers' message: President Obama, most notably, sounded like a well-dressed (but pissed off) Occupier in his 2012 State of the Union address—where he railed against the 1 percent and name-checked Warren Buffett's secretary—but so far, they've been unsuccessful. To date, the Occupiers remain an independent force.

Part of this is explained by demographics. Occupiers, as Jim Parsons and Mark Stacey will tell you, are mainly young people, and young people, for the most part, don't vote. Tea Party members tend to be older and they vote more than any other demographic. In their poll, the PRRI folks also found that, among those who identify with the Tea Party movement, more than one-third were white evangelical Protestants; a third of those who identify with the Occupy movement, on the other hand, had no formal religious affiliation whatsoever.

As noted, PRRI also determined that Americans who say they share the values of the Tea Party were overwhelmingly white, and a quarter of them were retired. But among the Occupier sympathizers, about 40 percent were non-white, and an equal number were under the age of 50. Naturally, the PRRI survey found that more than 70 percent of those who shared the views of the Tea Party identified themselves as conservative, while about 80 percent of the Occupy movement was made up of liberals and progressives. The Tea Partiers, then, were pretty stereotypical conservatives: they tended to be angrier, whiter and older. The Occupy movement—led, still, by amazing and thoughtful young people like Parsons and Stacey—is conspicuously younger, more diverse, and much more hopeful about the future.

That's an important distinction because it suggests why older conservatives still lead the values debate—in the main, they participate more actively in democratic contests than younger progressives do, so their values tend to dominate the discourse. They vote more, a lot more. Therefore, if your side is more actively involved in elections, it's only logical that your perspective on morality—mostly, that hoary conservative chestnut, the "family values" construct—will receive more media attention and the lion's share of political consideration.

As I wrote in my book about punk rock, *Fury's Hour*, young people represent the largest bloc of unclaimed voters in the United States, Canada and in most modern democratic states. Generally, out of all of the young people entitled to vote, as few as one in five regularly do so. In the United States, people from age eighteen to thirty represent 25 percent of the total American voting population, but according to Yale University's Department of Political Science (widely recognized as the leading expert on the depressing phenomenon), few of them vote. For example, only a third of them actually bothered to cast a ballot in the 2000 presidential election. Had they done so, George W. Bush would have been beaten—decisively—by the Democrats' Al Gore.

In Canada, the story isn't the same, it's *worse*: in the 2000 federal general election, within the younger eighteen- to twenty-four-year-old group, only a depressing 22 percent bothered to cast a ballot. And had more of them voted in the 2004, 2006 and 2008 general elections, conservative political parties—which were quite favourable to the war in Iraq and missile defence, but very hostile towards gay marriage and reproductive freedom—might not have been as successful as they were. In Britain, the situation is marginally better, but not dramatically so: there, only about a third of younger voters generally bother to vote.

It's a vicious cycle: political candidates routinely ignore young people because of their poor voter turnout, while young people—like the Occupiers—cite the establishment's political indifference as one of the principal reasons they don't vote. With each election, a bad situation gets worse.

As they studied the problem—a problem that, everyone should agree, has the potential to raze democracy itself—the experts at Yale discovered a number of things about young people and how they regard politics. For example, younger potential voters are much more interested in a candidate's position on the issues, and much less interested in their partisan affiliation. They like candidates who have been involved in issues at a community level, in a hands-on way, as Occupy has done. Young people care very little about a politician's appearance or style or manner, and are instead preoccupied with their record and experience and effectiveness. They are focused on *authenticity*, in particular.

Young voters want a candidate's attention and respect, because they feel (rightly) that they have been left out of the political process. They feel the system does not take them or their issues seriously, and they know when they are being patronized. They like candidates who listen, who show some kind of commitment. And most of all, they don't like fakes and phonies—they can spot those miles away.

A lot of it seems like common sense, in fact, or like the sort of things that older voters want, too. But the Yale studies have found that when a candidate actually spends time with young people, face to face, when a candidate is honestly more preoccupied by Occupy-style community activism than politics, when a campaign reminds young people about the importance of voting and helps them to do so—then youth turnout can be boosted by as much as eight percentage points. Eight percent may not sound like a lot, but it is: an extra 8 percent would have defeated George W. Bush. It would have kept Stephen Harper's Conservatives to a minority or even defeated them. Eight percent, in fact, is far more than the margin of victory enjoyed by most winning politicians in most electoral contests. It can make a difference.

And that, of course, is why conservative political interests are so nervous about serious efforts to mobilize young people to vote, and why they devoted so many resources to attacking—in some cases *physically*—the young people who make up the Occupy movement. That's why, in early 2012, Republican-dominated states started making it a lot harder for young people to register for the vote. They know that if campaigns like Occupy are successful, democracy itself will be changed. They know that if they don't subtly constrain attempts to get out the vote, as Harper's Conservatives did across Canada in 2011, then a lot of conservative politicians will soon be looking for other lines of work. For conservatives, declining youth participation in democracy and suppression of the youth vote are good for business.

Remember: the con voter base is smaller but more motivated. If conservatives can suppress the youthful progressive vote or keep it divided, they'll keep winning. Meanwhile, the Occupy movement—if it remains disinterested in direct participation in democracy, and if its members don't start coming out to vote for the progressive candidates who share their values—is actually the Right's best friend. They are, in a very sad way, the embodiment of a conservative's political fantasy: one, they're a group of mainly young people who have given up on democracy. Two, they're a group of mainly progressive young people who lack leadership and are divided on what their strategy and tactics should be.

For progressives in Canada, the U.S. and elsewhere, the Occupiers—and their "99 percent" credo—*must* be pursued. Their message, their values, are among the most popular anyone has seen emerge in politics in a long, long time.

If we progressives follow their lead, and we do it the right way, we can win again.

☆ ☆ ☆

"Capitalism, in its current form, has no place in the world around us."

Those are not my words, but a quote from a respected German economist named Klaus Schwab. For the many who are unlikely to have heard of Klaus Schwab before, rest assured: he's no socialist rabble-rouser. He's a well-to-do fellow, in fact, and the founder of something called the World Economic Forum, in snowbound Davos, Switzerland.

Prime Minister Stephen Harper was at Schwab's Davos gathering at the tail end of January 2012, as were dozens of other world leaders and billionaires. While Harper didn't perform the last rites on contemporary capitalism, plenty of others weren't nearly as shy. The capitalist "model" needs to be radically revised, said one billionaire, David Rubenstein. If we don't, he said, "we've lost the game." German Chancellor Angela Merkel, in the keynote Davos address, agreed: when it comes to capitalism, "we need to debate new methods," she said.

Davos 2012, therefore, was different from previous years. Among other things, it wasn't boring. It wasn't the usual orgy of self-congratulation, either. For the first time—and you can thank the Occupy kids for this—the masters of industry and politics acknowledged that, well, maybe they're not so perfect after all.

Don't just take this progressive's word for it, either. Ask Frank Luntz, the self-proclaimed conservative wordsmith. Remember what Luntz told Republican governors at that Florida gathering, just a few weeks before Davos: the public, he said in a moment of extreme candour, "think capitalism is immoral." *Immoral.* Therefore, Luntz said, don't attack the Occupiers. Say to the Occupiers and to the public: "I get it." Don't deny that there is inequality. Don't deny the need to "fix" the system, Luntz said. Agree.

Now, Luntz and his ilk aren't really interested in fixing an economic system that has effectively constitutionalized unfairness and inequity. They're just pretending to care, in the hope that the public will move on from their current tendency to favour the Occupier's point of view and start focusing on the weather again. Notwithstanding that, Luntz—and Schwab and Rubenstein and Merkel—are simply saying what, to many, is an unavoidable truth. When communism collapsed under the weight of its own sins, why did so many arrogantly consider that capitalism would be immune to change? It isn't.

It's a mistake to regard the surge in anticapitalist rhetoric as far-left polemics, but to dismiss critiques of capitalism—as the current Conservative Party and Republican Party leadership will perhaps always do—is a bigger mistake. The Tea Party movement demonstrated that one can be opposed to the squalid hallmarks of modern capitalism—twenty-five-year-old million-aire investment bankers driving BMWs, disgusting CEO pay-outs and perks, massive government bailouts—without being a communist. By coincidence, on the very day Davos was unfold-ing, I was talking with Occupy Newfoundland's Mark Stacey and Jim Parsons about whether they were (as obsequious con-servative pundits so often claim) old news. The obscene gap between the rich and the non-rich is still a message that needs to be heard, repeated Stacey: "We're sending the message to our governments and corporations that we will not rest until it has been corrected."

But everyone is saying you're old hat, I said. Parsons laughed. "It's winter," he said. "In the spring, we'll spill out again into public spaces, and start to attract more people again with our ideas." With their values.

If what we saw in Davos 2012 was any indication, some didn't wait for the snow to melt.

☆ ☆ ☆

Whenever we're in political trouble, progressives—Liberals and New Democrats in Canada, Democrats in the United States—will say we'd win more if only we *communicated* better. If only we had a better "narrative," we say, we'd beat conserva-tives more often. So, as noted, that young senator from Illinois, Barack Obama, called for and got a "new narrative" to wrest power back from conservative Republicans. Robert Reich, one of Bill Clinton's smarter guys, lamented that Republican conservatives win all the time because they "have mastered the art of political narrative."

Up here in the Great White North, you hear a lot of the same sort of kvetching. Shortly after he got his keester kicked in the May 2011 federal election, Michael Ignatieff told journalist Michael Valpy that he lost because he didn't "control the narrative." His successor, Bob Rae, said in a big vision speech at the Economic Club in Toronto that the "populist narrative" of Conservatives has been used to fool lots of folks into voting for Stephen Harper.

And so on and so on. Otherwise smart progressives yammer on about "narratives" and "framing" and "branding" and stuff like that. Up at the Liberal Party of Canada's mid-January 2012 convention, it was downright amazing to hear how many Grits were willing to vote for wacky resolutions. How come? "We need to change the frame," one delegate breathlessly informed me. "We need to change the narrative. If we don't make some dramatic policy changes, the media will say we didn't learn our lesson in the election."

"If that's true, the media can fuck right off," I curtly replied, but the bright-eyed Liberal delegate was undeterred. He and 75 percent of the delegates present then went ahead and voted to allow non-party members to vote for the next Liberal leader, thereby delighting (and astonishing) the NDP and Tory spinners present to observe the proceedings. It wasn't just dumb, it was insane: special interests—and malicious Dippers and Cons—would overwhelm the leadership selection process and leave us led by a dud. But *whatever*, said the narrative-seeking Liberals. It's different! It's new!

These days, my fellow federal Liberals are enthusiastic about storytelling, but they seem to be less preoccupied with how unhappily the story may end. Ignatieff, the former Harvard professor, was a terrific storyteller. In his campaign appearances, Iggy seemed to be styling himself as the national narrator, and he was pretty good at it. He'd stand at the head of the ersatz classroom (Canada, perhaps), and relate what he'd learned from what he called "ordinary Canadians" as he criss-crossed the hinterland.

Having had lots of classroom experience—unfortunately, almost exclusively in non-Canadian classrooms—Iggy was very effective at crafting a compelling narrative. Better, certainly, than Harper, who looked like he might fall asleep during the leaders' debates. But it didn't matter in the end. The compelling storyteller lost to the boring Tim Hortons guy, big time. Why? Because progressives—on both sides of the border—need to understand that pithy catchphrases and slogans aren't nearly enough. They never are. We need to go way, way deeper than that, into the values and morality stuff that is not easily expressed in words. Life and death stuff. Identity and purpose stuff. Into voters' hearts and not just their heads. The emotion-laden stuff that surrounds the 99 percent versus the 1 percent.

Thus, when I still read to him at bedtime, my youngest son got tired of books by Robert Munsch. Munsch is an acclaimed and bestselling writer of children's books. But my son was undeterred.

"But why?" I asked. "He's a great Canadian storyteller! He wins awards!"

"Because," my son said, "he always tells the same story in his books. It's boring."

Out of the mouths of babes, as another storyteller said.

☆ ☆ ☆

The mission, however, is not merely to tell tales. Michael Ignatieff and Al Gore did that, brilliantly, and they still lost elections to a pair of conservatives who couldn't craft a captivating yarn if their lives had depended on it. We progressives need to conjure up narratives that resonate deeply within the hearts of the people we are trying to reach and recapture. We need to show, and not merely tell. Facts tell, stories sell.

The values that permeate the Occupy movement provide useful guideposts for any progressives who are peering at the political map and desperately looking for a way out of the political darkness. Occupy's primary suggestion—that too few have too much of the power and too much of the wealth—strikes anxious conservatives at their core, because it is generally conservatives who hoard wealth and power, and it is conservatives who typically say to hell with everyone who is unlike them. It's significant, then, that the Occupiers' values set has become popular enough that the U.S. president, as well as billionaires and presidents and prime ministers at Davos, felt safe in asserting kinship with them. Captains of industry and leaders of nations, echoing the values of a bunch of leaderless, penniless, aimless, anarchic kids. Living in tents, down by the sea. It's amazing, when you think about it.

Capitalism—at least as it has how evolved in these conservative times—*sucks*, say the Occupier kids. We sort-of agree, say Obama and the giants of Davos. The expressed kinship of the billionaires and the presidents may be phony, it may be insincere, but it may also be a *start*. If progressives therefore embrace Occupy's morality, will there be (to put it crassly) a political payoff? Can the Occupiers' core message, about correcting the imbalance between the rich 1 percent and the struggling 99 percent, improve the fortunes of progressives?

Polls—and there has been no shortage of polls about the relative impact of the Occupy movement, as the mainstream media struggled to understand or vilify them—suggest the answer is an unqualified yes. Consider these findings:

- A CBS News/*New York Times* poll in October 2011 found a plurality of Americans—43 percent—agreed with the Occupy movement. Nearly 70 percent agreed with Occupy's basic premise, too, that money and wealth are unfairly distributed in America. A Nanos Research poll conducted in Canada the next month found nearly as many Canadians had a favourable view of the Occupiers, and among young Canadians, the approval rating was even greater: almost 75 percent of Canadians under the age of thirty agreed with Occupy's values.

- The results of a massive global poll by John Wright's Ipsos firm released at the start of 2012 suggest that, internationally, the Occupy movement was quite well liked, too. South Korea was the most sympathetic, at 67 percent, followed by Indonesia (65 percent) and India (64 percent). Meanwhile, said Ipsos, two in three North Americans had become very familiar with Occupy. (The firm had polled 17,678 adults in twenty-three countries in the first two weeks of November 2011.)

- Environics concluded in a January 2012 poll that, wherever pollsters checked, the attitudes and values of the Occupiers matched those of most voters. For example, two-thirds of Canadian respondents said the gap between the wealthy and everyone else is larger than it has ever been (only 27 percent said the gap remains the same). Environics also noted that their findings mirrored the opinions of Americans expressed in a November 2011 survey for the *Washington Post*.

- The October 2011 CBS News/*New York Times* poll further found that two-thirds of the American public said that wealth should be distributed more evenly in the country. Seven in ten Americans thought the policies of congressional Republicans favour the rich, and two-thirds objected to further tax cuts for the rich. Meanwhile, an incredible 89 percent of Americans said they distrusted government to do the right thing.

There's a message in those polls for progressives who are willing to listen. Mike McCurry says those surprising numbers offer possible salvation for progressives—but they also underline a key weakness.

"Look at Barack Obama," he says.

"There's a danger Obama faces," says McCurry as he sits in his modest Washington office, and as the sound of chanting Occupiers fades down Pennsylvania Avenue. "In 2008, and for the first time, I think, in ten presidential election cycles, more than half the electorate was under the age of fifty. That meant a substantial increase in participation by young people. The real fear that the Obama people have is that, if the Occupier crowd won't consider anything [that Obama's saying] to be exciting or relevant, they'll just check out.

"Young people tend to participate when they feel like something matters to them and their life. And when they hear politicians talking about other things, they'll say, 'Oh, that's not relevant to my life, and I'm not going to pay attention to this stuff . . .'" McCurry pauses. "They make a pretty rational choice, actually."

That is why, McCurry says, leaning forward at his desk, Occupy's message and values aren't unrelated to the political fortunes of Obama or any other progressive leader. Unlike the Tea Party, the Occupy movement has consciously and clearly rejected democratic participation. It is, quite literally, outside of all of that. As long as the Occupiers—or, more crucially, their voting-age peers who overwhelmingly back the Occupiers' values and goals—remain disdainful of politics and politicians, conservatives and conservative interests will benefit, says McCurry. He continues: "Rekindling their enthusiasm, and getting young people convinced that they can make an actual difference and end up gaining real political power—and being in a place where they can impact big decisions—I think that is something that has to be communicated way more effectively. We are not teaching the value of citizenship to young people. Why it's important to vote, why it's important to participate in democracy, why you should pay attention: that's your responsibility, as a citizen of your country."

But the Occupiers have explicitly rejected all traditional notions of citizenship, I say. They have even shown contempt for traditional society and its conventions, by moving themselves physically outside it. They hate what we have become, I say to McCurry, and maybe they're entitled to. "I think that's right," says McCurry, looking in the direction of the White House. "I don't think [the Occupiers] will be willingly co-opted by Obama or the Democratic Party. They would love to co-opt *Obama*, to turn it around, and sort of bring him inside their movement. But I don't think that's going to happen . . ." Pause. "Not yet, anyway."

☆ ☆ ☆

It couldn't have been a very good political fundraiser: none of us can now recall who was speaking. Most likely, it was a Conservative—because we were exiled to the furthest corner in the room, along with some of the other Liberals in attendance.

While the speaker wasn't at all memorable, the pleasant woman at our table was. She was employed by a mortgage broker association. Asked what was new in her field of work, she said: "Subprime mortgages. We're quite worried about them. If things unfold the way we think they might, it could be very, very bad."

How bad? "They could cause a new recession," she said.

Subprime mortgages, she explained, were home loans designed to help people who were high-risk. Smaller banks in the Southern U.S. loved them. The subprime mortgages had a higher rate, and were being given to people who didn't have jobs and couldn't make a down payment. That was bad enough, the mortgage association lady said. But what made the situation worse was that, as the housing bubble was bursting in the U.S., many of the people who had been given subprime mortgages were walking away—and the subprime mortgage debt was being picked up by bigger financial institutions and "bundled" with safer, more traditional mortgages. "It's like a virus," she said. "If it spreads, we're all going to get really sick."

That was 2006. Two years or so later, the virus had indeed spread, leaving foreclosures, defaults, bankruptcies, layoffs and wrecked lives in its path. Much of the civilized world is still grappling with the after-effects of the recession that was hastened, if not caused, by the subprime mortgage crisis. Full recovery, if it is to come at all, remains years away.

It's tempting to blame the subprime mortgage mess for all of our current economic woes. But ordinary folks, in their wisdom, know the identity of the real culprit. It wasn't just a high-risk lending practice in some poorly regulated regional U.S. banks. It was *greed*, pure and simple, practised at a historic scale. And the consequences of it continue to be seen in the body politic: anger, cynicism and—most of all—a profound distrust of those who wield power and control capitalism.

For more than a decade, the Edelman Trust Barometer has measured our confidence in financial institutions and government. This year, more than twenty-five thousand people in twenty-five countries were surveyed. Their conclusion? Trust in banks and financial institutions has never been lower—and trust in government has gone into an "unprecedented" decline. "Throughout the world, people blamed their governments for the financial and political crises they endured in 2011," said the report. "[Politicians'] credibility has taken such a beating that they are now the least-trusted spokespeople in the world." Said Edelman: "In 2008–2009, in the wake of a recession that saw large, global companies such as Lehman Brothers and AIG collapse, trust in business imploded. Government stepped in with bailouts and new regulations. But in 2011, government became paralyzed by the politics of extremism and endless haggling, and the public lost confidence.

"[The] Trust Barometer sees an unprecedented nine-point global decline in trust in government. In twelve countries, it trails business, media, and nongovernmental organizations as the least trusted institution. . . . Political brinksmanship on the debt ceiling in the United States, dysfunction on bailouts in the European Union, corruption in Brazil and India, and a natural disaster in Japan drove the downward trend. Business leaders should not be cheered by government ineptitude, especially as trust in the two institutions tend to move in sync. There is still a yawning trust gap for business."

While respondents don't trust governments, they want more government oversight of the corporate world. "[About half] of global respondents still want more regulation of business," concluded Edelman. Meanwhile, for the fifth year in a row, "[nongovernmental organizations] are the most trusted institution in the world." Conservative partisans don't want to hear any of this, but the 2,600 delegates at the World Economic Forum in Davos heard the message. Globally, citizens are fed up with what the experts dryly call "severe income disparity."

They're sick of greed.

"To increase trust levels," Edelman declared, "a combination of operational and societal factors is required . . . those that will build future trust are more societally focused. Listening to customer needs, treating employees well, placing customers ahead of profits, and having ethical business practices are all considered more important than delivering consistent financial returns. . . . We could go a long way to regaining trust by making the system more transparent, by clearing some of the obscurity that causes people to believe the system is a game rigged against their own interests."

From the Tea Party on the Right to the Occupy movement on the Left, Edelman suggests that ordinary folks have served notice that big political changes are needed. "The majority of countries surveyed do not trust their government to do what is right," said Edelman in its report. "Throughout the world, people blamed their governments, more than any other institution, for the financial and political crises they endured in 2011. In 17 of the 25 countries surveyed, government is now trusted by less than half to do what is right. In Europe, trust in government dropped by more than ten points in France, Spain, and Italy. In Latin America, Brazil experienced a 53-point plunge. In Asia, South Korea and China suffered declines of 17 and 13 points, respectively. In Japan, trust in government dropped by 26 points . . ." And so on and so on. Politics, and politicians, have rarely ranked lower. Businesses, meanwhile, remain loathsome to many, the world over. Shrinking disposable incomes, uncertainty about the future, hikes in consumer prices—all of these things have contributed to people's distrust of business and of businesspeople's values. But none more so than what Edelman blandly calls "intensified polarization of wealth." The gap between rich and poor, in other words. The Occupy credo.

The game has been rigged against those who have worked hard and played by the rules. It's a notion found in Bill Clinton's July 1992 nomination speech about hope (and his hometown, Hope, Arkansas). Clinton, even back then, brilliantly anticipated the Occupy mantra and placed it at the very centre of the most important speech he ever gave. "In the name of all the people who do the work, pay the taxes, raise the kids and play by the rules," Clinton said, "in the name of the hard-working Americans who make up our forgotten middle class, I accept your nomination for president of the United States." As Clinton then noted, average folks regard the cavernous fissure between the haves and the have-nots to be an issue of morality and values. It is the most telling commentary about our times extant. If citizens can be shown that conservatives have a well-documented lack of interest in the fundamental *immorality* of the gap, then progressives can win the values debate.

The system, as our mortgage broker predicted so many years ago, is sick. Greed and reckless behaviour—and lack of government oversight, principally during the George W. Bush era—spread through the system like a cancer.

Progressives, if they're smart, can offer a cure—and some prevention, too.

☆ ☆ ☆

If you are curious about how the recession could be so terrible in some places (like Florida), but less so in others (like Canada), take a look around Fort Myers. Once the playground of the affluent and the super-rich, coastal Florida was one of the first places to be hit by the global recession. It will also be one of the last places to exit it.

All around southwestern Florida, there are ugly scars, unmistakable signs that people are still struggling. Foreclosure notices are everywhere, as are ads for bankruptcy sales and bankruptcy help. Shuttered businesses can be seen wherever you look. Along a sunny stretch of beach once favoured by Floridians piloting big yachts, someone has planted some handwritten signs. "Our house for sale," they say. "EMERGENCY." While the experts will tell you the recession ended in the third quarter of 2009, residents of Florida would disagree. In 2009, jobs continued to be scarce, home prices continued to fall, equity was shrinking and the markets still hadn't recovered. A record number of foreclosures continued to be reported—with Florida accounting for a staggering one million foreclosures or home repossessions in 2009 and 2010.

Just east of Fort Myers's beach, lots of big single-family homes were being sold, with many of the transactions involving "mortgage acquisition" firms. Some prices even reached as low as $39,900—for a well-maintained home with four bedrooms and three bathrooms, no less. It was terribly sad to witness the economic misery that still persisted in such a sunny place. For folks visiting here from up north—and many of us Canadians still do, every spring break—we have to wonder: How did we largely avoid Florida's plight? Three reasons.

First, Canadians can thank my former boss, Liberal leader Jean Chrétien. When Chrétien refused to permit the big Canadian banks to merge a decade ago, he helped to preserve jobs—and most importantly, economic stability. Banks, and banking institutions, would continue to be subject to much more government oversight than in the U.S. Moreover, Chrétien would not permit the sort of rapacious subprime and zero-down mortgage lending that devastated Florida and much of the United States under the Republicans' watch.

Second, our lending institutions tend to be larger than many U.S. institutions, and more cautious in their approach— so widespread mortgage defaults, and the bank failures that follow them, are virtually unheard of in Canada. Jones Lang LaSalle, a firm that tracks global real estate trends put it this way: "Among the world's most transparent real estate markets, Canada differentiates itself on having a combination of a sound banking system, well-developed lending standards and stable property markets." The born-again progressives at the World Economic Forum agreed, noting we have a competitive advantage because of "soundness of banks" and "strength of investor protection." Liberals ensured that our banks remained secure by refusing to go along with the get-rich-at-all-costs policies favoured by the Bush regime.

Third, Stephen Harper's Conservative government was forced to govern in a decidedly *un*conservative way. To the annoyance of hard-core conservatives, who typically favour fiscal restraint, Harper was compelled in 2009 to act like a liberal and pursue a massive multibillion-dollar stimulus program. At the height of it, unrepentant conservatives at outfits like the Canadian Taxpayers Federation grumbled that Harper was "spending like a drunken sailor," or (even worse) like a liberal. But the unequivocally liberal stimulus spending worked. As the *Economist* noted: "[Others] might note that Mr. Harper has managed to govern for four years without a parliamentary majority, and that this has not prevented Canada from sailing through the recession."

Elsewhere, the sad story was the same, if not worse. Far from Florida—and far across the Atlantic—the vast majority of the governments in the EU are mostly found on the Right: after the election of David Cameron's Conservatives in Britain in May 2010, for example, the map of Europe became over-whelmingly conservative blue. But the conservatives who dominated the EU did little to prevent recession and its attendant misery. In fact, they made a bad situation worse. By late 2011, billionaire philanthropist and progressive George Soros said that the EU had become "ungovernable," noting that "a dynamic of disintegration" was tearing through Europe.

That fall, European leaders hammered together a deal of sorts to save the Union from ruin. The eleventh-hour plan addressed only the symptoms of the crisis, however, not its root causes. Greece had a debt level that was an extraordinary 150 percent of its gross domestic product. Conservative-led Italy, with a far larger and far more significant economy, had a debt-to-GDP level of nearly 120 percent. Ireland was deeply in recession, and there—as in Belgium and supposed conservative superpowers like Britain and Germany—the debt-to-GDP ratio hovered at or above 80 percent. The damage done to European economies had been mainly self-inflicted: their approach to basic fiscal policy had been the stuff of science fiction. They had done little or nothing to address the economic contagion that had spread throughout the continent.

Paying no heed to debt levels, conservatives handed out corporate tax cuts like candy. They were seemingly unconcerned about (or unable to deal with) the growing numbers of unemployed Europeans, and they governed like genuine conservatives: recklessly, without regard for future generations. For instance: Canadians avoided a Euro-style implosion because—as no less than arch-conservative Treasury Board President Tony Clement meekly acknowledged—we had stuck with liberal-style regulatory policies. So, in a little-noticed fall 2011 speech before the U.S. Chamber of Commerce, Clement lauded the government of Liberal prime minister Jean Chrétien for "rather remarkable" fiscal reforms in the nineties which have protected the Canadian economy ever since. Said Clement: "Successive Canadian governments, across political lines, faced the challenge square on, delivering fiscal reforms that started us on a path to balanced budgets. As a result, from 1997 to 2007, our country enjoyed a decade of strong economic performance, with Canada leading the G7 in economic growth."

He didn't say it, but I will: you can thank Liberals for that. Canada didn't do things this way, because for all but one year of the decade, Canada was governed by Liberals, not Conservatives. Stable governance, fiscal reforms: it's the Canadian liberal way.

Conservative politicians in Europe—and conservative politicians in sunny Florida, too—should give it a try sometime.

☆ ☆ ☆

Liberal class warfare: that's what conservatives call it when liberals argue that conservative values mean lousy governance and that conservative morals mean total indifference to the cosmic chasm between the rich and the reduced. That's what they'll say if we start to finally embrace the Occupy credo.

That's what they always do when they're cornered. You can almost set your watch by it. It's "class warfare" by "liberal elites," they say. Republican presidential aspirant Newt Gingrich, in particular, has elevated the use of the term to an art form since the mid-nineties, when every criticism of conservatives—however meek and mild—was labelled liberal-led class warfare. Gingrich still positively delights in using the term. Whenever someone had the audacity to suggest slashing taxes for billionaires was a bad idea, or that raising the minimum wage by a little bit was a good idea, Gingrich would screech about "liberal elites" and their proclivity for "class warfare." More recently, when President Obama talked about tax fairness in his 2012 State of the Union address, Gingrich dismissed it as "bash[ing] rich people." And if it isn't that, Gingrich asked, "What does he think class warfare is?"

Gingrich isn't alone. Other conservatives have taken note of the effectiveness of his fear-mongering and followed his lead. George W. Bush on defending tax cuts for the rich: Democrats, he said, were "ignit[ing] the great outcry of class warfare." Rep. Richard Armey on defending earlier tax cuts for the rich: it's "class warfare rhetoric." Rep. Paul Ryan on defending more recent tax cuts for the rich: "Class warfare makes for rotten economics." It goes on and on.

The best defence to this ancient conservative deceit, of course, is to simply throw it back in their well-fed faces. As New York representative Charles Rangel once did to his GOP tormentors so memorably: "Is it class warfare? You bet your life. But you [conservatives] declared it against the *working people of America!*" Even Lee Atwater, the fabled departed Republican strategist, agreed that the most effective response to the class warfare canard is to make his fellow conservatives wear it. Years before the Occupy movement, Atwater said: "The way to win a presidential race against the Republicans is to develop the class warfare issue . . . to divide up the haves and have-nots and to try and reinvigorate the New Deal coalition and to attack." Liberals are too often afraid to take Atwater's advice, however, because they are afraid of being outed as "liberals"—or, even worse, "elites." As Democrat communications director Brad Woodhouse admits, "The use of the word 'liberal' in this country is a pejorative. And the use of the word 'conservative' is totally different."

The best strategy, therefore, is not to get mired in conservative word games, which Luntz and his ilk resolutely adore. Don't talk about class warfare, much less acknowledge conservatives' use of the phrase. Don't get hung up on who is a liberal and who isn't; don't get into a debate about who may be part of an elite and who may not be. *Manage the dialogue*, as former Clinton advisor Dick Morris advises. And you do that—as another former Clinton advisor, James Carville says—by striking first. "It's hard for somebody to hit you when you've already got your fist in their face," Carville once succinctly observed.

In this epic battle between the 1 percent and the 99 percent, the stakes are very, very high. It's a war, in effect: it's a real war with real casualties. As in any war, and as in any political campaign, speed and accuracy are vitally important. So, too, is doing what Carville advises. In political campaigns, striking first is sometimes called "going negative." But it's not, really. It's never negative to tell the truth about your conservative opponents' absence of values and morals, and their near-total disinterest in helping those who need help. Years ago, I spoke to Carville about this very point. "Look," he told me, "the best way to do this game is to get all your information, and then get all your information out." Says Carville: "The voters deserve more information, you know? We're not in this business to be mean or negative. We're in it to draw distinctions, and to draw distinctions that favour our side. So we just go out and try and be very honest about these distinctions, these differences."

The most effective strategy is to tell the truth about conservatives and conservative "values." In particular, tell the story about the essential truth contained in the Occupiers' philosophy or the reality evoked in Clinton's 1992 nomination speech. To remind voters that those who have worked hard, and played by the rules, are being left by the side of the road. And those who are favoured by conservatives—the rich and the powerful—are taking more than they could ever possibly use.

Back in Occupy Newfoundland's camp, as the waves continue to crash against the harbour walls and the gulls lazily screech overhead, Mark Stacey says, matter-of-factly, "The growing trend that we see all over the world today is of the rich getting richer."

Conservatives say that kind of talk is class warfare. It's the chatter of out-of-touch liberal elites. Is that not true? Stacey is undeterred. "Of course, not everybody agrees with [us]— often because of muddled views on how our economic system works, or different views on what would constitute economic justice." He pauses, and it's apparent he's trying to be fair. "Income disparity is a very, very complicated problem. There is no easy fix for this problem, and the same goes for most other issues identified by the Occupy movement, like corporate accountability, or environmental preservation and global warming, or corruption, or lack of transparency, or undemocratic laws and regulations. We don't have a simple solution because there *is* no simple solution." The Occupier's critique of the way in which our society has evolved, however—that is as true as it is self-evident. It cannot be disputed, by any rational person, that there is a profound economic imbalance at the epicentre of our society.

The values that Occupy embodies, then—the morality and decency they speak to—can those things actually help to make existence, as grinding and as merciless as it is for so many, just a bit better? Can they truly make a difference? With the Occupy movement seemingly slipping away, as conservatives claim, does that not also mean that progressives' hope for reasserting our values is a lost cause, too? Mark Stacey concludes, quietly. "[Our] next chapter may not even involve a camp. I still think the camp will be back in the spring, but after that . . . who knows. The important thing is that we all continue, and that the discussion still takes place. I can't foresee an end to either of those any time soon.

"The future is in our hands."

HOW PROGRESSIVES CAN STEAL BACK WORDS

*Conservatives, and conservative lackeys, employ all manner of
deception and guile to disguise themselves in the wild, and endeavour
to appear as the friend of the common man and woman.
They make noises, slandering so-called elites and intellectuals, and they
will shame-facedly assert that theirs is a friendly ideology, at one with
Tim Hortons, white picket fences and Main Street. When, as has been
shown with incontrovertible facts and figures, theirs is the Party of
No, the Party of Fear, and their principal preoccupation is making the
rich richer and themselves more powerful than they deserve to be.
They claim fealty to the values of the family, when they value only
themselves and those who are kin to them.
Herewith, the means by which dedicated progressives and
liberals may dominate the field of discourse,
and show common folk that it is they, and not the conservatives,
whom they can and should trust.*

———

Politics and political communications are all about the
effective use of symbols, not words. Ask Jean Chrétien.
He'll tell you. Or, more accurately, he'll show you.

It was the long hot summer of 1993. The Canadian Conservatives had just picked former justice minister Kim Campbell as their leader, in a bid to sweep away the vestiges of the detested regime of former Conservative leader Brian Mulroney. Campbell was brainy but she also had a sense of fun: earlier, her advisors circulated a 1990 photo of the B.C. politician, in which a coiffed Campbell—bare-shouldered and possibly nude—holds her Queen's Counsel robes in front of her, with a hint of a smile playing on her face. The portrait (which photographer Barbara Woodley would eventually auction off for twelve thousand dollars) became a mini-sensation and ran in newspapers around the world.

One gushing account in Britain's *Independent*, under a headline that stated "A provocative picture may help Kim Campbell become leader of her country," read like campaign bumph: "She may read Tolstoy in Russian and play a mean Bach on the cello, but it was bare shoulders that put Avril Phaedra 'Kim' Campbell on a fast track to be Canada's next prime minister. Not since Pierre Trudeau was snapped sliding down a banister in Marlborough House—he was attending a Commonwealth leaders' conference shortly after being elected prime minister—has so much Canadian public attention turned on one photograph. . . . Ms. Campbell is being described as everything from Canada's Madonna to its Margaret Thatcher. The polls suggest that a Conservative Party led by her would double its support to more than 40 percent, enough to overtake the Liberals led by Jean Chrétien, who have topped the polls for the past three years. Much of Ms. Campbell's appeal can be traced to her cool, unstuffy handling of the media hullabaloo over the photograph: an arresting image of her standing, as if naked, behind a suit of lawyer's robes. It was taken almost three years ago, shortly after she became justice minister."

Fawning as it was, it was also true: a few weeks after her selection as Conservative leader, as the hot July of 1993 came to a close, polls showed that Campbell indeed had abruptly become the most popular prime minister in decades. She was new, she was exciting, and as the *Independent* had gushed, she was unambiguously different. Meanwhile, the Liberals were slipping in public opinion surveys and the sixty-one-year-old Chrétien was again being unfairly labelled "yesterday's man."

The epithet had been thrown at Chrétien from the very moment he won the Liberal leadership in June 1990. On that day, the CBC actually headlined one story "Yesterday's man voted today's Liberal leader." Then, in early 1991, the insult resurfaced when the Liberal leader needed to be hospitalized to remove a noncancerous nodule on his lung. Even when Chrétien denied being sick, many reported he was, anyway. Some of the anonymous (and gutless) acolytes of defeated Liberal leadership rival Paul Martin again hissed that Chrétien was "yesterday's man."

Chrétien, the media claimed, was in danger of losing the anticipated fall 1993 election to a woman many years his junior because his image was that of a fossil, while Campbell was a brilliant lawyer with a sense of fun. In other words, the fresh face captured in Barbara Woodley's remarkable photograph.

In the midst of all of this, on the August long weekend— just as Campbell was soaring to new heights of popularity in the polls—I was invited to the Stony Lake cottage of Swatty and Kitty Wotherspoon, two renowned Ontario Conservative Party activists. Pretty much everyone in attendance at the Wotherspoon retreat that weekend was a conservative. Some were Conservative Party staffers in Ottawa or at Queen's Park in Toronto; all were highly enthusiastic about Kim Campbell. As such, I received a lot of ribbing about my decision to leave my law practice and go to work for "yesterday's man." The assembled guests—like most of the political pundits and pollsters that summer—felt that Campbell was going to decisively beat my boss.

Early on Saturday, before everyone else was up, I went up to the Wotherspoons' main cottage, where Swatty had somehow been able to obtain a copy of that morning's *Globe and Mail*. As I walked in, he was shaking his head. He threw the newspaper on the table. "It's all over," he said.

On the front page of the *Globe* was something that even I hadn't known was coming. It was a photo of the Liberal leader by Canadian Press photographer Ryan Remiorz, taken at the Chrétien family cottage on Lac des Piles in Quebec. The CP photo showed Chrétien water-skiing—on one ski. The sun was shining through the arc of water created by Chrétien's wake, and he had a big grin on his face. "Wow," I said.

"Exactly," said Swatty Wotherspoon. "It's all over. He ain't yesterday's man anymore, the sonofabitch. You guys are going to win."

And so we did.

☆ ☆ ☆

Many years afterwards, Chrétien reclines in a chair at the law firm of Heenan Blaikie in Toronto. He's in a meeting room where small pencil portraits of him have been hung on the walls. He's still considered Canada's most successful living politician: the guy who won three historic back-to-back majorities; the guy who won was elected for a total of forty years in the House of Commons, ten of them as prime minister; the guy who repatriated Canada's constitution, stewarded through its Charter of Rights, and kept Canada out of George W. Bush's war in Iraq. After leaving political life, Chrétien signed on with Heenan's—where, many years before,

Pierre Elliott Trudeau had also worked—and he still maintains a busy practice, despite being past the age when most Canadians are understandably looking forward to retirement. He doesn't look at all like a guy past retirement age. In fact, he looks like a million bucks.

Notably, he certainly doesn't look like he's *dying*—which, in the early nineties, quite a few of his adversaries and media people were saying was the case. He laughs uproariously at the memory. "In 1990 I became the leader, and in 1991 I had a major operation. The press was writing that I was dying— and some of the guys who wanted to take over from me had already bought me flowers! I would tell the press that I wasn't sick and they would write that I was sick. If I was gone some- where for three days, they'd say I had gone somewhere for treatment. So how can you prove that you are not sick?"

That summer, Chrétien gathered with two of his oldest friends and most influential advisors, chief of staff and former Quebec City mayor Jean Pelletier and Montreal business exec- utive John Rae. Pelletier and Rae, along with being the closest to Chrétien, were giants within the long history of Canadian liberalism. They had a serious issue to discuss. Campbell, the three men agreed, was regarded as youthful and vital. Chrétien, meanwhile, was being derided as the opposite. So how does one prove one isn't dead or dying? How does one disprove such a falsehood, with an election just weeks away? Stretching out in his chair, Chrétien recalls: "I said I can do two things. One, I can do bungee jumping. And Pelletier said, 'If you do that, they will think you really *are* sick!'" He laughs again. "Or," he says, slyly, "I could do some water-skiing. On one ski."

He meant it, too. Chrétien grew up in the small Quebec town of Shawinigan and had been skiing and water-skiing with his family for years. All of us who worked for him knew he was in great shape, and he would regularly bound up the stairs in the House of Commons, leaving us younger guys gasping for breath. But the water-skiing stunt was a high-risk move. Even if he didn't fall, there was no guarantee that the photograph would run anywhere or that it would change anyone's mind. Asked why he thought it would work, Chrétien puts his hands behind his head and leans back. "Because it's *physical*. Because it requires a bit of skill, and it's not necessarily done by guys who are in their late fifties. I had to do something physical to prove that I was healthy." In politics, one's physicality—and one's willingness to physically express one's principles and values—is pretty important. There's a reason, for instance, why Franklin D. Roosevelt never permitted himself to be photographed in a wheelchair (after, historians will note, he acquired a paralytic virus during a vacation stop in Canada). Symbols, in politics, are critically important.

True enough. But Chrétien's water-ski photo represented a political gamble. What if—horror of horrors—he had fallen down? The enduring symbol would have been one of failure, not success. Chrétien shrugs. "I guess I'm the one who organized it," he recalls, thereby contradicting various publicity-seeking aides who, over the years, have claimed to have come up with the idea—and many other good ones. "I asked a guy from Canadian Press to come and take the picture. So I had to do well. When he arrived at the lake, I said: 'Let's make a deal. If I fall, you don't take the picture.' And he said: 'Sir, I'm taking the pictures. It's not me who will decide which picture Canadian Press will use. I will send them all the pictures I take.'"

The public, Chrétien says, know when something is risky and when it isn't. They attach political value to the former, because they admire risk-taking. They admire courage and conviction. Politicians and leaders who play it safe never make it into the history books. Chrétien therefore turned to his brother-in-law, who would be piloting the boat he would be skiing behind. "I said, let's do it! And I will pray I don't fall. So we did it with no fall, and it was a great picture. So [Remiorz] went and produced this famous picture of me on one ski, with a splash of water and the sun going through it. It's a fabulous picture that he did. That's when 'yesterday's man' went out the window. And it turned things around: my so-called health problem disappeared!"

That amazing photograph ran on or near front pages everywhere in the country that weekend—in both Vancouver papers, in the *Edmonton Journal*, the *Hamilton Spectator*, the *Toronto Star* and, in succeeding days, many other media outlets. Millions of registered voters saw it. It became, in short order, a highly effective repudiation of the main criticism that had been leveled at Chrétien in the three years since he had become leader of the Liberal Party. And it underlined how crucially important simple, compelling symbols—and not mind-numbing recitation of statistics—should be to progressives seeking to take back the public agenda.

Chrétien pauses, to emphasize a very important point, one that all progressives need to recall. "My words could not have convinced the press," Chrétien explains; "my *actions* had to convince the press."

In politics—in all effective communications, he says— words certainly matter. But they don't matter nearly as much as a memorable photograph or a dramatic bit of video. Nothing matters as much as the symbolism that is communicated by enduring images. Images, Chrétien suggests, echo the longest in a person's heart. They can go horribly wrong, too. He cites another example, that of one-time Conservative leader Robert Stanfield.

A former Nova Scotia Conservative premier, Stanfield became federal Conservative leader in 1967. Often referred to as "the greatest prime minister Canada never had," Stanfield was an upright, cerebral man, but a bit awkward. At two crucial points, Stanfield made grave errors. Neither, in and of themselves, should have been consequential—but for a comparatively little-known man seeking the highest office in the land, they were fatal. They were no more than fleeting images, but they became symbols. The first was a photo of Stanfield lounging in a chair in September 1967 at Maple Leaf Gardens in Toronto. As he serenely awaited the results of the voting that would see him anointed Conservative leader, Stanfield took bites out of a banana. And, as one Facebook group bearing the same name amusingly observes: "No one looks cool while eating a banana." Stanfield, from the very beginnings of his leadership, looked decidedly uncool when compared to his rival-to-be, Pierre Trudeau. It wasn't fair, and it possibly wasn't accurate, but it became the reality.

The second photograph, however, was even more damaging. In fact, it's widely acknowledged that it cost the Conservative leader an election campaign which up until that point had been his to lose.

One sunny day in May 1974, as the Grits and Tories battled for electoral supremacy, the Conservative campaign paused at a rest stop near North Bay, Ontario. An aide brought out a football, which Stanfield started throwing around. Many times, Stanfield successfully caught and threw the football, and the well-regarded photojournalist Doug Ball snapped those moments some thirty-six times. But then—just once—Stanfield fumbled. It was to be the biggest fumble in Canadian political history. Ball later described the excruciating scene: "Knock-kneed, hands clasped awkwardly, grimacing as a football slipped between his bony fingers." That was what Stanfield looked like, to millions of voters.

Tellingly, perhaps cruelly, it was also to be the most enduring symbol of Robert Stanfield's long political career. For Canadians, it became more than a photograph: it became an epitaph on the

career of a man who, by most accounts, was thoroughly respectable and much more of a progressive than a conservative. Immediately thereafter, the *Globe and the Mail* ran Ball's photo on their front page. The headline said it all, rhetorically: "A political fumble?" No newspaper—not a single one—ran one of Ball's many other shots showing Stanfield actually *catching* the ball. The picture, which would win Ball a National Newspaper Award, was a perfect example of conservative broadcasting magnate Roger Ailes's most enduring political axiom, the Orchestra Pit Theory: "If you have two guys on a stage and one guy says, 'I have a solution to the Middle East problem,' and the other guy falls into the orchestra pit, who do you think is going to be on the evening news?"

Chrétien grins again, and nods a bit on hearing Ailes's pithy truism. These ephemeral images—and the powerful symbols that result—are mostly accidents, he says. The ones that stick in people's minds are the ones that are the hardest to map out in advance. Says Chrétien: "Some are phony and succeed. Others are sincere and don't succeed. It's difficult to measure. But if you ask me, I never planned these things. The only one thing I ever planned was water-skiing, the rest just happened."

But how do these symbols, planned or otherwise, have such a tremendous impact? And how is that so many people remember them for so long, like the immortal Stanfield football and banana photographs? Chrétien thinks for a moment. "People are visual," he says, finally. "They look at things as much as they listen to things. If you want to know if you trust somebody, and he's on TV, you turn off the sound and just look at his body language. The body language doesn't lie. People and the media, they feel it and sense it. Like, if you are giving a speech, you need to be expressing something that is coming from *inside* of you. You need to feel it." He pauses. "To do that, you must be yourself."

Other famous symbols come to mind: Bill Clinton playing the saxophone, while wearing shades, on the Arsenio Hall Show in 1992. Pierre Trudeau making a pirouette at Buckingham Palace in 1977 (captured by the apparently ubiquitous Doug Ball). Dwight D. Eisenhower at Cypress Point in 1952, swinging a golf club like a pro—which he practically was. And, of course, Jean Chrétien applying the "Shawinigan handshake" almost two decades ago. The resulting image became a symbol that, many years later, many, many Canadians still recall with amusement—and quite a bit of admiration.

Chrétien settles in to tell the story of that unforgettable winter day, coyly relating some facts that haven't ever been made public before. "It was not something that was planned at all," he says. "I just had a human reaction."

It was February 15, 1996. Chrétien, some aides and his RCMP security detail were across the river from Ottawa in Hull, Quebec, to celebrate National Flag Day. It was sunny but bitterly cold. As Chrétien attempted to speak to the assembled crowd, some self-styled antipoverty activists yelled and tried to force their way to where the Liberal prime minister was standing. The speeches had to be cut short, and as Chrétien made his way to leave, two protestors—one the son of a millionaire bank executive, the other menacingly waving around a metal bullhorn near a group of children—stepped in his path. The whole scene felt like a riot in progress, Chrétien recalls.

Chrétien tells the tale, as only he can: "What happened is there was a bunch of young kids in front of me. I was signing autographs. The kids were there with Canadian flags, and they asked me to autograph their flags. So that's why the [RCMP] bodyguards were behind me at that particular moment, to permit me to have access to the kids.

"Some of these kids had been pushed around by these protesters, and it was reported later that some even had to go to the hospital. So, the event had been disrupted, and we had cut down the speeches. [After the speeches and autographs,] I was going back to my car, and these two guys rush towards me, shouting. One had a steel bullhorn. He was screaming things, it was not highly complimentary. So when the first one arrived, I grabbed him by the neck and flipped him over. But the press didn't ever report that, with the other guy—the one with the steel bullhorn. I pushed down the bullhorn, too, right after I flipped the first guy over. Then an RCMP guy flipped the [bullhorn-waving protestor] over." He pauses, and shrugs. "I had to grab the guy by the neck and flip him. So I did."

Even for those who don't follow Canadian politics very closely, it was a pretty memorable event: a prime minister had taken hold of a crazed protestor by the neck and tossed him aside like he was a rag doll. The resulting image, captured by cameraman Phil Nolan, would go on to win Photo of the Year. It showed Chrétien, impassive, with his hands around the neck of gnome-like protestor Bill Clennett, who looked distinctly (and understandably) unhappy. Nolan's snap would run in newspapers everywhere. Assorted Conservatives, predictably, expressed outrage. Former Conservative leader Joe Clark called on Chrétien to apologize, and in the House of Commons, right-wing MPs like Chuck Strahl and Deb Grey attacked Chrétien for what he had done. Chrétien-hating French media pundits, in particular, chastised him. Amnesty International condemned him, too.

One long-time Parliament Hill reporter, Susan Delacourt, seemed to suggest the Liberal leader had somehow planned the whole thing: "You see the pictures, his teeth are gritted, he seems angry," Delacourt said on one TV panel. "He looked like he was out to prove a point." Out to prove a point? Not quite, but Delacourt wasn't alone. Over at *Maclean's* magazine, two journalists gravely opined that "the incident could not have come at a worse time" for the government, and that it had "left lingering doubts" about the Liberal leader. Picking up on the refrain a few days later, one senior advisor to Chrétien leadership rival Paul Martin piously intoned on CTV's Canada AM: "I think the prime minister, just like every other Canadian, regrets what happened last week."

Except that, well, he didn't. Neither did "every other Canadian," either. At all.

"Yes, some people were nervous," Chrétien recalls. "Some were even saying I would have to resign, because they had listened to too much of the negative press. They said that I can't stay in the job of prime minister, [because] I'm a guy who can't control himself. So I said we will wait and see."

Never make a decision in the heat of the moment, Chrétien would always advise his staff. Wait until the dust settles a bit. And never, ever buy into the consensus of the conservative elites and media. That, he says, is a big mistake—because the conservative consensus is almost always wrong.

"You know my technique," he says to me. "I will not watch TV after these things, I let things calm down. My press people will eventually report to me. [The confrontation] happened on a Friday, so one of my press people called me on the Saturday morning."

The forty-four-year-old protestor named Bill Clennett, Chrétien was told, had broken his dental bridge in the scuffle. He wanted to be compensated for it. "Don't worry," the assistant jokingly said. "We will pay for it using the [government's] infrastructure program." The two chatted some more. Eventually, the aide revealed that a Toronto radio station had conducted a quick survey about the Flag Day fracas. Fearing the worst, Chrétien preferred to put it off: "I said to him, 'Don't give me the results until I'm back at work on Monday.'"

The aide replied: "Mr. Prime Minister, we won't tell you on Monday, in any event."

"Why?" Chrétien asked, genuinely puzzled.

"If we tell you," answered the press secretary, "we're afraid you will go out and grab another protestor by the neck. It's gotten an 85 percent approval rating!"

Canadians—then and now—were highly amused by what happened. They weren't mad at Chrétien at all. Men, in particular, loved it. There are, accordingly, two pretty important lessons to be learned from the Shawinigan handshake controversy—and they are lessons many smart conservatives have already learned.

First, Main Street is where the votes are—not Wall Street or Bay Street. Populism works: if the media and the elites are against you, it's often a good thing. In the early days after the Shawinigan handshake, it was impossible to find a media maven or a member of the chattering classes who didn't think Chrétien had done himself irreparable damage. When they eventually got around to soliciting the input of the public, however, they were astonished to learn that the throttling of Bill Clennett had made Jean Chrétien *more* popular, and not less so. The 99 percent are not, and perhaps never were, preoccupied with the views of the 1 percent.

Second, nothing communicates better than an image, particularly one that evokes an emotional response. Not speeches, not talking points, not a stage-managed quip in a press conference. Chrétien explains why. "I was a populist," he admits. "I still am. I wanted to be a man of the people; that's where I came from. A small town. I've always been an anti-establishment candidate, in a way. The intellectuals and the conservative business crowd always looked down on me for two reasons. For the fact that I didn't always speak English very well, and I had a very strong French accent. And because I wasn't what they considered an intellectual type of guy. So the intellectuals claimed I wasn't sophisticated enough, or not bright enough, or whatever it was.

"But it suited me pretty well, because it made me even me closer to the people. The *people* felt that Chrétien was a man of the people. I never wanted to lose that."

I describe my theory that HOAGs are more successful at politics because average people can visualize themselves having a beer with them at a family barbecue. There are exceptions, of course, like Pierre Trudeau, who wouldn't hesitate to quote classical philosophers in the House of Commons. But Trudeau, Chrétien observes, was *courageous*. He took risks. Voters saw that, and they admired it, even when they passionately objected to the deceased Liberal prime minister's policies. Trudeau wasn't a HOAG, but he unquestionably wasn't a wimp, either. He was tough, but he clearly loved ordinary people and the country itself, Chrétien says.

Asked to name an American president who was similar— one who was an intellectual, but who loved people and innately understood the power of symbols in political life, Chrétien doesn't hesitate. "My friend Bill," he says. "Bill Clinton. Oh, yes, he was good."

Clinton was the first U.S. president to have been a Rhodes Scholar. He attended Oxford University. He has a law degree from Yale. He had won numerous scholarships, and could— like Trudeau—quote the classics. But he was a populist, too, Chrétien recalls, and he had a very big heart.

It was known that the former U.S. president and the former Canadian prime minister were friendly, but less known was the full extent of their closeness. During their respective mandates (Clinton 1992–2000, Chrétien 1993–2003), the pair were in regular contact, sometimes daily, on everything from politics to sports (the pair famously played together golf dozens of times, and Clinton would joke that the fiercely competitive Chrétien would even let him win sometimes). At crucial points, the Democratic president was hugely helpful to the Liberal prime minister—most notably in the fall of 1995, when Canada very nearly broke up during Quebec's referendum on sovereignty. At a crucial moment, Clinton chimed in, expressing the preference of the United States for a united Canada. The statement was seen as hugely provocative by infuriated Quebec separatists, but it was a key factor in ensuring that Canada stayed together. Many Canadians, as a result, have a deep and abiding affection for Bill Clinton.

Early on, too, Chrétien developed a fine appreciation for Clinton's approach to political symbolism. "I watched him on TV, like everybody else," Chrétien says. "He was one of the best. I remember one time, he came to Ottawa and we had discussions. I said to Aline [Chrétien, the former prime minister's wife], 'Why don't you take Hillary skating on the Rideau Canal, she's from Chicago.' That produced a hell of a good picture, with Hillary Clinton skating on the canal with my wife." It was another symbol, an easy, folksy photo of the friendship between two nations. While the two women skated, surrounded by cheering crowds, the president and the prime minister waited at a popular (but, importantly, not upscale) Ottawa restaurant on the canal, called the Ritz. Chrétien continues: "So [Aline and Hillary] both arrived and there was a big crowd. And the two of them did what Bill and I were doing naturally. Aline would take one side of the hall, I would take another side of the hall, and Clinton would take both sides—Hillary, too. And they shook hands with people."

Later on, Chrétien watched the coverage the event got. "To me, it was a sign that they understood the need to be comfortable with real people. Clinton always looks comfortable—but some [conservative politicians] don't look comfortable at all.

Some do not express themselves easily. I think they are built like that. I think Harper is like that. I watch him, he is not comfortable when moving in a crowd.

"You have to speak the language that is the language of the people. Bill did that. I did that," Chrétien concludes. "Is that symbolic? I don't know. But it works."

☆ ☆ ☆

We were in an unremarkable Toronto boardroom in the fall of 2008, a few weeks before Michael Ignatieff would become interim leader (and then leader) of the Liberal Party of Canada. Gathered in the Yorkville boardroom were Ignatieff's effervescent wife, Zsuzsanna Zsohar, plus most of his senior advisors. I was the only one wearing a T-shirt (an Obama T-shirt, incidentally).

My friends Ian Davey and Liberal MP Paul Zed, two of Ignatieff's closest advsors, had asked me to attend to provide Iggy with some candid advice. "How candid," I asked? "Let 'er rip," they said. So I did, and I started with what I consider to be one of the key considerations in picking a president, prime minister or future spouse: *authenticity.* Ignatieff looked inauthentic, I related, as the assembled folks audibly inhaled. His physicality and his appearance, in particular, made him look a bit like a phony. "You look like John Kerry," I said, to stunned silence. "You know, the head, a bit too skinny. Big eyebrows. Looks too patrician and egg-headish."

It wasn't that Ignatieff wasn't highly articulate and engaging in either official language, I suggested. He was. And the former Harvard professor was perhaps the most learned Canadian political leader since Trudeau. But there was an artifice to it all. In scrums, in press conferences, in speeches, he seemed affected, like he was acting. I heard that a lot—and from people who were Grits, too.

After he won the Liberal Party leadership, I'd watch Ignatieff as he spoke, my insides churning. It wasn't that he'd make lots of verbal flubs or say things that were inappropriate. Instead, he simply seemed programmed. He'd almost never make mistakes; he looked and sounded too slick. "Just once," I told Davey and Zed, "I would love to see him lose his temper with a journalist, and tell them to go fuck themselves. Just once. It'd be the best thing that ever happened to him."

Davey and Zed agreed. The most celebrated example of the kind of thing we were discussing took place in January 1988, when CBS News anchor Dan Rather interviewed Vice President George Bush Sr. The interview was supposed to be a presidential candidate profile of the type that CBS had been broadcasting for weeks. In reality, Rather and his producers intended to go after Bush aggressively about his role in the Iran-Contra Affair. Even Bush's critics later agreed that it was a nine-minute on-air ambush. But the way in which Bush handled Rather helped win him the presidency. Here's a snippet from the Rather-Bush clash:

RATHER:	I don't want to be argumentative, Mr. Vice President.
BUSH:	You *do*, Dan.
RATHER:	No . . . no, sir, I don't.
BUSH:	This is not a great night, because I want to talk about why I want to be president, why those 41 percent of the people are supporting me. And I don't think it's fair . . .
RATHER:	And Mr. Vice President, if these questions are . . .
BUSH:	. . . to judge my whole career by a rehash on Iran. How would you like it if I judged

	your career by those seven minutes when you walked off the set in New York?
RATHER:	Well, Mister . . .
BUSH:	. . . Would *you* like that?
RATHER:	Mr. Vice President . . .
BUSH:	I have respect for you, but I don't have respect for what you're doing here tonight.
RATHER:	Mr. Vice President, I think you'll agree that your qualification for president and what kind of leadership you'd bring to the country, what kind of government you'd have, what kind of people you have around you . . .
BUSH:	Exactly.
RATHER:	. . . is much more important that what you just referred to. I'd be happy to . . .
BUSH:	Well, I want to be judged on the whole record, and you're not giving me an opportunity.

The Bush-Rather interview-cum-ambush became so pivotal, so much part of U.S. political history, that C-SPAN would sell recordings of the confrontation on its website. Bush himself came to regard it as the moment his political fortunes turned around. Other journalists—including some who were traditional antagonists of Bush, or even CBS colleagues of Rather—were meanwhile highly unimpressed by the behaviour of the star reporter. Sam Donaldson, no pussycat in interviews, said, "Rather went too far." Mike Wallace, a CBS leading light in his own right, said, "The style was wrong. Dan lost his cool."

In their encounter, Bush is clearly frustrated and even angry. He stumbles over words, he doesn't complete sentences. But it is *because* of that, not despite it, that the Republican vice president seems most truthful. Given the nature of Rather's interview, it is apparent to everyone watching at home that Bush has not practised or received any special media training to deal with Rather. He stammers, he loses his patience, he is anything but smooth—and, therefore, he comes across as authentic. No longer would he be regarded as an East Coast Ivy League wimp. The confrontation with Rather catapulted Bush ahead in the polls and helped to win him the presidency.

Why? Because the most elusive commodity in leadership politics—the Holy Grail of any campaign for a candidate or a cause—can be reduced to a single word. *Connection*. Does the leader connect with the people they hope to lead? Do average folks feel the aspiring leader understands the day-to-day reality of their lives? What the connection is, of course, is difficult to define. Like values, you often cannot put it into words, but you are keenly aware when it's present and you know when it isn't. If there is a connection between the leader and the led, it is often a winning campaign.

In any political cause I've assisted, I've observed that the politicians who come from humble beginnings—the ones who have been on public transit, who have worried about putting bread on the table, who have lain awake at night wondering where the next rent or mortgage payment will come from—are always the most successful. They are the ones who are seen as authentic.

Allan Gregg, a brilliant Canadian fellow who used to be a conservative pollster, recently gave a speech about all of this. It's worth quoting. "Whatever else our leaders' shortcomings, this strikes me as their most systematic failure—they have not picked up on the electorate's craving for *authenticity* nor adjusted their behaviour to conform to this new reality," said Gregg. "For most of my adult life, I have worked with political and business leaders and have never ceased to be amazed at how different they can be in private compared to their public personae. Time and time again, I have witnessed otherwise funny, thoughtful, caring men and women walk from the wings of the auditorium to the podium, only to be transformed into nothing less than a big, blustering bullshitter—in effect, offering up a 'performance' and a caricature they think they should be playing.

"Typically, these performances range from pillorying opponents with hyperventilated allegations of failings; feigned outrage at what others would consider modest grievances; taking exaggerated credit for accomplishments that are better shared; and avoiding any direct and honest engagement of difficult subject matter that has the potential to cause media controversy." Gregg recalled a poll he'd done with his firm, Harris/Decima. "Asked how often a typical politician would tell the absolute truth when making make public statements, four out of ten claimed less than 50 percent of the time. One percent believed politicians are absolutely truthful all the time! Think about this!"

It's worth thinking about. Bill Clinton, Jean Chrétien, Ronald Reagan: all of these politicians were successful because, most days, voters felt they weren't phonies. They made missteps, they made mistakes—for instance, Chrétien's verbal flubs became the stuff of legend (my favourite: "A proof is a proof. What kind of a proof? It's a proof. A proof is a proof. And when you have a good proof, it's because it's proven.") But these political leaders were successful because voters innately sensed that they understood the reality of their daily life—that, at one time, these men had "been there." While these leaders often end up being very well-to-do at the back end of their lives, voters trust them because, at the front end, they had experienced the pitiless, terrifying reality that is a regular person's life. They've led what real people consider to be an authentic existence. And unlike the bullshitters Gregg describes, they remained true to their roots, too.

Political parties spend untold millions to connect their leaders with the everyday reality of people's lives. But, as in love, you can't *buy* that kind of relationship. You can claw your way to top of the political heap—and the likes of Mitt Romney and Stephen Harper have certainly both done that—to snatch the brass ring. But that doesn't mean regular folks think you in any way deserve it. As Edelman's and Allan Gregg's research shows, and as the genesis of the Tea Party and Occupy movements demonstrates, most citizens don't believe most of the things politicians have to say, these days. That, more than anything else, is why certain politicians— despite all of their hard work, despite the Herculean efforts of supporters labouring in the backrooms—still have not *connected* with Joe and Jane Frontporch. Conservatives in Canada, and Republicans in the U.S., have laboured mightily to craft populist personas for Stephen Harper and Mitt Romney. They have expended a few fortunes to convince you that hockey rinks and Tim Hortons franchises (in Canada) and log cabins and factory floors (in the U.S.) are the summit of all populist wisdom, and that Harper and Romney are most at home in such places.

But that, of course, is bullshit. In New Hampshire, during the primaries, Romney actually said that he, too, had feared getting a "pink slip" more than once—but the only private sector pink slip Romney's ever handled are the ones he's delivered, not received. (Romney was most authentic, para- doxically, when he confessed on CNN that he doesn't care about the "very poor." *That* was authentic. It just wasn't the kind of authentic Romney needed.) Up north, meanwhile, if anyone can produce·a single undoctored photograph of Stephen Harper lined up for a double-double at a Tim

Hortons franchise prior to the 2004 election campaign, I'll happily post it everywhere on the Internet and issue the requisite *mea culpa*. But they can't. The Tim Hortons thing and the pink slip thing—just like every other political affectation that preceded them—are the invention of boys in the backroom. They're false. *Ipso facto*, conservatives like Romney and Harper don't connect.

At this point, naturally, a partisan conservative will shriek that Harper and Romney *do* connect—they *are* authentic. How else to explain Romney's hard-fought victory in Tampa in August 2012, when he finally seized the Republican presidential nomination? How else to explain Harper's electoral triumph in May 2011, when he finally captured his much-lusted-after parliamentary majority? The answer is simple enough: Romney and Harper owe their respective victories to their opponents, who came across looking and sounding even less authentic than they did. When facing off against the likes of Newt Gingrich or Michael Ignatieff, it isn't hard to look more authentic.

But that doesn't make you authentic, does it? Nope, it doesn't.

☆ ☆ ☆

Keep it simple; show it, don't say it.

If you are trying to sound authentic in what you want to communicate, that's what you need to do. But too often, progressives don't. For example, some Democratic Party strategists participated in a *Christian Science Monitor* panel a few years back. James Carville, the Ragin' Cajun, was one of them. As is his wont, Carville made one pithy observation that all progressives should remember: "[We] need a narrative. It's tough to beat a narrative with a litany. And that happens to us again and again and again."

Progressives—be they Democrats in the U.S., or Liberals and New Democrats in Canada—too often make things overly complicated. Instead of promoting just a few memorable campaign planks, as the likes of Ronald Reagan or Stephen Harper have done, progressives and liberals always come up with litanies of stuff. That is, mind-numbing laundry lists of policies and prescriptions. Among other things, it invites suspicion. When you're not being economical with your words, it suggests to your audience that you are being economical with the truth. Or, as Chuck Berry once observed: "If you can't say it in two minutes, it can't be said."

If you have too many policy priorities, you don't have any. So, in the historic 2006 federal election campaign, Harper had just five: make government more open, cut the sales tax, reduce health-care waiting times, give parents cash for child care and impose tougher sentences for gun crime. Nothing more. His Liberal rival, Paul Martin, had his platform leaked before its official release, and it contained nearly two hundred priorities. The Liberal document was bursting at the seams with weasel words like "work with," "work closely with," "work to develop," "work towards," "work to increase," as well as lots of fuzzy promises about "reviews" and "dialogues" to consider, study, encourage and explore. Blah, blah, blah.

The necessity of simplicity, to a smart guy named David Shenk, is beyond dispute. If your messages—if your policies—are too numerous or too complicated, then you have lost the war before it even begins. Shenk wrote a wonderful book about a related subject some years ago, called *Data Smog*.

"Data smog" is a pithy phrase that accurately describes what life has become for too many of us: we are bombarded by hundreds of thousands of words and images every single day. We are smothered by veritable mountains of useless information—on the Internet (and on its bastard children,

Facebook, Twitter, Tumblr and the like), on TV, in emails, on the sides of buildings—all the time. Information, to Shenk and Postman, does not equal knowledge. It is, as Shenk writes, mostly worthless garbage: "One of the most vivid consequences of the information glut is a culture awash in histrionics. As the competition heats up, we do what we have to do to make our voices heard. We TALK LOUDER. Wear more colour. Show more cleavage. Say shocking things."

The solution, it should be said, is not to dumb everything down to the lowest common denominator. Instead, we need communications that are simple, visual and true. We need the right information, not simply more of it. As Shenk notes: "We are bathing in information, and while this is often a very good thing, there is the danger of drowning in it." Information, to cite another wonderful Shenk metaphor, was once doled out like caviar; now, there is so much of it, it is as familiar as potatoes. Some communicators, though, always know how to break through the data smog, however thick it may be.

Ronald Reagan was one of them. Reagan was called The Great Communicator for good reason. More than anything else, he knew that complexity was fatal to political success. In his 1988 farewell address, he said, "I won a nickname, 'The Great Communicator.' But I never thought it was my style or the words I used that made a difference: It was the *content*. I wasn't a great communicator, but I communicated great things."

Reagan was being typically self-effacing, which is another hallmark of the great political communicators. Modesty, simplicity, authenticity, clarity: these are the characteristics of the very best political communicators. Reagan often called it "plain talk."

Plain talk isn't something we Liberals and Democrats should disdain. Plain talk isn't the preferred lingo of the simple-minded. It is, instead, the approach of those who are respectful of voters. As I say in my book *The War Room*, communicating in an uncomplicated way, as Reagan so often did, isn't condescending. It doesn't suggest that you think your audience is slow or poorly educated. On the contrary, fellow progressives: taking pains to ensure that your message reaches the greatest number of eyes and ears—doing all that you can to ensure that you are understood—isn't merely considerate. It is, in point of fact, the very essence of democracy.

It's democratic because it acknowledges your obligation to win the support of the greatest number, and not just a select few. It's democratic because it acknowledges that (again) victory is always found on *Main* Street, not *Wall* Street. If voters and consumers have a problem arising out of the new media revolution, it's not that they are unintelligent. It's that they lack the information they feel they need to make an intelligent choice.

That's why the simplest and most visual narrative is so important. In snowy February 2012, Stephen Harper capped a five-day trade mission to China by hugging a giant panda bear being loaned to Canadian zoos. Later on, he met with Chinese Communist boss Bo Xilai. As Harper told an impassive Bo: "More people in Canada will notice the pandas than anything else."

It worked, too. People noticed it, and they remembered it—certainly more than anything else Harper did on his Chinese trade mission.

Words tell, pictures sell.

☆ ☆ ☆

Whenever they are desperately casting about for an authentic, connected, winning message, political types—be they conservative or liberal—will often start blathering about the need to have a better "brand." The American Marketing

Association, which knows a thing or two about brands, defines them as a "name, term, design, symbol, or any other feature that identifies one seller's good or service as distinct from those of other sellers."

But if that's so, then *people* can't be branded. To be sure, politicians and political campaigns are often likened to soap, something to be hawked to political consumers. But the last well-known person to try to brand themselves with a symbol was the musician Prince, who in 1993 came up with an unpronounceable hieroglyphic. Everyone thought he was being nutty, and his record sales started to slump. For a while, he even became known as "the artist formerly known as Prince." Eventually, in 2000, he acknowledged defeat and went back to being what he was before, which was plain old Prince. Branding a person, then, isn't the best strategy. It doesn't really work. With companies, of course, it can work.

One company that is synonymous with highly effective branding is called Apple. You may have heard of it. With its iPhones, iPods, iPads and iTunes, it's one of the most successful companies on the planet, and it makes more money than God. It has an instantly recognizable logo and company name, to be sure. But it is Apple's products, its substance—not some Madison Avenue agency's touchy-feely ad campaign or clever tagline—that have built its great reputation.

Another example: Classic Coke. Back in 1985, Coca-Cola decided to change the taste of the beverage that is sold more than a billion times daily around the world. It also decided to call the resulting beverage New Coke, with a different logo. That, as things turned out, was a mistake of gargantuan proportions. An immense consumer backlash ensued, but not about the name that was on the can. Cola drinkers didn't like what was *in* the can. The company hurriedly reverted to the old formula.

Voters, too, are much more preoccupied with what politicians *do* than with what they *look like*. In 1993, the governing Canadian Conservative Party thought otherwise: they mocked Jean Chrétien's facial paralysis in TV ads and were accordingly reduced to near-extinction, partly for their "face ad." Internal polling we federal Liberals had done showed that some people were, indeed, preoccupied with how Chrétien looked and sounded. But far more Canadians considered Chrétien's plans and priorities to be of greater consequence.

What you say, and what you do, therefore, is what matters most. Not branding a person, in the way that a consumer product is branded. There are some lessons, though, that we can learn from the branding experts. For instance, it is indeed possible to associate one political choice with an attribute that another political choice lacks. And when communications-savvy conservatives face off against unlucky liberals, it is often the "elite" brand versus the "anti-elite" brand. As it was in the Canadian federal election of 2006.

In that year, as in every election year, the font of all wisdom was the local hockey rink—so sayeth Sarah Palin and Stephen Harper. (Or, depending on where you live, the football field, the soccer pitch or the baseball diamond.) Parents huddled on cold benches, clutching cups of coffee, swapping stories about their kids, shaking their heads about those dummies in Ottawa or Washington. Being hearty, plain-talking North Americans.

Back in November 2005, while watching my daughter play at a hockey rink in the Leaside neighbourhood of Toronto—the same rink allegedly haunted by Stephen Harper as a kid, coincidentally—I posted something to my website suggesting that the election was going to be about hockey moms and dads versus the elites. With Harper championing the former, and a Westmount millionaire named Paul Martin personifying the latter. Was I right? Well, I can now reveal that—immediately after I posted that observation—I received emails from two senior Conservatives in the party's war room. They swore me to secrecy, and then told me that this was exactly what they hoped to do.

And it's exactly what they did. With every photo op (particularly the one showing the Tory leader taking his kids to an Ottawa hockey rink), with every positive statement (Stephen Harper stressing his middle-class roots), with every critical statement (the continual references to Martin's millions and his decision to fly his tanker ships under foreign flags), the Tory campaign was all about the revenge of hockey moms and dads. It was a clever and highly subtle branding campaign: it likened political choices to simple, and simplistic, everyday consumer choices.

It wasn't about Left versus Right. It wasn't about urban versus rural. It wasn't about East versus West. It was about Tim Hortons versus Starbucks: regular folks versus the elites. The classic conservative frame. Stephen Harper won because he told the story regular folks want to hear. We federal Liberals had lost touch—with Canadians, with each other—and we deserved to lose. (To continue the metaphor, we deserved some time in the penalty box, and, unfortunately, we're still in it.)

Harper's whole campaign was about what political types call "retail"—street-level, pocketbook stuff, aimed at average people. In his case, however, it was almost quite literally retail—one type of coffee over another. His advertising campaign was deliberately market-driven, too: in one much-seen spot, shot inside a Tim Hortons–like coffee shop, ordinary folk could be seen shaking their heads about Liberal perfidy. It intentionally wasn't fancy or complicated, and it did the trick. The Tory leader proudly left the glossy, rich-looking Madison Avenue bafflegab to the Liberals. He went for the authentic, homespun hockey rink stuff. It worked. It usually does.

The photo of Harper taking his kids to a rink in the family van was the beginning of the end for Martin. Canadian parents identified with that image and, at the same time, they started to suspect that Paul Martin had never struggled to balance mortgage payments or pay a utility bill. Harper's campaign wasn't consumed by complaints about Liberal spending scandals or their wacky environmental plans. The Conservatives, instead, devoted themselves to making the case that their leader lived the life of a typical person—as they would again in 2008 and 2011. And they made the case that his Liberal opponents—Paul Martin, Stéphane Dion and Michael Ignatieff—didn't.

"Our campaigns," said one of my anonymous Conservative correspondents, "have been about making voters feel that Harper isn't a radical, that he doesn't have a hidden agenda. That he is trustworthy. Most of all, that he is *authentic*, when he says he is just an average Canadian.

"That, more than anything else, is what they want."

☆ ☆ ☆

In this election year, in any election year, *the* political question is this: Who is the most authentic? Who's the real deal?

Who has a simple, clear and winning style, and is best able to express all of that visually? This year, particularly, the question is: Does Barack Obama still have it? Can he win, with conservatives everywhere looking better funded and better organized? Mike McCurry ponders that last one carefully. He's a lifelong Democrat, and he supports the president without reservation. But . . .

"Essentially, I don't think it's [Obama's] vocabulary or the speech," he says, choosing his words with care, "so much as it's action and result. Part of the problem that [Democrats] have had with Obama is that he has been very good at articulating a case, but not so good at delivering any fundamental results. So I think people still have to be convinced." The fact that Mitt Romney, Newt Gingrich and Rick Santorum spent more of 2012 attacking each other than the president hasn't helped Democratic fortunes as much as one would think, or hope. Sure, Romney said that he doesn't much care about the "very poor" in America. Sure, Santorum said that because female soldiers have certain "types of emotions," they shouldn't be assigned combat roles. Sure, Newt Gingrich said that laws prohibiting child labour are "truly stupid." But to Bill Clinton's brilliant former press secretary, Democrats shouldn't get too cocky. The problem for the president, McCurry suggests, is that the very thing that won him the White House—his authenticity—is now regularly, and unfairly, called into question. "[Democrats] see the same stagnation and gridlock, and it's very, very frustrating," admits McCurry. "It kind of leads the temptation for some of them to say: 'Screw it, why should I get involved?' So I think we Democrats need to get better at delivering tangible results."

When it's suggested to McCurry that Obama *has* delivered some positive results—ending the wars in Iraq and Afghanistan, delivering health care to thirty million Americans who didn't have it before, leading the U.S. through a brutal recession and on to modest economic growth—he doesn't disagree. "Obama put enormous political capital behind some very large propositions," McCurry says. "But a lot of it got marginalized. It really hasn't produced any real results for a lot of people."

The solution, he says, may lie in doing less, not more. Voters have become profoundly wary, and weary, of progressive politicians who come down from the mount, waving around the latest political commandments and promising monumental change. They've seen that movie too many times before, and they recall that it usually ends badly. After frittering away the first two years of his first mandate on trivialities, Clinton learned this lesson well. To be regarded as effective, McCurry says, a political leader needs to do those things that are (a) doable

and (b) measurable. That is, capable of being seen and evaluated by the people whom politicians serve.

"Clinton, in my day, took a lot of heat for what we'll call
the small things," recalls McCurry. "You know, the little
micromeasures. Like, we're going to have a federal program
where we give tax breaks to schools that have school uni-
forms. Some people said that was ridiculous. And it wasn't the
biggest thing in the world, true, but it worked. And that's the
sort of thing [Obama] needs."

In high-stakes politics, in any communications battle, it's
not enough to wait for your opponents to screw up. You need
to show them results, however modest. "A lot of the American
public has checked out on Obama," McCurry says . "He's got
a lot of things going against him right now." For instance,
in the week I conducted this interview, the papers were full
of the sorts of stories that can make Democratic blood run
cold. On a three-day bus tour through Virginia and North
Carolina—two states he must win to be competitive in the
presidential election—Obama encountered little of the mania
that attended his every move in 2008. At one rural North
Carolina barbecue joint, in fact, some diners took the opportunity to give the president a finger-wagging talking-to.
Incredibly, others didn't even bother to stand up to greet him
or shake his hand. The president of the United States!

"Yeah," McCurry nods his head at the mention of the
unhappy three-day tour. "He's just not a tactile politician.
Clinton, he was. If someone was upset, he'd put his arms
around them and give them a big hug. Obama is a good dad.
He's got a lovely wife. But he has to do a better job at connecting with people. He just isn't *connecting*."

In the business of politics, failing to connect with voters
isn't necessarily always fatal (Stephen Harper)—but it usually
is (Michael Ignatieff, Mitt Romney). When times are tough,

particularly, citizens want to feel that their leaders understand what they're going through. They want someone to share their pain. Obama, some feel, doesn't.

McCurry reflects. Obama is capable of delivering speeches with power, grace and credibility. The president is calm when under fire, perhaps more so than any in recent memory. He radiates intelligence and integrity. But, acknowledges the former Clinton confidant, none of that matters so much in 2011. Voters want *results*. Obama's health-care reform was diluted by the for-profit health conglomerates until it was virtually meaningless. And the Bush-era wars took far too long to come to an end.

Worst of all, says McCurry, Obama's White House let the president be defined by the Tea Party–dominated Republicans in Congress. "He let the other side paint him as a big-government liberal. When he isn't."

Beset by economic woes, battered by a perception that he hasn't delivered the "hope" he promised, what is Barack Obama to do? "A presidential candidate comes into your living room every night via the TV. There has to be an emotional bond between the candidate and the voter. It's crucial that you establish that rapport."

It's an open question, therefore, whether Barack Obama— the candidate who changed history, the candidate who convinced Americans that "Yes, we can"—can reestablish that rapport, and whether he can recapture what he has seemingly lost. As of now, there is no time left to start delivering results and to reconnect with millions of Americans—many of whom feel disappointed by unfulfilled promise.

One of Obama's confidants, Democratic Party spokesman Brad Woodhouse, insists that Obama can indeed deliver what is needed. Obama, he says, is one of the most trustworthy politicians ever to set foot in the White House. And it's a mistake to read too much into ill-starred turns like the one through Virginia and North Carolina. Says Woodhouse, ever the Democratic soldier, "I'm from North Carolina, and I was thrilled he was in the state. I think it's good, first of all, for the president to do this type of thing. It's energizing for him. And it gets him outside of the bubble here in Washington. I think it has worked, and you'll see more of it from him, soon enough."

Woodhouse rejects the notion that Obama is a little less authentic these days. Being president in America's present circumstances, he says, is extremely difficult—and the GOP has been determined to make it even more difficult. "Look, the Republicans are hell-bent on not letting the president win any victories between now and the election," Woodhouse says. "But they're not going to prove anything. They're not going to win anything. As he moves around the country, the polling has shown that his jobs plan is becoming increasingly popular.

"We can't let this election simply become a referendum on the president because then, yes, that would be a very tough election. What we have to do is convince people that there really are two visions to choose from. It's a choice not just between two candidates. It's a choice between two different sets of *values*. One of the reasons the president's personal popularity has been resilient over the course of his term is this: people share his values. The polls show that, too. And it can't just be that we're better on Social Security or that we're better on Medicare. I mean, what does any of that mean? And he's pretty damn good at communicating, and describing to people what that all means. He's good at *showing* it."

Some distance away from Washington, Jean Chrétien—who knows a thing or two about running countries, and about getting re-elected—listens to a recitation of Barack Obama's visit to the North Carolina BBQ and how some people wouldn't shake his hand. "Yes, yes," he says, but he doesn't agree that Obama lacks the common touch, the ability to connect with people. "For me, I enjoy shaking hands with people, I still enjoy it. But I'm not surprised by what happened to [Obama]. When I'm on the street, people come to me. But if people are in a restaurant, they won't always get up. So the press was wrong, I think, to go after Obama." He pauses, then acknowledges: "I'm trying to defend Obama."

Chrétien thinks for a moment, then continues: "Because politics is people, you see. You have to convince the people that you are better than the other guy to serve them. You have to keep in mind that you need them—and that you will serve them. They are not there to serve *you*. You are there to serve them." All the best communicators know how to use a symbol to make a point, Chrétien says. They know how to speak the language of the people. They know the crucial importance of authenticity—of being themselves. Obama needs to remember this. They know that, when facing adversity, saying nothing isn't much of a solution. The solution, Chrétien says, lies with remembering that, at the end of the day, there are a hell of a lot more votes on Main Street than Bay Street.

"Obama's good. He's got it," Chrétien says, finally. "I know what he's trying to do. So do the people."

CONCLUSION

HOW TO FIGHT THE RIGHT
(AND KICK ASS)

Conservatives, previously despondent, are now a species triumphant.
With deviousness and cunning, they have taken hostage language, as
well as values, to tower above the political landscape. They are utterly
without scruples, but neither are they dim.
Herewith, in the final lesson, how clever conservatives have seized
control of the media to propagate their views and values—and how
progressives and liberals, fighting for all that is good and pure, shall
take it back and, verily, fight the Right!

———

Conservatives, whether we progressives like it or not, now
dominate politics in Canada, the United States and Europe. And they haven't done so by being dummies. They've
done it by being *smart*.

As Ragin' Cajun James Carville and plenty of others have
cautioned, our side of the political continuum too often dismisses conservatives as red-necked, mouth-breathing knuckle-
draggers. (I've been guilty of it myself, and more than once, too.)
But that's been a big strategic error, for a couple of reasons.

One, it plays into the conservative strategy that sees progressives depicted as snobby, latte-sipping elitists who profess kinship with ordinary folks—but who wouldn't want to actually live next door to them. Moreover, it validates the conservative narrative that they, and not pointy-headed liberals, are the real populists. That is, that they are the ones who are closest to the hopes, aspirations and values of average citizens. Not liberals, who are out of touch and high and mighty—and who mock the everyday concerns of Joe and Jane Frontporch. Mackubin Thomas Owens, a conservative commentator, zeroes in on this tendency, noting that liberals "yammer on ceaselessly about 'tolerance' and 'diversity' [but] don't seem inclined to extend those concepts to many of their fellow citizens, whom they portray as religious bigots, racist rednecks and generally stupid people." (Owens then goes on to describe critics of the Right as "ungodly," but that doesn't obscure his broader point. He's right, at least, on that.)

Mocking our conservative adversaries as "religious bigots, racist rednecks and generally stupid people" is a mistake for another reason: it seriously underestimates our principal adversary. We should never underestimate the power and effectiveness of the conservative propaganda machine.

Take a look at Sun News and my good conservative friend Kory Teneycke, for example.

☆ ☆ ☆

In 2006, I was hired to promote the use of ethanol in gasoline. Among other things, my clients—many of them grain farmers whose corn was used to make ethanol—wanted to get government to legislate that gas should be partly made up of their product. Using ethanol as a fuel additive is good for the environment, they told me, because it reduces tailpipe emissions like carbon monoxide. That's why countries like the United States and Canada now use it.

But back then, people were only just beginning to understand the benefits of ethanol in gasoline. So a renewable fuels association hired me to help them out, and one of its members was a gangly, big-eyed fellow named Kory Teneycke.

Teneycke hailed from a grain farm in rural Saskatchewan, and he knew a lot about agriculture. In his teens, he got the political bug toiling on provincial conservative campaigns, where he learned a thing or two about losing—as well as winning. He was widely seen as pretty sharp, and later on, he headed east to render advice to Ontario Conservative leader Mike Harris and federal Reform Party leader Preston Manning.

When we finally met, Teneycke didn't seem all that conservative. Despite his pedigree, I—the arch-liberal attack dog—found that he was a very likeable guy. When no one else was around, he would express to me views that were categorically liberalish. And it couldn't be denied, I told skeptical progressive pals, that aggressively promoting ethanol—and thereby making the planet less polluted—wasn't an activity you would associate with a stereotypical conservative.

Teneycke still isn't stereotypical. He's easygoing, he's sensible, and he has an intimidating intellect. We enjoyed working together—and we ended up winning, too. Ethanol became a required additive to gasoline in Ontario, despite the efforts of petroleum industry lobbyists to stop it.

Eventually, Teneycke headed up to the big leagues in Ottawa, where he became Prime Minister Harper's research director, and then in 2008, his director of communications. During his tenure, Teneycke was a senior member of the Conservative campaign team, and among other things, he helped to drive the Liberal Party of Canada to its worst showing in history. After leaving Harper's office, he appeared on CBC television as a Conservative spinner, where he tormented NDP and Liberal mouthpieces (me included). He seemed restless, however. A lot of us wondered where he'd end up next.

In June 2010, we found out. With the backing of conglomerate Quebecor, Teneycke had developed a plan to create a conservative television network for Canada. While Quebecor stressed that the new network wouldn't simply be what some were calling "Fox News North," its mainstream media competitors were unconvinced. Speaking on a CTV political talk show in Ottawa after announcing the creation of the network, Teneycke dismissed the claim. "We're calling it Sun News, the Sun TV News channel. I think too often you don't see a raw debate. You don't see the kind of debate that you would see in real life, whether it's around a kitchen table at an extended family gathering, around a coffee shop. You're seeing a lot of news where the commentary around it . . . simply has the edges filed off. I think Canadians want to see debate that's sharp, that's intelligent, that's controversial, and I think there's more space for that . . . we see an opportunity." He continued: "The moniker of Fox News is something that our competitors try to paste us with as a label. This is going to be a controversially Canadian channel. It's Canadian owned, the content will be Canadian, so I think trying to pigeonhole us in that way, they want to smear the network before it gets out."

The Fox News North moniker, however, stuck. And when Sun News competitors unearthed U.S. Justice Department filings showing that Teneycke and Harper had met quietly, in Manhattan in March 2009, with Fox News owner Rupert Murdoch and its president, Roger Ailes, some felt they had stumbled across evidence of a full-blown conservative conspiracy. It's *Fox News North*!

"The media already blast Canadians with a steady chorus of right-wing ideas," *Toronto Star* columnist Linda McQuaig warned. "A Fox-style network here—if Harper gets his way—would turn that into a deafening cacophony." Her *Star* colleague, Heather Mallick, called the yet-to-broadcast network the "illegitimate child" of Fox News. The Fox network, she wrote in one wonderfully vivid column, "celebrates hate and ignorance" and is "a poison tree" and "a news cartoon." Like Fox News, Sun News may well "hate women and blacks, Muslims, Mexicans," declared Mallick, who was once (she freely confessed) employed by Quebecor herself. Sun News might just be, like Fox, "a malign force bubbling with rage." There may not be a corporate connection between Fox News and Sun News, conceded Mallick—but there was a "visceral connection." She concluded the column by approvingly quoting a British dramatist who had expressed a desire to assassinate Rupert Murdoch.

Ouch! There was a lot more of that sort of commentary in the days following Teneycke's announcement (although not too many outright calls for his, or Murdoch's, assassination). Kory Teneycke was undeterred. He got to work on doing what no one had done in Canada in decades—building a TV network out of nothing. So, the day before announcing the creation of the Sun News Network in Ottawa, Teneycke, an inveterate user of Facebook, sent me a brief message. "Looking for commentators," he wrote, never being one for blandishments. "Curious if you would be interested in writing for the Sun."

When I read Teneycke's note, I didn't exactly fall off my chair. As a Liberal who grew up in Alberta, I wasn't unused to being surrounded by (and even occasionally liking) card-carrying conservatives. Later on—while writing for the union-bashing *Calgary Herald*, as well as the Liberal-hating *Ottawa Citizen* and *National Post*—I was typically one of the few lefty voices to be found in the papers. When I was recruited to write freelance opinion pieces for the *Citizen* and the *Post,* I had been promised that I was free to express my opinions. But that was a lie.

After a year or so writing for the *Citizen*, one of the paper's editors, Scott Anderson, said they were discontinuing my column because it was "too liberal." And later, at the *Post*, I received one too many emails like this one in December 2006 from their self-professed "free speech" editorial advocate, Jonathan Kay: "Warren—we can't run your column. We're not in the business of praising the likes of [*Star* columnist] Rick Salutin, [CBC radio host Anna Maria] Tremonti, etc. I checked with [*Post* editor-in-chief Doug Kelly] and it's a no-go." Shortly afterwards, I quit writing for the *Post,* after being forbidden from filing some positive words about human rights.

What I was uneasy about at the Sun, I told Teneycke, wasn't being surrounded by conservatives. As an Alberta Liberal, and as someone who had written for Canada's overwhelmingly conservative news media, I was pretty used to that. What I was concerned about was being prevented from saying and writing what I really believed, as had been the case at the free speechies the *Ottawa Citizen* and *National Post*. Teneycke simply told me I would be encouraged to write about whatever I wanted, however I wanted to do it, twice a week.

He was true to his word. With the exception of one appearance in December 2011—when I got into a heated on-air battle with Sun News TV host Brian Lilley about sex education (he's against it, I'm for it), and when Lilley briefly ordered that my microphone be cut off—nobody at Sun News has ever tried to prevent me from saying what I think. They ask me on-air all the time, and they've even brought me in to host the odd show. They're mostly conservatives, and they hardly ever agree with anything I have to say, but they don't ever try to stop me from saying it.

Which suggests that, as advertised, Sun News honestly favours what Kory Teneycke once called "raw debate." And, just perhaps, that conservatives like Teneycke know that—when it comes to the news media—the dominant voice is now unapologetically conservative, and that they need not worry so much anymore about liberal loudmouths like me.

☆ ☆ ☆

Kory Teneycke, one of the smartest conservatives you'll ever meet, muses.

I've just asked him where the idea for Sun News came from. He says plainly, "It came from me. It was certainly not an original idea, but it came from me in the sense that I put together the initial proposal and found a company to invest in it. [It was] something I have had an interest in for a number of years. Canada has had many strong conservative voices on radio, in print and more recently on the Internet. I shared the frustration of many conservatives that we seemed to be locked out of television. I have always thought there was a market for a conservative television voice in Canada. Just look at the popularity of conservative talk radio hosts—why not bring that form of populist conservatism to television? It certainly worked for Fox."

Was it easy, I ask, or did things go wrong along the way? He laughs. "I could fill a book on that one. The first obstacle was finding a partner that saw the same market opportunity that I did and was willing to make a huge investment to make it happen. I didn't start with Quebecor. I actually approached [Western Canadian broadcasting firm] Shaw first. They were polite, but it didn't progress to a second meeting."

So he kept trying. The communications director to former Conservative prime minister Brian Mulroney, Luc Lavoie, offered a key introduction. "I was introduced to Pierre Karl Péladeau by Lavoie. I did not know Luc well at the time, but the role he played in getting the network launched was critical and equal to mine. Without getting into all the details, Péladeau was interested enough to hire me to put together a business plan. That process took the better part of a year. [Péladeau's] company is infused with an entrepreneurial spirit [that is] rare in such a large enterprise. By that I mean a willingness to take risks, like launching Sun News, [which is a risk] most widely held companies would never take . . ."

Something that made the entire undertaking even riskier was Avaaz. A U.S.-based group of activists, claiming some thirteen million members worldwide, Avaaz was founded in 2007 by Res Publica and MoveOn.org, and had Sun News in its sights months before the network had even broadcast a minute of programming. In the summer of 2010, Avaaz launched an online petition, Stop Fox News North, and declared its opposition to the notion that Prime Minister Harper wanted to "push American-style hate media onto [Canadian] airwaves." Eventually, the petition garnered thirty thousand signatures, some of which were delivered to Canadian broadcast regulators.

Booker Prize–winner Margaret Atwood signed the petition, too, and became an early critic of the network-to-be. Said Atwood: "Some people signing the petition object to the expected content. I object to the process. It's the [prime ministerial] pressure on yet another civil servant that bothers me. These folks are supposed to be working for the taxpayer, not the PM." A few days later, Teneycke wrote an op-ed that suggested Atwood was "[putting] her political agenda ahead of principles and patriotism." He also noted that the Avaaz petition contained the signatures of nonexistent people.

Avaaz said that it had investigated the phony signatories, and declared that most of the fictitious petition names emanated from a single IP address in the Ottawa area. Shortly after Avaaz forwarded its findings to the Mounties and Ottawa police, Teneycke resigned from his position at Quebecor and

Sun News (though he has since returned). Teneycke said that the licensing of Sun News had become too controversial, and that he hoped his departure would lower the temperature. He took the blame for much of the controversy, saying it had gotten out of hand. "Broadcasting, like so much of the Canadian economy, isn't exactly an open, free market. Anyone can produce television content, but to get distributed to millions of homes requires reaching accommodation with [broadcast regulators] and the cable/satellite companies. Some have described this set-up as a legally sanctioned oligopoly, others say it is corporatism or crony capitalism. Regardless of what adjectives you use, it is ugly.

"We had opposition from incumbent media interests at every stage of the process—starting at the CRTC with our licence application, and then more opposition in the boardrooms as we tried to negotiate access to the market. Some of this was ideological, some of it was naked financial self-interest, and some of it came from within the government itself." He pauses. "Regardless, it was, and continues to be, a tough process. At this time, the nature of our licence and carriage agreements mean we are only in four out of ten Canadian households. Our competitors are in every household."

The network, therefore, isn't anywhere near where it needs to be, according to Teneycke. Many years of hard work lie ahead before conservatives, or anyone, can characterize it as a success. "Despite new media, television is still a very powerful medium," says Teneycke. "It is the great legitimizer of public opinion. For an idea to be taken seriously, it has to be a part of the debate on television. It is how we get to know our politicians and our commentators. In an earlier time, something was true because Walter Cronkite said it was. Today in the United States, guys like Bill O'Reilly cut a huge wake in public opinion, not because of their books or columns, but because of their nightly cable shows. Television lets people get to know you in a way that the printed word never can."

Since April 2011—when it launched, too early from Teneycke's perspective, in the middle of the federal election campaign—Sun News has been headquartered on the east side of downtown Toronto. One studio is found in an older building that was previously occupied by a failed mainly-movies channel; the other is across the street, and in a newer complex that houses the *Toronto Sun* newspaper, as well as a grocery store and some other businesses.

Not everyone at the Sun News network is a conservative. Following just about every liberal-loving column I produce— and I write for the national Sun chain twice a week—I almost always receive emails from staff within the Sun or Quebecor agreeing with me. Or even if they don't agree with me, they are glad that I am with the Sun. I've never felt as welcomed by a bunch of conservatives.

The on-air talent is mostly conservative, certainly, but no more so than some of the folks I have worked with at Global News or CTV News. Some of them come across as hard-core right-wing when on the air. But when the cameras aren't on, they aren't nearly as strident. What became apparent to me, a few weeks after the network got going, was that the network's on-air personalities weren't strong conservatives quite so much as they are strong *personalities,* offering up what one executive told me was "infotainment." The core Sun News group—no more than about a hundred employees, as compared to the many thousands who work for the CBC—still consider themselves outsiders, even when the likes of me point out that conservative voices increasingly dominate the media universe.

But Teneycke dismisses my claim that the news media now mainly tilt Right. "As a conservative, I would say you *still* need to fight for space everywhere," he says. "As a media executive,

I would say in a thousand-channel-plus universe, it is good business to narrow your target audience—be it Left, Right, or by some other attribute."

But it shouldn't ever be just the sound of one hand clapping, he adds. Among other things, that's *boring*. "I think it is important to have strong conservative voices represented in left-wing media, just like it is important to have strong progressive voices on conservative channels. Prior to working for Quebecor I was the token conservative on the CBC. As you can attest," he says to me, "it can be a lot of fun to play that role. It is very punk rock." He laughs, knowing my passion for it.

"I don't care what kind of news channel you are running," he says. "You really can't have a real or good or interesting debate without having powerful arguments on both sides." In his own case, Teneycke says, he'll listen to CBC Radio One, or tune in to Chris Matthews on MSNBC, to elevate his blood pressure. By the same token, he insists, some of the most dedicated viewers of Sun News are on the Left. "When it comes to editorial opinion, I support media outlets staking a strong ideological claim. It is good for media diversity and good for democracy. If it isn't this way, a lot of stories will not be covered; a lot of debates of interest to a lot of people will not be aired. The most common form of media bias is the decision of what *not* to cover. You only have so much space, and so editors and producers cover what they think will engage their audience. Needless to say, the CBC and Sun News make very different decisions on what to cover every day, which is good!"

When I ask Teneycke how conservatives have achieved political dominance by dominating values and language, he contends that this is only partly true. "In an age where the failure of the modern welfare state is leading the news everywhere," he says, "the Liberal narrative is still centred on big government programs. Conservative values are dominating because they seem to ring true to a greater number of Canadians."

The reason progressives are struggling, Teneycke maintains, is that they are attempting to redefine what values and policies will make up the foundation of their movement. Are those values, that intellectual foundation, popular enough to win elections? It's fine to have some policies that are more for urban constituencies than rural ones, Teneycke says. "But if all your policies are like that you are in trouble. Conservatives are used to being locked out of cities and ethnic communities. [We've] adapted and found ways to fix that. The Left is now locked out of rural and small urban markets—almost everywhere, at almost every level of government. That's a problem. The ideas are the tough part. Picking the right words to describe them is pretty straightforward."

The sort of renewal progressives need to do, Teneycke says, is the same sort of exercise that the conservative movement went through in the nineties and earlier. There are no shortcuts, he says. "Just a lot of hard work—and most of it done in obscurity, too."

While, like most ardent conservatives, Teneycke doesn't believe (as I do) that the Right dominates the punditocracy, he does believe (as I do) that the Left needs to get its collective act together. First and foremost, he says: "Show up. Fight for your point of view to be heard. Never turn down a chance to debate. I have often wondered why so many activists on the Left are so unwilling to directly engage with critics, including the conservative media." He tells me I am one of the few lefties who will agree to debate a prominent voice on the Right; I demur. "[But] there are lots of smart people on the Left who won't go near a real debate. That is a shame. I think conservative commentators in Canada are far more comfortable to engage in a heated debate in the media, irrespective of the media outlet. [Most] conservatives would happily engage in a debate almost any time and anywhere. Once again I credit all those years in the wilderness.

"Sparring makes you stronger," he concludes. "Sparring against strong opponents makes you better still."

So, I ask, should we progressives fight the Right?

My conservative friend laughs. "Yes! Fight the Right!"

☆ ☆ ☆

But how?

If progressives are to fight the Right, and win, we need to pay close attention to their successes—to how conservatives have quite literally burglarized the liberal homestead, and made off with populist values and symbol-laden language. Because, make no mistake: while liberals and progressives slept, conservatives did indeed break in and swipe the recipe to the political secret sauce. And that's the irony presently seen at the heart of the Left's frantic efforts to locate a winning narrative and a captivating set of values: we had *both*, and we let them go.

Since the late 1960s, we progressives and liberals have been scrambling to locate what we once indubitably had. That's not to say that we have been completely incapable of winning in the interim, of course. Jean Chrétien, Bill Clinton and Barack Obama have shown that we can, when the circumstances are right, beat back conservatives. But if we are honest with ourselves, we should acknowledge that recessions and a fractured Right certainly didn't hurt our chances. In 1992, Clinton benefited greatly from the candidacy of Ross Perot and a recession; the following year, Chrétien reaped the political rewards of the same recession, and the federal Conservatives splintering into three camps (Reform, the PCs, and the Bloc Québécois). In 2008, Obama arrived as the literal embodiment of change as the Western world slipped into a calamitous recession that had been mostly authored by Republicans (and about which establishment Republicans, and their bastard Tea Party progeny, continue to squabble to this day).

Mostly, however, the Right has been winning and the Left has been doing the opposite. Back in the early 1960s, we had the better ideas. We knew what we had to say and how to say it, too. That's because we had the likes of Tony Schwartz.

Never heard of him? Many haven't. He was an exceedingly modest man, and because he was agoraphobic, he rarely even left the brownstone where he lived and worked in Manhattan. He didn't seek publicity; he shunned it. When many, many others sought credit for his work, he didn't contradict them. I caught up with him a few years before his death in 2008, and when he came on the phone to chat for the first time, he expressed surprise that someone from Canada had ever heard of him.

I had. For a lot of us who work on progressive and liberal campaigns, Tony Schwartz was a giant, a star. Before many of us were even born—and long before far-right snake oil purveyors and mendacious con men took control of the airwaves and the legislatures, driving discord and division—Tony Schwartz transformed modern politics, and in just sixty seconds. He did in one minute what it takes other progressives lifetimes to learn. He defined the conservative adversary before they could define themselves. He created a symbol, one that endures nearly fifty years later. He connected with the hearts and minds of average people, using language that spoke to their values, their identities and their lives. For progressives, he changed everything.

When we spoke, Tony Schwartz was unfailingly polite and self-effacing, and he would dispute all of the accolades I offered up. That was the kind of guy he was: a kind and gentle soul, but one who knew how to craft memorable (and occasionally very tough) messages that spoke to the values of millions of

Americans. He was a magician. The most dramatic example of his wizardry, most feel, came on September 7, 1964, when Schwartz conceived and produced a single Democratic Party TV spot which, among other things, won Lyndon B. Johnson the presidency—a spot which radically revised the way in which advocacy and campaigns were thereafter done. (Along with writing about it enthusiastically in a couple of books, I even named my company and my dog after it.)

"Daisy," as it is universally known, is filmed in grainy black and white. It starts off with a little girl, about four or five, standing in a field. There's a breeze, some birds are chirping, and she is wearing summertime clothes. She has long, blondish hair, and she's looking at a flower—a daisy—as the commercial begins. Almost singing, she is counting as she plucks petals from the daisy. "One, two, three, four, five," she says, quietly. She gets her counting wrong: "Seven, six, six, eight, nine, nine—"

Abruptly, the girl stops and looks up, surprised. The mood changes. A man's voice is suddenly heard, echoing and harsh and loud, and he's counting, too. As he does so, the camera moves in on the little girl. "Ten, nine, eight, seven, six, five, four," he barks, and all that can be seen are the child's eyes, which are now clearly afraid. "Three, two, one . . ." The shot moves into her iris, and suddenly there is an explosion: the screen is filled with a gritty image of an atomic bomb being detonated. The girl is gone. As the mushroom cloud reaches upward, filling the sky, another voice is heard: the voice of Lyndon B. Johnson, president of the United States and the Democratic Party's candidate.

"These are the stakes," he says in his Texan twang, and without emotion. "To make a world in which all of God's children can live, or to go into the dark." There's a pause. "We must either love each other, or we must die." The screen goes black, and a few words appear in white: "VOTE FOR PRESIDENT

JOHNSON ON NOVEMBER 3." Then there's another male voice: "Vote for President Johnson on November 3. The stakes are too high for you to stay home."

Daisy ran only once as a paid TV ad, during Gregory Peck's *David and Bathsheba* on Monday Night at the Movies. An estimated fifty million Americans saw it. Even now, so many years later, it is incredibly powerful and dramatic. Even though its production values are prehistoric when compared to what can now be seen on TV, it still beats everything. It can send shivers down your spine.

It created a "revolution," the *New York Times* would write decades later. It was, the *Times* continued, "the most revolutionary television ad in history during its first and last broadcast." It had "an undeniable impact," and it was "the most negative political ad in American history." When the results were announced early on November 4, 1964, Lyndon B. Johnson won by a landslide. Barry Goldwater, meanwhile, barely won his home state, by less than 1 percent. Out of fifty states, the Republican nominee took only six. Daisy, most felt, had helped to demolish the conservatives' campaign.

The effect it had on Americans, too, was as immediate and as overpowering as the explosion that ends it. Within moments, the White House switchboard lit up with hundreds of calls from those who wanted to protest the ad. The Republican establishment screamed in outrage. One Republican politician furiously complained to the National Association of Broadcasters; the chairman of the Republican National Committee filed a fiery objection with the Fair Campaign Practices Committee, calling the spot "a libel against the Republican [presidential] nominee." Hundreds of people called the Republicans themselves to register their objections to Daisy, including, allegedly, a Virginia mother who said the spot had reduced her four-year-old to tears before bedtime.

The background to Daisy, Tony Schwartz explained to me many years later, was simple: conservatives of Goldwater's ilk scared people. Even before he won the Republican Party's presidential nomination in a nasty fight at the Cow Palace in San Francisco in July 1964, the hard-line conservative had alienated many Americans with words and deeds that were inarguably extreme. In fact, near the end of his acceptance speech, Goldwater resolved any doubt about that, when he hollered: "I would remind you that extremism in the defence of liberty is no vice! And let me remind you also that moderation in the pursuit of justice is no virtue!"

With those words, and with his well-documented willingness to deploy nuclear weapons to halt the spread of communism, Goldwater had made himself a target for Tony Schwartz. When Schwartz was summoned to a meeting at the advertising agency of Doyle Dane Bernbach, the small agency behind the brilliant early Volkswagen Beetle ads, he was already alarmed about a possible Goldwater presidency. When one of the DDB admen held up a photograph of LBJ, and asked Schwartz, "Would you work for this product?" Schwartz didn't hesitate. He agreed on the spot—even though he had never before toiled on a political campaign.

Schwartz was from New York City, but he wasn't part of the Madison Avenue advertising elite. In the house where he lived with his wife and two sons—and where he would later receive pilgrimages by Democratic presidential and senatorial candidates—he built a soundproof recording studio, filled with top-of-the-line cameras and editing machines. He was a bit of a curiosity to Madison Avenue, in fact. Schwartz had an interest in recording children at play, as well as in what he called "the world of numbers."

Long before Daisy would change the course of the 1964 presidential campaign, Schwartz said, he "wanted to do a record essay on numbers without any narration, just the world of numbers. . . . The most complex use of numbers was the countdown on the atom bomb or a rocket blast-off. The simplest use of numbers was a child counting from one to ten. I started fooling around with [that]."

Schwartz was a political neophyte, but he was also a quick study. Schwartz told me what he had learned about the process, and what progressive types could learn from it as well. "A political ad is about things that are *important* to the people, at the time the election is taking place," he said, noting that the possibility of nuclear war was uppermost in many minds at the time. "The Daisy ad was an interesting thing, the way it came about. They asked me to do the sound for six or seven spots for Johnson, and I said okay."

The Democrats and the DDB team told Schwartz they wanted a spot to emphasize the fact that, as president, Goldwater would have his finger hovering above the nuclear button. Schwartz immediately told them he had something that might work. "I told them I had it all done already," he said. "I had done a Polaroid spot for Doyle Dane Bernbach with my nephew, counting up to ten and getting all mixed up as kids will at his age—four or five." He had also produced dozens of spots and radio essays for WNYC, the New York affiliate of National Public Radio. In one of them, he had an idea. "I added [to the spot featuring his nephew] a countdown from a rocket blast, and a bomb sound going off. And then I had an announcer say, 'In a world of nuclear weapons, we have to have a strong United Nations.' So I took that and played it for them. They flipped. Find a child, I told them, picking the petals off a daisy. And I'll produce it."

The little girl—a four-year-old, Monique Luiz, whom DDB found through a city talent agency, and who would grow up to be an architect in California—was filmed with her flower while in a field near the Henry Hudson Parkway, north of the city. President Johnson's audio track came from one of his Rose Garden speeches.

Most Americans were watching NBC that Monday night, but many later claimed to have seen it. (The same phenomenon often happens after televised leaders' debates—people who do not watch the debate at all will insist that they saw it, in order that they may give their opinion to friends and family.) Many Americans also claimed that Barry Goldwater had been named in the spot. But he wasn't, not at all. Said Schwartz: "We never mentioned Goldwater. The type on the end said, 'Vote for President Johnson' and so on. But Goldwater's name was never mentioned in it. Now, for years, this was called the beginning of negative political commercials. But it wasn't." At first, Goldwater dismissed the ad. But within days, he and his Republican advisors saw the damage that Daisy had wrought, and Goldwater lashed out, bitterly calling it "electronic dirt," and saying those behind it made him "sick to my stomach." But it was too late.

The powerful words that Johnson spoke actually belonged to the British poet W.H. Auden. Years later, members of the Auden family tracked down Schwartz and asked him how the New York City adman had persuaded the poet to write for a political commercial. He laughs at the memory, but Auden himself, apparently, had not been amused. A White House speechwriter had partially appropriated some language from Auden's most famous poem, "September 1, 1939," written about the growing storms of war. When Auden finally saw Daisy, he was livid. "I pray to God that I shall never be memorable like that again," he said, giving orders that the poem not reappear in any collections of his work.

But that's all history, now. What matters to this day is why Daisy—a TV spot that was only broadcast once, nearly a half-century ago—still resonates. Daisy was effective, Schwartz said, because it confirmed the public's suspicion that Goldwater favoured the use of nuclear weapons, while Johnson did not. When the commercial came on, he said, Americans asked themselves, "Whose finger do I want on the nuclear trigger? The man who wants to use them, or the man who doesn't?"

That's part of it. But Schwartz was, characteristically, understating Daisy's power and significance. It ended a conservative extremist's presidential campaign, to be sure. The Daisy spot still echoes through the years because it represents possibly the last time that values and language came together, perfectly united, in a progressive political campaign.

In his book *The Responsive Chord*, Schwartz suggests that Daisy was effective because it stirred up powerful, unarticulated emotions among those who saw the spot. It went deep, deep into the collective psyche of Americans and spoke to values. "The best political commercials are similar to Rorschach patterns," he writes. "They do not *tell* the viewer anything. They surface his feelings and provide a context for him to express those feelings."

The point of Daisy, he explains, is not merely to develop a communications strategy, or to try and get one's message across. Those ad agency clichés don't begin to capture what Schwartz wanted to achieve. The best messaging—values messaging—begins with messages that *already* have resonance in a person's emotional makeup. Values that are already there. The objective, he says, is not simply to order one's words in a beguiling way, or to invoke the word "values" without ever fully understanding what it means. It can't be emphasized enough: with values messaging, the objective is to stir up deeply felt feelings that are now (and likely have always been) present in a person's deepest psyche.

Schwartz told me he called it "evoked recall" in one of his

two books; it's also what he calls "resonance." That is, we need to look for a person's deeply emotional, and profoundly motivating, past memories and feelings. When the words in a commercial or a speech connect with those memories and feelings, we connect with more than a person's values—we connect with their *identity*, their innermost self, in a direct and highly authentic way. Aristotle, Schwartz says, knew about all of this long ago—he called it "empathematic" to communicate with a person in such a profoundly emotional way that meaning isn't actually created until that person receives it and approves of it. In effect, it's communicating at the level of the unconscious, and building a bridge to a deeply felt emotion or memory. Conservatives are good at it.

"What Democrats and liberals need to do," Schwartz told me, "is understand that feeling is more important than thinking. Trying to connect with people, you find out what they feel, and you work backwards from that." As Schwartz also notes in his (wordy, but eerily accurate) work of media prophecy, *The Responsive Chord*: "In developing a set of useful principles for communicating, it is necessary to abandon most of the traditional rules we were taught. A resonance approach does not begin by asking 'what do I want to say?' We seek to strike a responsive chord in people, not get message across. This involves, first, examining how stored experiences are patterned in our brain, and how previous experiences condition us to perceive new stimuli. Second, we must understand the characteristics of the new communication environment, and how people use media in their lives. Only at the final stage do we consider the content of a message, and this will be determined by the effect we want to achieve and the environment where our content will take on meaning."

It's ironic, and unfortunate for liberals, that it was conservatives who learned Tony Schwartz's lessons the best. On right-wing talk radio, on Fox News and Sun News, on whatever bully pulpit they possess, conservatives can still be seen and heard making an emotional appeal before they will ever make an intellectual one. Progressives heap scorn on all of this, of course, and they regularly mock conservatives' anti-intellectual inclinations. But that, again, is foolish. By belittling simple, evocative messages, progressives help make the case that it is conservatives—and not progressives—who are the true populists. Along the way, they render themselves effete intellectual snobs, while the conservatives win the hearts of voters.

Conservatives learned well the lesson that Tony Schwartz had taught them so dramatically in Daisy. After 1964, they rarely strayed from the emotional appeal and a message array that is immersed with everyday values.

"That's 'the responsive chord,'" one conservative said on a PBS talk show a few years ago, after Schwartz had passed away. "I was taught that by Tony Schwartz, one of the top Democratic media consultants, the guy who created Lyndon Johnson's famous advertising campaign from '64. He's the guy who taught me that sometimes you ask a rhetorical question [to] which there is no answer."

He had made a pilgrimage to sit at the feet of Tony Schwartz, the conservative confessed, and he listened very carefully to what the Democratic communications guru had to say. Said this prominent conservative: "So you can criticize me for doing that, for teaching these techniques to politicians and to CEOs." But, the conservative makes clear, he doesn't care about the criticism.

The conservative's name?

Frank Luntz.

☆ ☆ ☆

If progressives are hoping to beat conservatives in the quest to dominate the language of everyday political discourse—and we *should* be—then we desperately need to identify what Francis Fukuyama calls "the alternative narrative." If we don't, the fight against the Right is lost even before it truly begins.

But smart conservatives like Kory Teneycke and Frank Luntz stand in the way. While their ratings, some days, may not seem all that big, Sun News, Fox News and conservative talk radio have played a pivotal role in ensuring that the Right's values, and the Right's words, crowd out the Left. As Geoffrey Nunberg wrote in *Talking Right*: "The Right's stories are echoed and amplified by the broadcast commentators who fill the airwaves with Right-wing chatter . . . people have never before had access to a 24/7 stream of the stuff: Right-wing talk radio and Fox News are the first media in history to turn political indignation into a successful business model. If you care to, you can hear more political talk in a single week than anyone in the Nineteenth Century could experience in an entire lifetime."

That's not all. The media's conservative commentariat take liberal outrages—real or imagined, big or small—and market the hell out of them. Whatever the misdeed, whatever the misstep, voices on the Right will always devote themselves to depicting the Left as corrupt, or clownish, or both. Whenever I am asked to appear on Sun News, I know in advance that the subject matter will be about something liberals did wrong. My task is to defend the entire Left, about anything and everything. It ain't easy, believe me.

But it must be done! If the Right has taught the Left anything, it is that being remiss in defending and championing our values, and our words, is a huge strategic error. And if, as James Carville says, we are usually right and they are usually wrong, it is more than bad strategy. To refuse to fight—to choose discretion over valour—is to be fully complicit in the Right's wrongs.

What, then, should be the alternative narrative that Fukuyama and others call for?

Jean Chrétien, who crafted winning campaign narratives at the national level for forty years—and won three back-to-back majorities—agrees that the best narrative for progressives is the one that could be seen in virtually every North American and European city in the summer and fall of 2011: the 1 percent versus the 99 percent.

"I will tell you a very sad story," says Chrétien. "I work with big business people. I'm a populist, but I have to deal with big shots all the time. My work leads me to some pretty big files, and I have to go to Wall Street a lot. I know a person that I met there about seven years ago. Some clients took me to New York, and I met this guy and I liked him. He was working for one of the big banks there. He had a very good personality and he had good values. He was complaining about the war in Iraq, the cost of it, in terms of dollars and human lives. He was making a lot of money, working for a good company, but it was obvious to me he had a good liberal conscience.

"Later on, he went out on his own. He became very successful on his own, and suddenly he started to make lots and lots of money—and he changed completely. He became . . ." Chrétien trails off. "He had become extremely *greedy*. A man who was a Democrat before, was telling me now that Barack Obama, this great man, was a communist. I was shocked because he was not the same man anymore—the man with great liberal values and a great personality. To me, this was a sign he had fallen into the trap—and he believed now there were no limits to how much money you can get. But there *is* a limit! There is a line—and it is a line that capitalism cannot cross without penalty. There is a wall, there.

"The Occupy kids out on Wall Street knew that, too. They were a great example of that. [Occupy] was impressive—some of these kids were saying the same thing Warren Buffett said. Buffett said that he was paying less taxes than his secretary, and he shouldn't be." Chrétien pauses a last time. "This thing, the 99 percent thing, can become an issue in the next election. It can be very big. And I believe this is what Obama is going to say."

Brad Woodhouse, the Democrat's lead unelected spokes-man, admits that he is impressed by what Chrétien has to say. "I have a lot of respect for Mr. Chrétien," he says. But there is a risk in the Occupy mantra, it is suggested. Is the alternative narrative to be found in the 99 percent versus 1 percent—or isn't that simply serving up what Republicans and Conservatives deride as class warfare?

"I think what the president did in 2008," Woodhouse says, "was to really connect to Americans' values. It wasn't: 'Do you want to support the candidate that favours Wall Street, or are you going to support the candidate that favours Main Street?' It wasn't that simple. What it was, instead, was: 'Do you want someone in the Oval Office who values the contribution the middle class makes, and the struggles that they go through? Then and now, it isn't just a class warfare thing. It's more about *identifying* with people. It's about sharing their values. And I think the president has done that—and it's one of the reasons his personal popularity has been resilient over the course of his presidency. People *do* believe that he shares their values. The polls show that."

What about the need to show results? What about Democrats who say he hasn't delivered nearly enough? Woodhouse doesn't sound worried. "Sure. Sure, it does have to attach values. It can't just be: 'We're better on Social Security, we're better on Medicare.' It has to be: 'What does that *mean?*' And he is still pretty good at describing to people what that means. And

I thought Bill Clinton did that, too, you know? Gore and Kerry didn't. So is it class warfare? No, it's about fairness. And, frankly, class warfare *is* about fairness."

When I ask Mike McCurry for his final words, he suggests that ascertaining the alternative narrative isn't ever an easy task. "In your book, I think it's important to look at whether or not we have a much more polarized political culture now. Is the distinction between the Left and the Right sharper now? Because, let's face it, we now have a fundamental debate about how do you use government—and what is the proper role of government? How do you use government as a tool to improve people's lives? I think we may have an election in 2012 that's way more about *that* fundamental proposition, which would be kind of interesting." The differences between the respective parties' economic and social policy plans are typically matters of degree, he says. So, too often, the choice comes down to who the voter likes, and who they don't like. Better to have, à la Occupy, a values campaign.

"I think we might have a real question around, well, values and fundamental philosophy," says McCurry. "Can government be a force for good or not? Is government the problem, or is government something we can use to make life better? You've got two different points of view here—now *choose*."

That is, indeed, the choice. And all three—Chrétien, Woodhouse and McCurry—are winners, and progressive winners, too (a rare species, these days). And they all suggest that the Occupy hypothesis—the few with too much, as against the many with not nearly enough—is perhaps the best one. It's the most authentic, and therefore the most effective, progressive message anyone has seen since Tony Schwartz put together Daisy in the summer of 1964.

"That's it," says Chrétien, pointing a finger at his great big heart. "That's it, because people feel it. That's it, because it's true."

☆ ☆ ☆

Early in 1983, the Carleton University Students' Association, of which I had just been elected president, hosted former U.S. president Gerald Ford. My predecessor had invited the thirty-eighth president to give a paid speech, which—at the time—set off quite a lot of controversy. When he finally arrived on campus, surrounded by a phalanx of Secret Service agents, Ford seemed much like his reputation: he was an inoffensive sort of fellow and certainly no extremist.

When compared to Ronald Reagan—then occupying the White House and busily ballooning the deficit and defence spending while cutting taxes for the rich—Ford seemed very much what we Canadians call a "progressive" conservative. He wasn't a maniac, even if he shouldn't have pardoned Richard Nixon.

Ford spoke to us in our gymnasium. Thousands of students and professors were on hand to hear what he had to say. But partway into his speech, a group of people I'd never seen before suddenly appeared at the back, waving signs and hollering. Among other things, the group was protesting Ford's alleged role in facilitating the bloody 1975 invasion of East Timor by Indonesian forces. The group got louder, and it became apparent their objective was to silence the former president. It got tense, but Ford eventually got to the end of his remarks. When it came time for the question and answer session, I stood up at a microphone. Like now, I was no conservative, but along with lots of others, I was interested in allowing him a platform—conservative or not. And I certainly wasn't interested in seeing him shouted down by some people who were clearly from off campus. So I said to Ford that I wished people had extended him the courtesy of letting him speak. Carleton was a hotbed of student radicalism in those days, but my words got a lot of applause.

Later on, some of us were invited to meet and speak with Ford at the university's Faculty Club. My father was in town for a medical conference, so I brought him along as my date, and at one point, we both got an opportunity to speak with the former president on our own. He revealed himself to be a genial and kindly man, much like his reputation made him out to be. He seemed to be genuinely interested in our questions, and answered each one thoughtfully. At one point, I tried to explain to him the ongoing tensions between separatists and federalists in Quebec, and also between the franco-phones and anglophones who lived there. "Anglicans?" Ford asked, and then laughed when my dad and I corrected him. He wasn't embarrassed.

The conversation turned to U.S. politics, and the tremen-dous success Reagan was having over Democrats. I told Ford that my family was made up of hard-core liberals, and we found it frankly amazing that Reagan remained so popular when so many of his policies weren't, at all. How did he do it?

Ford looked off towards the Faculty Club windows, mea-suring his words carefully. It was evident that he didn't want to say anything that would sound remotely critical of his Republican successor.

"The president is an amazing communicator," he said, finally. "And that is what this game of politics is all about, really. I think he's also been successful because he knows how to get inside people's hearts, and not just their heads. They understand him."

And that remains as true now as it was then. Even though things were decidedly a mess on his watch, Ronald Reagan—a conservative deity still, nearly a decade after his death—showed everyone that, when you have the right words, and the right values, you will continue to win. As Reagan again would, him-self, in 1984. With his use of symbols, with his alignment with the little guy, with—more than anything else—his *authenticity*, Reagan indeed became The Great Communicator.

He showed conservatives how to defeat liberals and progressives, even when the prognosis was grim. He showed conservatives that, when they come together as a disciplined and unified force, they can persuade average citizens to vote for them. Even when voting for conservatives is against the best interests of those same citizens. Even when defining "conservative" is hard to do.

Gerald Ford, former leader of the Republican Party, eyed me a bit warily.

"You know," he said, smiling, "you liberals could learn a few things from us conservatives. You might even end up beating us, you know."

We can—because we *must*.

Fight the Right!

ACKNOWLEDGEMENTS

Political people, like me, are weird. Normal people read books from front to back; political folks do it backwards. That's because they always check the index (or the acknowledgements) to see if they are in the book. If they are, they'll buy it.

As such, I intend to thank everyone who was interviewed for this book, or anyone who has ever offered me their political insights in the past. That way, I not only get to offer them my sincere thanks, but I potentially get them to buy it, too. (Some folks named below may not want to be thanked, but they only have themselves to blame. They shouldn't have associated with me.) So here goes.

In the Far West, I learned from the likes of Gary Collins, Gord Campbell, Clark Roberts, Greg Lyle, Stew Braddick, Ted Olnyk, Luigi Perna, John Eisenstat, Irv Epstein, Raymond Chan, Paul Fyssas, Ross Fitzpatrick, May Brown, John Kenney (RIP), Don Williams, George Taylor, Royce Frith (RIP), Judy Kirk, Gord Robson, Steve Kukucha, Bill Brooks, Erin Berger, Patrick Wong, Celso Boscariol, Kent Scarborough, Dave Wizinsky, Jay Straith, David Plewes, Heather Dunsford, Alan Shuster, Herb Dhaliwal, Martyn Brown, Diana Hutchinson, Alex Pannu, Dennis Prouse, Murray Dykeman, Pam McDonald, Fraser Randall, Andre Gerolymatos, Tim Morrison, Martin MacLachlan, Svend Robinson, Mike McDonald, Dirk Ricker,

Jen Reid, Stuart Pelly, Jonathan Ross, Ed Barnes, Jim Sullivan, Lorne Burns, Mark Reder, Chuck Strahl, Greg Walker, Don Millar, Renate Bublick, Mark Marissen, Mike Brooks, Adam Korbin, Prem Vinning, Elliott Poll, Joseph Spears, John Nuraney, Stan Winfield, Ted Nebbeling and Neil Sweeney. Special thanks go to Brad McTavish, Mark Brady and Naina Sloan. And I am also immensely grateful to Toby Ward for his judgment, his loyalty and his friendship, all of which I value a great deal.

In the Nearer West, my home, I was enlightened by Stephen Carter, Hunter Wight, Alison Redford, Nick Taylor, John Cordeau, Steve MacAdam (RIP), Colin MacDonald, Joyce Fairbairn, Sheldon Chumir (RIP), Lloyd Axworthy, Paul Anderson, Derek Raymaker and his amazing parents, Raj Chahal, David Asper and his dad Izzy (RIP), John Harvard, Ginny May, Harley Schacter, Ron Duhamel (RIP), Ken Boessenkool, David MacInnis, Cos Gabriele, Mark Igglesden, Tom Bagley, Hugh and Scott McFadyen, Martin Egan, David Morley, Lee Hill, Rey Pagtakhan, Ethel Blondin-Andrew, Mark Johnson, Catherine Lappe, Dan Nearing, Jim Keelaghan and Bob Haslam. Always standing by me when I was battling western separatists and/or kooky right-wingers were my parents, Lorna and Doug; my brothers, Lorne and Kevin; my sisters-in-law, Barb and Annette; my nephew, Troy, and his wife, Melisa; and the two guys who have been allies the longest, Rockin' Alan Macdonald and Ras Pierre Schenk.

In Godless Central Canada, where my brood and I currently reside, there are about a million people to thank, and to whom I owe much, whether they know it or not. The list will only be partial, for which I offer *mea maxima culpa* in advance. There is James Villeneuve, Jen Norman and Dave Pryce, Tom Allison, Gordie Brown, Rick Anderson, John and Peter Wilkinson, Beth Clarkson, Eugene Bellemare, Andy Stein, Senator David Smith, Wendy Iwai, Matt Maychak, Ben Chin, Gordon Prieur,

Jeff Ryan, Jo Reath, Richard Patten, Percy Downe, Angelo Persichilli and his wonderful family, Sheila Copps, Jane Taber, Pierre Marc Johnson, John Hayter, Benoit Chiquette, Malcolm Lester, John Hinds, Michelle Bishop, Joan Bryden, Pete O'Neil, Gordon Ashworth, the McGuinty family, Justin Trudeau, Jim Peterson, Herb Gray, Emond and Heather Chiasson, David Peterson, Robert Houle, Dennis Mills, Dale Lastman, Rod Phillips, Aaron Lazarus, Andrew Steele, Dwight Duncan, Chris Benner, Manuel Prutschi, Mark Quinn, David Gourlay, Jeff Steiner, Patti Munce, Shannon Deegan, Marc Laframboise, Gabor Apor, Hugh Segal, the Fearless McGuinty War Rooms '07 and '11, Charlie Angelakos, David Zussman, Bob Murdoch, Mark Poole, Jack Warren, Bruce Drysdale, Stevie Cameron, Beatrice Raffoul, Adrian Montgomery, Phyllis Bruce, Paul Godfrey, Gary Clement, Duncan Dee, Ian MacLeod, Val Poulin, Dan Dunlop, Sharon Smith, Randy and Luba Pettipas, Dominic Agostino (RIP), Greg Wong, Mark Stokes, Peter Gregg, Bob Nault, Heather Armstrong, Taras Zalusky, Stan and Bernie Farber, Eric Johnson, Nick Nelson, Alice Willems, Jonathan Goldbloom, Isabel Metcalfe, Grant Kippen, Doug Wotherspoon, Greg Schmidt, Pat Neri, Monique Bondar, Sean O'Connor, Sheila Ward, Aaron Dobbin, David Caplan, Laurel Broten, Doug Melville, Greg Tsang, Tony Knill, Kevin Lee, Rob Trewartha, Murray Campbell, Cal and Darrell Bricker, Jerry Yanover (RIP), Chethan Lakshman, Nathalie Gauthier, Helen Burstyn, Claudette Levesque, John Chenier, Johanne Senecal, Joe Belfontaine, Krista Scaldwell, Earl Stuart, Joe Ragusa, John Baird, Paul-Emile Cloutier, Gerald Butts, Ron Drews, Jean Pelletier (RIP), Phillip Gigantes (RIP), Priya Suagh, John Parisella, Deb Roberts, Christine Hampson, Titch Dharamsi, Tenio Evangelista, Jack Siegal, Rob Ritter, Hugh Scott, Don Boudria, Mike Pearson, Scott Hutchison, Joan Lajeunesse, Tim Barber, Chris Bentley, Peter Lauwers, Alister

Campbell, "Marc the Ninja," Eme Onuoha, Dan Rogers, Kevin McGuire, Dan Hays, Pete Tuinema, Coralie D'Souza, James Wallace and Glenn Garnett and Lorrie Goldstein and Kory Teneycke and Brian Lilley and Krista Erickson and everyone at the *Toronto Sun*, Bill Fisch, Joe Volpe, Denise Costello, Joe Comuzzi, Chris Bingham, Dan Rath, Bill Fox, Hugh Blakeney, Chris Clark, Scott Sheppard, Peter Cathcart, Paul Pellegrini, Mary-Ellen Kenny, Helen Burnstyn, Steve Kelly, Jim Anderson, Christine Albee, Patrick Muttart, Brenda Leask, Debbie Gowling, Ruby Dhalla, Julienne Racicot, Con Di Nino, Bob Chant, Louise Harris, Maryse Harvey, Lina Bigoni, Scott Lovell, Dan Miles, Kevin Bosch, Ian and Catherine Davey, Dan Cook, Ray Heard, Cindy Boucher, Derek "Deeks" Kent, Gen LeBlanc, Jill Fairbrother, Karim "Special K" Bardeesy, Ralph Palumbo, George Young, Herb Metcalfe, Christine Hampson, Claudette Brown, Diane Gemus, Jim Munson, Jean-Marc Fournier, Neil Campbell, Mark Cameron, Beryl Wajsman, Mark Fung, Deb Davis, Ron Atkey, Sandra Pupatello, Patrick Parisot, Tim Powers, Alexis and Dawn Levine, Dan McCarthy, Rob Steiner, Nicole Lovell, Michel Frappier, Greg King, Paul Genest, Nicki Holland, Declan Doyle, Megan McGillicuddy, Barry McLoughlin, Kassandra McMicking, Rarihokwats, Adam Radwanski, Big City Lib, GritChik, Rick and Angie Bartolucci, John Mraz, Sergio Marchi, Jean Carle, Arnold Chan, Greg Owen, Dan Brock, Stephen Taylor, Fred Gaspar, Peter Milliken, Dan Tisch, Paul Zed, James Bowie, Tracey Sobers, Mike O'Shaughnessy, Cam Carpenter, Rob Granatstein, Rick Smith, Monte Kwinter, Katie Telford, Stephen Rouse, David and Chris Collenette, Scott Sellers, Christina Blizzard, Tel Matrundola, John Harding, Kelly Rowe, Chris Fleck, Karl Belanger, Kathleen Wynne, Randi Rahamin, Maurizio Bevilacqua, Christine McMillan, Leslie Noble, Kate Malloy, Noble Chummar, John Duffy, Johnny Z., Eddie Francis, John

Tory, Jimmy Warren, Richard Cleroux, Scott Bradley, Monte Solberg, Ted Betts, Andre Ouellet, Jorge Gomez, Tony Macerollo, Pam Waeland, Lou Clancy, Justin VanDette, Duncan Fulton, Yves Gougoux, Nick Parker, Dan Hayward, Sean Plummer, Mike Miner, Martin Cauchon, Carole Coté, Conrad Winn, Brad Lavigne, Matt Guerin, Ajay Chopra, Michael Kleinman, Allan Strader, Phil Goodwin, Omar Alghabra, Derek Nighbor, Pierre Tremblay (RIP), the Calgary Grit, Mike Duffy, Hilary Linton, Jerry Grafstein, Rudy Griffiths, Chaviva Hosek, Joan Fraser, Pat Gossage, Sonia Clement and countless others. Special thanks go to my best friend and Canada's best libel lawyer, Brian Shiller; my other friend and lawyer, Clay Ruby; Jim Watson for many years of support and "shameless" photo-mongering; Bruce Hartley and Randy McCauley for political smarts far beyond their collective years and great friendship; my blogging co-conspirators and regular commenters on www.warrenkinsella.com; my Ontario Liberal family, Don Guy, Laura Miller, Brendan McGuinty, Dave Gene, Chris Morley, Bob Lopinski, Alicia Johnston, Brian Clow and Fahim Kaderdina; my pal Bob Richardson, who is one of the sharpest political strategists around; my similarly addled band mates, Rolf Dinsdale, Rayman and David Shiller; and my partners and colleagues at the Daisy Consulting Group, Katherine Fidani, Paulo Senra, Jason McCann, Destiny D'Andrea, Byrne Furlong and Josh Hollenberg.

In the Far East, I have learned much from the likes of Shona Kinley, Kirk Cox, Allison MacNeil, Paul Sparkes, Tim Powers, Brian Tobin, Kevin Fram, Willy Moore, Steve MacKinnon, Jean Lepine, Greg MacEachern, Lawrence Macaulay, Al Graham, Meredith Naylor, and Carl Gillis, whom we all miss so much still. Most of all, I have had the privilege to have learned at the knee of the great Roméo LeBlanc, one of the most decent men to ever set foot on Parliament Hill. God bless his memory.

Beyond our borders, I am grateful to George Lakoff, Geoffrey Nunberg, Mike McCurry, Paul Begala, James Carville, John Rowley, Betsey Wright, Haley Barbour, Rod Shealy, Phil Noble, Lynda Kaid, Tony Schwartz, Dick Morris, Lucianne Goldberg, Tobe Berkovitz, Pippa Norris, Mark Mellman, Dane Strother, Scott Howell and many others.

For those who went above and beyond the call of duty to get this book in your hands, I offer the most sincere thanks of which I am capable. Included in this small group is Destiny D'Andrea, for overseeing interview transcripts and keeping me organized. There is also former prime minister Jean Chrétien and his wife, Aline, who have stood by me when many others did not.

Thanks, too, to my agent, Helen Heller. She's the best there is. My publisher and editor are Anne Collins and Paul Taunton, respectively, who displayed saint-like patience in dealing with me. Also, thanks to my brother from another mother, Scott Sellers, publicist extraordinaire.

Most of all, my deepest gratitude to Lisa, who understands me better than anyone ever has, for giving me help and support and love to get this one done, and more ("WDYHM?"); and to my children, who are my reason for living: Emma, Ben, Sam and Jake.

Thanks to one and all.

INDEX

WARREN KINSELLA is a lawyer, pundit, political consultant, and a newspaper and magazine columnist. He is the author of *Kicking Ass in Canadian Politics* and the bestselling *Web of Hate*. He lives in Toronto, is a Dad to four amazing kids, still plays in a punk band and is the president and founder of the Daisy Group, a political consulting firm.